The World After GDP

To Damiano and Lukas, wishing them all the best as they grow up in a post-GDP world

The World After GDP

Economics, Politics and International Relations in the Post-Growth Era

Lorenzo Fioramonti

polity

The right of Lorenzo Fioramonti to be identified as Author of this Work has been asserted in accordance with the UK Copyright, Designs and Patents Act 1988.

First published in 2017 by Polity Press

Polity Press
65 Bridge Street
Cambridge CB2 1UR, UK

Polity Press
350 Main Street
Malden, MA 02148, USA

ISBN-13: 978-1-5095-1134-1
ISBN-13: 978-1-5095-1135-8(pb)

A catalogue record for this book is available from the British Library.

Typeset in 10 on 16.5 Utopia Std by
Servis Filmsetting Ltd, Stockport, Cheshire
Printed and bound in Great Britain by Clays Ltd, St. Ives PLC

The publisher has used its best endeavours to ensure that the URLs for external websites referred to in this book are correct and active at the time of going to press. However, the publisher has no responsibility for the websites and can make no guarantee that a site will remain live or that the content is or will remain appropriate.

Every effort has been made to trace all copyright holders, but if any have been inadvertently overlooked the publisher will be pleased to include any necessary credits in any subsequent reprint or edition.

For further information on Polity, visit our website:
politybooks.com

Contents

Acknowledgements

Most books are, directly or indirectly, the outcome of collective efforts that take many different forms. This book is no exception. My theoretical framework connects different strands of scholarly literature in the natural and social sciences, from institutional, ecological and evolutionary economics to complexity science and sociobiology. It also deals with governance, innovation and technological progress. Such an eclectic approach is the result of many collaborations, discussions and debates that I have had with a long list of colleagues and friends. They are too many to be mentioned here. Accept my apologies if, because of brevity, your name is not included below.

I would like to begin by thanking my 'partners in crime' at the Alliance for Sustainability and Prosperity (www.asap4all.org), especially Robert Costanza, Ida Kubiszewski, Enrico Giovannini, Kate Pickett, Kristín Vala Ragnarsdóttir, Lars Fogh Mortensen, Roberto De Vogli and Richard Wilkinson. My ideas about systemic change and collective action have also benefited from conversations I had with colleagues such as Mark Swilling, who co-directs the Centre for Complex Systems in Transition at the University of Stellenbosch, John Boik from MD Anderson Cancer Center at the University of Texas, Patrick Bond from the School of Governance of the University of the Witwatersrand and Dirk Helbing, the Chair of Computational Social Science at ETH Zurich.

While writing this book, I met with governments, organizations, companies and groups of citizens advocating for a shift to a post-GDP system of accounting. My journey was accompanied by many friends who share the same concerns about this number and the power it has acquired in contemporary societies. These individuals are Katherine Trebeck, Martin Whitlock, Alfred Tolle, Yannick Beaudoin, Otto Scharmer, Julia Kim, Lew Daly and Cylvia Hayes, as well as all participants in the Global Wellbeing Lab. My role on the task force coordinated by the Initiative for Policy Dialogue at Columbia University was also essential to introducing some of the concepts of this book into the policy debate. Thus I would like to thank Joseph Stiglitz, Akbar Noman and Ravi Kanbur for inviting me to join their initiative.

I would also like to acknowledge some colleagues at my home university. In particular, my team at the Centre for the Study of Governance Innovation, who were willing to take on more managerial roles while their director spent days typing relentlessly in his office, my co-director Ward Anseeuw, who leads some of our most innovative projects on distributed data generation, and Bernard Slippers, a professor of genetics, with whom I collaborate to foster trans-disciplinary research and collective science leadership through a new project called 'Future Africa'.

Finally, I want to thank my wife, Janine, who shares this critique of the GDP world and works energetically with me to turn our home, our family and our communities into the dynamic core of a new economic and political system.

Figures and Tables

Figures

Tables

Introduction

Nauru is a tiny island in Micronesia, the smallest nation in the Pacific. With 21 square kilometres of surface, it is the third-tiniest state in the world, behind only the Vatican and Monaco. It is completely surrounded by coral reefs, which emerge out of the ocean to seamlessly erect steep cliffs reaching over 70 metres above sea level. The island is immersed in a humid and hot climate, due to its proximity to the equator. Its name derives from the Nauruan word *anáoero*, which means 'Let's go to the beach'.[1] When Captain John Fearn of the British whaling ship *Hunter* reported the presence of Nauru to the outside world in 1798, the place was so pretty that he called it 'Pleasant Island'.

Until the mid-twentieth century, Nauru was a remote outpost of colonial empires, first German and then British, with a short period of Japanese control during the Second World War, and later it became a protectorate of Australia and New Zealand. Unknown till then, what eventually catapulted Nauru onto the global scene was its unparalleled development trajectory. Why? Because this island nation boasted the highest gross domestic product per capita in the world between the 1970s and the mid-1980s, overtaking financial paradises like Luxembourg and Liechtenstein and oil-rich Arab states.[2] Its economic 'boom' was due to the exploitation of one of the world's purest and most extensive reserves of phosphate, a key ingredient for the industrial production of fertilizers. When the country acquired

1

independence in 1968, the New Nauru Phosphate Corporation intensified extraction and introduced innovative chemical treatments, with the support of foreign experts. With an unprecedented 91 per cent of purity, Nauru's phosphate exports travelled beyond the conventional Australian and New Zealand markets to reach several Asian economies, from Indonesia, to Japan, the Philippines, South Korea and Taiwan. As of the early 1980s, the peak of extraction was around two million tonnes a year, at a market price of about US$60 per tonne. Unable to construct a deep-water harbour because of its coral reef surroundings, the government built gigantic cantilevers sticking out of the mines, transporting the brown powder for hundreds of metres through conveyer belts connected to ships stationed offshore. Out of the overall proceeds, less than US$3 per tonne would go the landowners' fund, with another US$12 destined for long-term investments, including purchasing a fleet of Boeing aeroplanes and commercial ships, a chain of international hotels and a 52-storey skyscraper in central Melbourne, the tallest building in that city. After some spending on a host of social programmes, the remaining profits would stay with the local government council, which controlled the phosphate industry. Landowners shared in about U$1.4 million every three months, with the sums paid to each individual owner reaching as much as US$360,000. This meant an astonishingly high income by the standards of the Pacific atolls 'where most people exist on subsistence agriculture and fishing, seldom seeing more than a few hundred dollars in cash in a year's time'.[3]

Then things began to fall apart. In its rush to 'development', the Nauruan government over-exploited the phosphate mines, destroying the natural habitat supporting indigenous flora and fauna. Revenues plummeted in the late 1980s when most mines became unusable, and the government defaulted repeatedly on international payments.[4] In a scramble to keep generating revenues, Nauru turned into a tax haven in the 1990s and was included in the list of 'non-cooperative' nations by the Financial Action Task Force on Money Laundering. For some time, the government adopted a number of questionable policies, including issuing passports to foreign nationals in exchange for a fee. With no arable land left and no other source of income, the country eventually accepted aid from Australia in 2001 in exchange for hosting the Nauru Regional Processing Centre, a de facto detention camp for asylum seekers, widely deplored for harsh conditions and ill-treatment of residents.[5]

As reported by Nauru's former president Hammer DeRoburt, the strategy of digging into debt to fund the extractive infrastructure was 'advised by economists', despite some locals raising objections about the extravagant expenditures.[6] When the president reached out to the Asian Development Bank in the 1980s to seek support for his industrial project, the request was turned down, 'declaring that Nauru's high per capita income made the government ineligible for assistance'.[7] In a report to the United Nations (UN), Nauru's leaders recognized that phosphate mining resulted in 'drastic land degradation', 'removal of natural vegetation' and 'the almost total modification of the landscape of the topside' of the island. The report concluded: 'This is by far the most widespread and visible environmental concern in the country – an impact that has had a direct and/or indirect influence on all other environmental impacts and cultural change over the past 90 or so years.'[8]

Even the weather pattern has drastically deteriorated, so much so that present-day Nauru suffers from continuous heat rising from the mined-out plateau, which drives away rain clouds and leaves the sun-baked island plagued by constant drought. Water is so scarce that the island runs dry for most of the day, with households relying on a desalinization plant to satisfy their needs. When, in the late 1980s, the government won a case before the International Court of Justice against Australia's mining operations, it invested the US$75 million of the settlement to restore some of the lost ecosystems 'in hopes of coaxing pandanus, mango and breadfruit trees to grow again'.[9] But to no avail.

With no viable economic opportunities, broken infrastructure, ecological mayhem and a dishevelled education system, mass emigration is the only long-term option for Nauruans, most of whom have sought better economic opportunities in New Zealand and Australia. As a traditional culture of fishing and garden plots was replaced by imports of western-processed foodstuffs, the dietary profile of Nauruans has also worsened to unparalleled levels worldwide, leading to a widespread health-care crisis. According to body mass index statistics published by the World Health Organization, Nauruans are the most overweight people in the world, with 97 per cent of men and 93 per cent of women being obese as of mid-2000 data.[10] From 'Pleasant Island', Nauru has become one of the world's capitals of cardiovascular diseases, kidney failure and type-2 diabetes, a diet-related chronic illness that has affected 40 per cent of inhabitants since the 1990s and has also claimed the life of former President DeRoburt.[11]

A 1995 report about the island published in the *New York Times* reads: 'While Nauruans may be among the world's most affluent people, they are also among the most sickly, racked by diabetes, high blood pressure and obesity brought on by a diet of fatty, imported food. Few Nauruans live much past the age of 60.'[12] Nauru's vicissitude is arguably an extreme case, yet it is coherent with the rules underlying contemporary approaches to economic prosperity as a function of the gross domestic product (GDP). I will provide a more thorough explanation of 'what is wrong' with GDP in chapter 2, but a few pointers are in order here. First of all, GDP only measures material output, without considering the value of natural and human inputs that are 'depleted' in the process. It conceptualizes progress as a continuously growing set of market transactions, regardless of whether these are beneficial to society or not. Undesirable conditions like diseases, traffic jams, disasters, pollution and crime do trigger economic transactions, for instance, by requiring more medical treatment, anti-smog devices, higher insurance premiums and larger jails. Thus they count positively towards GDP, but are certainly not evidence of prosperity. In many ways, the massive exploitation of phosphates in Nauru was consistent with its GDP trajectory, as none of the associated costs on the environment and society mattered to economic advisers and government officials, let alone foreign investors. A country that depletes its energy sources and destroys the environment to prop industrial output is seen as productive by GDP. By contrast, a country that preserves nature by curbing exploitation and consumption may very well be classified as 'underdeveloped' and in need of drastic reform. Moreover, GDP only counts transactions that occur within the formal economy, hence disregarding all economic activities that are informal, voluntary in nature and are performed within the household, thus driving societies to commercialize social life, reduce leisure and free time and support large corporate-driven industrialization. As remarked on the website of the Organization for Economic Cooperation and Development, 'If ever there was a controversial icon from the statistics world, GDP is it. It measures income, but not equality, it measures growth, but not destruction, and it ignores values like social cohesion and the environment. Yet governments, businesses and probably most people swear by it.'[13]

As a limited geospatial entity, with no capacity to externalize damage to the rest of the world, Nauru's dramatic parable was an accelerated version of what is happening to our planet due to the convergence of social, economic and environmental crises. After a century of accelerated growth, the global economy has now become a closed-loop system, in which the externalities of GDP are stifling development itself, endangering not only prosperity in the long term but also the very survival of the human species. The financial crisis, rising inequality, the depletion of non-renewable energy and climate change deeply question the current model of economic globalization, demanding an urgent reorganization of our societies. As economic, political and ecological instabilities affect populations around the world, we see new waves of migration spanning the globe: desperate people who flee their homelands like Nauruans abandoned their sinking island. No matter how many fortresses some may try to build, it is becoming painfully clear that nothing can stop men, women and children running away from oppression and ecological disasters. At the same time, deprivation sits side by side with conspicuous consumption. As migrants desperately make their way across deserts, seas and armed border posts, millions of tourists leisurely criss-cross the sky and invade hitherto pristine natural ecosystems. As beggars scavenge through trash on the streets of the new shiny megacities, the super-rich have hardly any time to enjoy their sumptuous penthouses, busy as they are jetting across continents to follow their money. Never before has humanity enjoyed so much connectedness, technological advancements and longevity. Yet this has come with a huge cost not only in terms of ecological impacts, but also in terms of social cohesion and equitable development. Through a misleading set of development policies and incentives, we have built a system of social organization replete with contradictions, now threatening to push our civilization to the brink of collapse.

This book's main argument is that changing the economic 'rules of the game' can lead to profound political and social transformation. While this may sound like a nightmare to the staunch defenders of the current industrial and economic model, there are many reasons to believe that we may be on the verge of an historic transition to a more equitable, sustainable and happy society. As I will discuss in the following chapters, the economy should be seen not as a separate societal sphere which exists on its own, as the idea of the 'market' seems to suggest. Rather, the economy is nothing other than a system of rules contributing to human coordination. As a consequence, the modification of its modus operandi is likely to activate a cascade effect throughout society, leading to a different social order. By focusing on pioneering research about alternative metrics of progress, governance innovation, institutional change, complex systems, collective action and international relations, the following chapters will take the reader through a thorough analysis of the many flaws of the current global order based on GDP growth and will describe the incredible potential for change made possible by the convergence of top-down reforms, bottom-up pressures and new distributed technologies.

I am completely aware that changing a number will not, per se, change the world. For the latter to happen, we need a concerted effort by various sectors of society: a global movement committed to challenging the status quo and the interests behind it. As I will show in the book, however, dethroning GDP can trigger a cascade effect. Our entire development model rests on the way in which we measure prosperity, development and ultimately success. It is GDP that gives authority, influence and widespread social acceptability to the growth model that is intoxicating the planet. GDP sets the standards, the guidelines for policy as well as the corporate drive for consumption that virtually all societies are currently imitating and replicating. It drives a suicidal race to the cliff, which imposes stressful lifestyles, generates irrational desires and threatens to tear the world apart, while undermining the very social and natural foundations that make life possible.

Not only does GDP set the rules of the 'growth game': it automatically disqualifies all alternative development approaches, which are routinely sidelined, ridiculed and dismissed by policy makers, business leaders and the media. In this context, eroding the power of GDP means more than just changing a statistic: it means re-inventing the 'lens' through which we define prosperity and the policy goals for achieving it. Classical economic analysis in the eighteenth century showed the unproductive nature of the ancient regime's political order, dominated by hierarchies of kings, aristocrats and landlords. Coupled with innovative technologies that shifted energy away from horses and into factories, modern economic thinking paved the way for the affirmation of industrial capitalism and the resulting bourgeoisie-dominated revolutions. Similarly, post-GDP measures demonstrate the fictitious nature of contemporary economic growth, questioning the alleged productivity and efficiency of the corporate-dominated market. Not only do they reinforce a policy shift towards climate-compatible development and greater equality, but they also embolden those social actors traditionally marginalized by mainstream economic thinking, from small businesses to households, civil society, local communities, environmental advocacy groups and alternative energy movements. Like at the dawn of capitalism, policy reforms and societal pressures are now being reinforced by a technological revolution, which is providing unprecedented opportunities to create value by collaborating across networks, thus augmenting the pressure for institutional transformation. I believe that a shift towards a post-GDP system of development is the glue that unites these factors in one coherent narrative, with the potential for a multiplying game-changing effect. Connecting top-down reforms, bottom-up pressures and technological innovation may thus facilitate a transition to a 'horizontal' economy, founded on localized forms of production and consumption, in which citizens rather than consumers will be the key driving force of human development. As I will argue throughout the book, the shift to a post-GDP economy may also have an impact on contemporary politics, affording new opportunities for participation. As GDP is the benchmark via which the global pecking order is defined, new global powers may emerge and a different international system may be forged.

Structure of the book

In chapter 1, I will outline the theoretical underpinnings of this book's thesis, showing how GDP is not just a number, but a powerful institution supporting the current economic system. This statistic guides preferences and behaviours and ensures predictable outcomes through a dominant logic of appropriateness and consequence. In many more ways than we often recognize, this number influences what we do, how we do it and why we do it. In this part of the book, I connect various theoretical approaches to institutional and social change to show the potential ramifications of a post-GDP system of governance. My intention is not to describe a utopian world: rather, it is to demonstrate how change can be achieved by harnessing the complex interconnectedness of governance processes, social pressures and technological evolutions.

In chapter 2, I will tell the story of GDP's institutional evolution, from its inception before the Second World War to contemporary governance. In particular, the Bretton Woods Conference of 1944, which redesigned the world system and instituted international financial institutions such as the International Monetary Fund (IMF) and the World Bank, sealed GDP's footprint on world politics by elevating it to the global parameter of success. Since the turn of the millennium, however, the critique of GDP has left academic circles to enter the global public debate. A loose 'post-GDP' movement has been triggered by researchers, intellectuals, commissions, task forces and popular campaigns.

In chapter 3, I will explore what types of change might be triggered if a post-GDP system of metrics were introduced in economic governance. By building on an institutionalist approach to collective action and highlighting the possibility of convergence for top-down reforms and bottom-up pressures (this is what I call the 'sandwich' model), the chapter will outline how alternative metrics of economic performance can generate different economic and/or reputational incentives, as well as galvanize alternative types of business activities which develop horizontally and 'scale across' society rather than vertically through traditional forms of corporate governance. The chapter will show how metrics that 'internalize' the externalities of economic activities are likely to affect the political and public perception of large companies (especially the most polluting ones) by accounting for their costs to society, ultimately undermining their licence to operate. At the same time, small businesses and the 'sharing' economy will see their contribution to wealth and progress amplified (as their contribution to societal well-being normally goes beyond the limited monetary impact captured by GDP), thus encouraging both policy makers and citizens to shift their preferences towards a new type of economic growth. The post-GDP production system is likely to operate like a 'horizontal economy' based on customization (as opposed to mass production and economies of scale), on producing what we need (as opposed to generating waste) and on local production cycles (as opposed to comparative advantages and globalized transportation). The new economy would be more likely to achieve full employment, as it will entirely re-invent the concept of work, and it would markedly increase social well-being by reconnecting people to their local needs and natural ecosystems. Importantly, the new economy would assign a crucial value to households and communities (which are entirely neglected by GDP), given that the post-GDP system of performance will portray this social 'core' as the precondition for a functioning and dynamic economy.

Chapter 4 will focus on political transformation. For the GDP ideology, all the activities we perform in our households, in our local communities and in the vast informal economy (including small-scale farming and the non-profit) are of no value. When we care for another, when we look after our common resources (from water to natural ecosystems) and when we participate in the public sphere, we are of no consequence for the GDP paradigm. Here, too, the interaction between new metrics and shifting popular demands may produce radical changes. Post-GDP indicators will indeed reveal that the social unpaid activities we perform every day not only constitute most of our waking time but are also the backbone sustaining the very existence of the formal economy, a fact confirmed by research conducted also by institutions such as the Organization for Economic Cooperation and Development and the International Monetary Fund. When global rankings are revised to account for social capital, community work and household activities, many allegedly poor countries appear quite wealthy, while many rich economies fall down the ranks. Post-GDP metrics are likely to affect the preferences and behaviours of policy makers, some of whom may simply use them to acquire global status, as Italy did, for instance, in the 1980s when it estimated the scale of its informal economy to surpass the United Kingdom as the world's fifth-largest economy.[14] Civil society would be able to exploit this too, advocating a shift away from the 'growth' society to the 'well-being' society. Just as the post-GDP economy will be based on the prosperity generated by collaborative 'horizontal' entrepreneurial initiatives, post-GDP politics will also promote sharing and cooperation in political processes. Representative forms of participation, such as traditional political parties, may change profoundly and ultimately give way to local governance structures based on direct participation. This shift will also contribute to eroding the primacy of the nation-state, with more powers devolved to the local level. Local governance systems may emerge as pioneers in post-GDP transitions, due to their proximity to citizens, and cross-border cooperation among institutional units (e.g. local administrations, provinces, etc.) may become more common.

Chapter 5 applies the same framework to world politics. In international affairs, power and status are intimately connected with the size of a country's economy. No surprise, then, that GDP has colonized the very lexicon of global governance. International clubs such as the G7 or the G20 have been defined according to their members' contribution to global economic output. The concepts of 'emerging markets' and 'emerging powers' are also dependent on a nation's current and projected GDP growth, as well as the ambiguous distinction between the developed and the underdeveloped (or developing) world. This chapter will show how the shift to a post-GDP scenario, having contributed to economic and political change, may also result in a major reorganization of international relations.

The post-GDP system of performance does not happen in a vacuum but in an already battered global economy. Shrinking energy sources make a recovery of the globalized economy, in which one can shift production around the world searching for cheap labour, much less likely. The Sustainable Development Goals (SDGs) ratified by the United Nations in 2015 call for a more nuanced approach to economic success, making the case for a different set of metrics. Climate change demands a radical switch to renewable and less polluting forms of energy, which – unlike coal and oil – can be found anywhere but can hardly be transported, thus empowering local energy production. As new environmental regulations will be introduced to align with the SDGs, deal with climate change and shift the energy basis, globalized markets will become less profitable in the long run, which means that business activities may refocus from the global to the regional/local level to seek new profits. In the post-GDP system of performance, it will be much harder to show the economic benefits of a global trade agenda, due to the massive externalized costs. At the same time, such a transition to localized forms of production and consumption does not necessarily mean a resurgence in national protectionism. The post-GDP economy will indeed need to be embedded in the geographic, climatic and ecosystemic conditions of each territory: therefore, national borders will stay porous. As a matter of fact, regional cross-border exchanges may very well become more common than they are now. For instance, by exchanging energy locally, contiguous communities across national borders may push for further integration. Similarly, small businesses would find it attractive to pursue regional avenues for sustainable development, and local governments may establish partnerships with regional equivalents. This drive for regional integration may be particularly strong in large nations, where distances from the periphery to the centre are larger than those between cross-border peripheries. Territorial continuity will matter a great deal, which means that geographically homogenous areas will have an incentive to build common infrastructure, regardless of whether they reside within the same nation or cut across multiple countries. A new set of highly connected and ecological sustainable 'bioregions' may constitute an emergent form of polity, with nation-states transiting from being monopolists of regulation to being facilitators of bottom-up integration.

In the conclusion, I will reflect on a post-GDP world as a possibility. Current trends in accounting and policy planning are important factors but are unlikely to trigger systemic change unless the critique of GDP becomes a lens through which we frame the various malaises of our contemporary society and experiment with ways to innovate our political and economic order while building pressure from above and below. By discussing the power of numbers as institutional tools, this final section will argue in favour of a 'democratization' of accounting with a view to exploiting the opportunity presented by the SDGs to demand popular consultations on the definition of social progress. Indeed, for as long as societal performance systems are decided by specialists and technocrats, there is the risk of change being 'hijacked' by conservative forces. Ultimately, there is no sustainable well-being, nor democratic accountability, without the capacity of citizens to decide what the ultimate goals of political and economic life should be.

1

The Making of a Post-GDP World

GDP influences our governance systems more than we realize. Politicians are rated on their GDP achievements, which can make or break elections. Countries that boast high rates of GDP growth get invited to join exclusive global clubs, from the G20 to the Organization for Economic Cooperation and Development (OECD), which includes the world's 'wealthiest' countries. Business leaders are expected to increase output because this is captured in GDP and counts towards national economic success. Investment choices are predicated on GDP's present and future projections, as the power of international credit ratings has demonstrated: countries, companies and other organizations can be irremediably broken by a negative rating motivated by low GDP growth.

As remarked by economist Robert Repetto and his colleagues in 1989, 'the national income accounts are undoubtedly one of the most significant social inventions of the twentieth century':

> Their political and economic impact can scarcely be overestimated. However inappropriately, they serve to divide the world into 'developed' and 'less developed' countries. In the 'developed countries', whenever the quarterly gross national product (GNP) figures emerge, policy-makers stir. Should they be lower, even marginally, than those of the preceding three months, a recession is declared, the strategies and competence of the

administration is impugned, and public political debate ensues. In the 'developing' countries, the rate of growth of GNP is the principal measure of economic progress and transformation.[1]

Since the Bretton Woods Conference of 1944, which redesigned the world economic system, GDP has become much more than a statistic: it has been the overarching parameter of success and a fundamental ordering principle at the global and national level, establishing the economic and political 'rules of the game'. This has been true for all varieties of socialism and capitalism in the twentieth century, as the consensus on GDP growth was eminently cross-ideological and, therefore, more pervasive than any other political ideology.[2]

Yet the convergence of economic, social and environmental crises has reinvigorated a debate on the usefulness of this instrument for the twenty-first century. Since 2009, when the first 'post-GDP' commission led by Nobel laureates Joseph Stiglitz and Amartya Sen was established in France, the critique of GDP in mainstream political and economic debates has grown from strength to strength.[3] The same year, both the OECD and the European Union promoted a new initiative by the name of 'Beyond GDP'.[4] In 2012, several African countries joined forces to pledge a shift away from GDP maximization, arguing that the protection of natural resources against depletion and overuse should become a leading parameter for economic development.[5] A few months later, the Rio+20 Earth Summit provided a global platform for most of these institutional reforms to be discussed. Various alternative indicators were presented, discussed and formally launched, and a long series of commitments to redefine a system of governance in harmony with social and ecological well-being were made. The World Economic Forum has been featuring 'beyond GDP' high-level panels over the past few years, with the chief economist Jennifer Blanke publicly admitting that 'something is clearly missing and we need to move beyond GDP to get there'.[6] Even the *Economist*, a liberal free-market magazine, has been publicly advocating a move beyond GDP, after having published several reports and a full issue dedicated to the topic of 'remeasuring prosperity' in 2016. Against the backdrop of a growing popular discontent with the type of governance decisions shaped by this mainstream approach to societal success, the UN Secretary-General Ban Ki-Moon has called for a post-GDP framework for the world: 'Gross Domestic Product (GDP) has long been the yardstick by which economies and politicians have been measured. Yet it fails to take into account the social and environmental costs of so-called progress. [. . .] We need a new economic paradigm that recognizes the parity between the three pillars of sustainable development. Social, economic and environmental well-being are indivisible.'[7]

The ratification of the SDGs in September 2015 is arguably the culmination of more than a decade of evolving discourse at the global level. Interestingly, this policy process is currently being met with an increasing dynamism throughout society. Social movements advocating a post-growth society have proliferated in the past few years. International conferences dedicated to the concept of 'de-growth' have become a regular appointment for scholars and activists worldwide. A 2014 event in Germany saw the participation of more than 4,000 scholars, local government officials, activists and small businesses.[8] So-called 'transition initiatives', which help communities adopt 'energy descending' low-consumption political and economic strategies, have spread across the world since they were launched in the mid-2000s.[9] Civil society campaigns opposed to international trade agreements, austerity policies, financial speculation and investment in fossil-fuel energy infrastructure, which are largely justified by governments and businesses as strategies to enhance GDP, are mushrooming not only in the so-called global North (or West) but also among the nations of the global South.[10] Many companies have committed to reforming their practices by integrating alternative indicators of success focusing not only on profit but also on ecological footprints and social parameters.[11] Natural capital protocols, which require companies to account (and pay) for the depletion of natural resources, have become increasingly popular. If the SDGs are to have any impact on society, then we should expect a serious international commitment to reaching a comprehensive agreement on climate change in the wake of the Paris conference of December 2015, which will require (or, at the very least, nudge) nations to implement alternative development policies and reform governance processes. This will open further space for additional bottom-up pressures towards radical transformation.

This is of course no foregone conclusion. There are entrenched interests, both in the political and economic realm, which may resist change. The fact that there is limited knowledge of a potential post-GDP system is likely to weaken the push for radical shifts, especially if conservative forces make strategic use of this lack of evidence to convince society, as has been in the past, that 'there is no alternative' to the status quo. Against this backdrop, it is paramount to investigate how a post-GDP economic and political order may look and how it may be brought about. The goal of this book is to show the implications that a post-GDP system of governance would have on our economies, our political systems and the international order.

A new narrative for the twenty-first century

Needless to say, this is not the first book projecting how current trends may affect the social, economic and political order in the future.

Scholars of social sciences have traditionally offered alternative scenarios, some of which have been characterized by optimistic projections while others have largely embraced pessimism.[12] The end of the Cold War, for instance, triggered a series of 'visionary' accounts of a post-bipolar international order. One dominant account – associated with political scientist Francis Fukuyama – depicted the triumph of western capitalism over the socialist experience in the East as ushering humanity into 'the end of history', that is, a phase of stability, homogeneity and rampant growth.[13] Such thesis viewed the dominance of markets and the push towards economic globalization as evidence of a post-ideological global melting pot dominated by limitless consumption streams. A second account, much to the contrary, maintained that the end of the bipolar order would open up the possibility for fragmentation and the resurgence of cultural and religious conflicts. In his bestselling *Clash of Civilizations*, Samuel Huntington anticipated much of the inward-looking demands put forward by social groups inspired by cultural cleavages as well as the resurgence of terrorism and religious fundamentalism underpinning such political claims. The attacks on the World Trade Center on 11 September 2001 powerfully exemplified these two opposite visions, with the symbol of global market globalization directly targeted by forces inspired by religious fundamentalism, thus questioning the apparent uniformity of the new global order.

Broadly speaking, trying to predict social transformations (and analysing what may cause them) has always been the ultimate ambition of social scientists. Not only political breakthroughs, but also development trajectories have inspired a considerable number of writings outlining risks and opportunities for the future. Famously, in *An Essay on the Principle of Population*, the British political economist Thomas Malthus predicted that demographic growth would make consumption habits unsustainable, resulting in social instability and hampering poor people's hopes to achieve higher living standards. By predicting famine, war and extermination if population growth was not kept in check, he went down in history as the prototypical advocate of restrictive economic policies. The biologist Paul Ehrlich resumed the demographic theme almost two centuries later, in the 1960s, with the bestselling book *The Population Bomb*, which predicted large-scale global starvation and a series of ecological crises if consumption levels and demographic trends were not brought to lower, more sustainable and equitable levels. The *Limits to Growth* report to the Club of Rome published in 1972 applied a similar perspective to a variety of economic sectors, concluding that resource depletion, environmental degradation and economic collapse would have been inevitable without reforms that limited consumption levels and restrained countries' economic growth.[14] Geographer Jared Diamond popularized such a perspective through his work on the success or collapse of previous civilizations, showing how ecological dynamics matter a great deal in determining social order and resilience over time.[15] Intellectuals affiliated with the 'de-growth' movement have often linked their critique of a consumption-based society with the design of different social orders built on community life and reciprocity.[16]

The 'limits' literature has had a fundamental impact on contemporary social psyche and public debate (e.g. *Limits to Growth* sold more than 30 million copies, Diamond won the Pulitzer Prize and Ehrlich remains one of the most cited ecologists of our time). Since then, the world's leading scientific journal, *Nature*, has published a series of research papers focusing on planetary boundaries and ecological thresholds, while civil society organizations like the Ecological Footprint Network have designed global indicators to assess the extent to which societies operate within natural limits, with other groups complementing such ecosystem focus with indicators of social needs.[17]

This research work significantly contributed to building environmental awareness in the population and strengthening public regulations in terms of conservation policies, safeguard mechanisms and precautionary principles. At the same time, this ecological turn was met with hostility from economically conservative camps, especially among supporters of neoliberal economic policies. For instance, in the 1980s, Ehrlich's thesis was publicly challenged by economist Julian Simon. What came to be known as the Simon–Ehrlich wager occurred in the pages of the journal *Social Science Quarterly*, where Simon challenged Ehrlich to bet on the future prices of rare commodities, such as copper, chromium, nickel, tin and tungsten, as indicators of imminent resource depletion. Eventually, Ehrlich lost the bet as the price of these five commodities declined between 1980 and 1990, thus running counter to the depletion thesis, although subsequent studies showed that Ehrlich's argument would have been victorious had other commodities been included in the bet or had the time frame been extended by another twenty years.[18]

Simon's chief argument – that human beings are naturally prone to innovation and will always find new ways to replace depleted resources with new discoveries – has become quite prominent among defenders of the inherent virtues of the market economy, in particular as it has provided a powerful reason to deregulate the economy and support the expansion of capitalism globally.[19] More recently, these arguments have been put forward by a number of opponents to global climate change agreements, who believe that accelerated economic growth is the best way to advance technologies and discoveries that will help humanity in the future.[20] Advocates of green economy transitions have straddled both camps, arguing for industrial transformations but mostly through harnessing business innovation and entrepreneurship rather than top-down regulations.[21]

The focus on technology has animated a lot of debate recently, particularly among those interested in the intersection between technical shifts and economic structures. In many ways, this debate is reminiscent of Schumpeter's classical argument that 'creative destruction' is a fundamental component of capitalism, ultimately allowing it to continuously re-invent itself. In his book *Capitalism 4.0*, former business expert at the *Economist* Anatole Kaletsky argues that the 2007–2008 financial crises challenged the neoliberal global economic order, but not capitalism per se. The crises indeed triggered shifts towards a new form of capitalism, dominated by both government control and market innovation. Others take the argument about the capitalist order even further. Jeremy Rifkin, for instance, has postulated that the convergence of internet-based communication systems and renewable energy sources is triggering a new industrial revolution, leading to profound changes in corporate strategies, the demise of fossil fuels and the possibility for individuals and households to produce energy and share it across smart grids.[22] Former *Wired* magazine editor Chris Anderson agrees that new manufacturing technologies are challenging conventional industrial systems, especially in so far as they allow micro-producers to compete with large corporations through ever more sophisticated 3D printers.[23] In a 2015 book called *Post-Capitalism: A Guide to Our Future*, journalist Paul Mason describes how a 'sharing economy', based on peer-to-peer collaboration, is gradually supplanting conventional corporations organized along the principles of competition, economies of scale and mass production and consumption. According to Rifkin, these technological changes are challenging the very nature of the capitalist order and have the potential to bring about a new social, political and economic system based on open access and sharing.[24]

My book builds on these debates by moving the argument to the next level. Ecologists are right about the environmental (and, by extension, the planetary) boundaries that must not be violated by human actions, lest tipping points may be reached and cascading destruction activated. Similarly, economists are right about the capacity that human beings have to innovate and re-invent the structures in which they operate. Technologists are equally correct in pointing out how new inventions are fundamentally altering conventional production and consumption processes, opening up unprecedented possibilities.

What all these accounts neglect is the role played by institutional systems in guiding or hampering social change. Companies are rewarded exclusively for the profits they generate, with little or no regard for their impacts on ecosystems: thus managers have an incentive to exploit resources even when their conscience would dictate otherwise. Governments are expected to do anything they can to achieve good investment ratings, which are based on questionable econometric parameters and considerations of financial returns: thus they push for more consumption, extraction, exploitation and appropriation of natural resources, even when most citizens would favour socially and ecologically sustainable policies. Those communities, families and individuals interested in social and ecological change are constantly faced with a paradox: they recognize they need for new models of equitable and sustainable development, yet they operate according to old rules designed to do the opposite. This makes the transaction costs associated with change extremely high, with most people becoming complacent about the status quo despite their level of ecological consciousness, propensity to innovation and appreciation for technological advancements. All these paradoxes are fed by the institutional system based on GDP, which hampers change even now that all critical conditions seem to be present. This is why replacing GDP through a new institutional data system would not just be a statistical reform: it would be the crucial institutional trigger we need to make change happen by connecting the push for an ecological transition with the immense potential for human innovation and the radical applications afforded by new technologies. The wind of change is mounting, but to sail we need to remove the institutional ropes that are still keeping the boat tied to the shore.

Unlike other books, which have imagined the technological transition to sustainable development or have produced pure manifestos for new economic progress, *The World After GDP* focuses on both the economic and the political implications of a 'post-GDP' system of governance. This is a realistic scenario, based on new systems of accounting for countries and businesses, current demands by social innovators and civil society and pragmatic proposals largely shared by major international institutions from the OECD to the World Bank. This is not a critique of economic growth per se, as some advocates of 'de-growth' have undertaken; it is, rather, an analysis of how our politics and economics have been affected by the GDP-based narrow definition of growth and how the future may need us to re-conceptualize growth and progress in a way that is compatible with our aspirations and challenges in the twenty-first century.

An institutional approach to power

It is commonplace to think about the economy as something separate from the world of social relations. The idea of 'the market' as a geographic location has contributed to this perception: the economy has come to be understood as a space outside the state, family, community and the public in general. The classical concept of supply and demand, which is common to all economics textbooks, has also reinforced the notion that the economy is a somewhat special sphere where prices are indicators of value. According to this perception, the economy's unique task is to generate wealth, which the 'outside' world can benefit from. Even a Marxist perspective identifies the economy as separate from the rest of society. While it recognizes that the forces and relations of production (what Marx calls the base or infrastructure) have a fundamental impact on the social superstructure, it does not fully capture the importance that economic rules of interaction have on structuring order throughout society.

The dominant view of the economy as a separate reality has also been instrumental in motivating free market reforms. It is indeed evident that, if we accept the fact that the economy is nothing other than a space where supply meets demand for the creation of value, then its autonomy should be respected and nurtured. If we accept that the economy is a separate sphere characterized by a specific objective (value creation), then we would also agree that it should be run according to its own rules, in full autonomy from other spheres of collective action.

Such a representation of the economy is comforting to many as it implies that economic systems are nothing less than technical tools for value creation, devoid of social, cultural and anthropological bias. The reality, however, is that the economy is a vague concept, mostly fictitious, and its 'borders' are an arbitrary abstraction at best.[25] For instance, the separation between for-profit and non-profit activities is extremely fuzzy, and so is the assumption that public and private interests can be easily disentangled. This book argues that the economy is not a separate sphere or space but a complex decision-making system. The economy allocates and distributes resources, attributes roles and responsibilities, generates incentives for compliance and ultimately creates order by guiding collective action. In this regard, it is not different from politics or from any other form of social coordination.

As a decision-making system, it affects the rules that guide behaviour in general, thus contributing to shaping political and social dynamics too. The idea of separation is confusing because it assumes that the economy is neutral to the type of social order in which it takes place. It is also misleading because it suggests that political and social institutions can evolve with an equal degree of autonomy, regardless of processes underpinning the functioning of the economy. The separation approach is, of course, blind to the fact that economic actors can actively influence political choices and social preferences, a well-known problem in many so-called democracies. What is more concerning, however, is that this approach neglects a subtle yet powerful phenomenon: the very rules driving the economy also contribute to shaping, at times directly and at times indirectly, the rules governing society at large. As a matter of fact, economic rules are generally more powerful than political decisions at establishing social order. For instance, most people spend more time behaving like workers and consumers than they spend being voters, community members or families. Day-to-day actions, including time management, individual and social schedules, food choices, resource allocations, as well as a myriad of activities that occupy centre stage in a person's life, such as shopping and household maintenance, are deeply influenced by economic parameters and considerations, probably more so than they are guided by political or cultural beliefs. In his book *Capitalism 3.0*, Peter Barnes makes a similar argument, comparing the economy to a computer's leading software, the operating system:

> An operating system is a set of instructions that orchestrates the moving parts of a larger system. The most familiar example is a computer operating system that coordinates the keyboard, screen, processor, and so on. Operating system instructions are

written in code that can reside in electrons (as in a computer), chemicals (as in genes), or social norms and laws. Frequently, parts of the code can be expressed mathematically. [. . .] I like to think of our economic operating system as analogous to the rules of the board game *Monopoly*. It defines such things as starting conditions, rules of play, and the distribution of rewards and risk. It defines them partly through law, and partly by assigning fictional things called *property* and *money*.[26]

The economy as a decision-making system is therefore a powerful contributor to social order. In modern societies, most people's behaviours are moulded by direct and indirect incentives as well as logics generated by the economy. The collective coordination we experience every day is largely an effect of economic decisions that we have internalized more or less consciously: we go to work, pitch up in time for meetings, produce and consume in a predictable fashion and develop preferences among a variety of choices mostly because of the economic rules that have been embedded in our collective behavioural code. This is true for any type of economic system. Whether centralized or distributed, enforced through command and control or through utility and self-interest, all economic systems have a profound influence on people's individual and collective attitudes and preferences, ultimately determining human behaviour in a variety of ways. As the political economist Karl Polanyi argued, the human economy is nothing else than 'an instituted process'.[27] In the words of Moses Abramovitz, one of the early critics of GDP, 'an economy is a mode of social cooperation based on a system of rewards and incentives.'[28]

In the contemporary economic 'operating system', GDP is a powerful ordering principle. Like software, it decides which activities and objectives can 'run' on the system and which ones cannot, by setting very arbitrary but influential production and asset boundaries. Whatever function is performed through an alternative 'code' is simply not registered by the system: the file is corrupt and cannot be read. In a word, it does not exist. For instance, the food cooked at a restaurant and purchased by customers is registered as part of a nation's economy, while the same food cooked at home and shared with family and guests is not. Chopping and selling trees adds to the economy, but growing them does not. GDP equates value with money, thus representing the economy as a set of transactions regardless of whether these make a positive contribution to development. Health-care costs, insurance payments for accidents and post-disaster reconstruction are considered of economic value. Prevention and resilience are not. GDP also hides the so-called 'externalities', which are surreptitiously eliminated from considerations of economic performance. Consequently, the pollution and waste, as well as the social disruptions caused by the dominant industrial model, are conveniently obscured or even counted as positive drivers of growth when they trigger public or private expenses. Similarly, the positive non-monetary contributions of small businesses and cooperatives, which are notoriously less polluting and more socially integrated than large corporations, are not given any relevance in the economic rules of the game. As only GDP-based transactions count, the operating system is titled in favour of large wasteful production at the expense of shared economic activities.

Against this background, can the shift towards a post-GDP system of economic governance help build a new operating system for society? The answer is 'yes', provided that we understand GDP as a powerful institutional framework which has shaped incentives, policies, perceptions and behaviours. Understanding GDP as an essential cog in the economic machine establishing the current 'rules of the game' opens up enormous possibilities for institutional change. Indeed, by reframing current definitions of economic growth and profit, by redesigning the role of business, by connecting formal and informal production, by identifying the actual drivers of sustainable prosperity and well-being, the post-GDP operating system may provide a major opportunity for progressive forces in society to pursue alternative governance processes not only through moral and social justice arguments, but also on sound economic grounds.

From a theoretical perspective, this book builds on the new institutionalism approach popularized by the economist Douglass North, recipient of the Nobel Prize in Economics in 1993, and pioneered in political science by scholars such as James March and Johan Olsen. According to North, institutions are 'the rules of the game in a society' or, more formally, they are 'humanly devised constraints that shape human interaction'.[29] What is meant by rules is 'the routines, procedures, conventions, roles, strategies, organizations forms, and technologies around which [. . .] activity is constructed'.[30] The particular power of these rules is that they 'structure incentives in human exchange, whether political, social, or economic'.[31] A vast array of behaviours and actions we observe in governance processes every day simply reflects the routine way in which 'people do what they are supposed to do': 'Simple stimuli trigger complex, standardized patterns of action without extensive analysis, problem solving, or use of discretionary power.'[32]

The realization that a certain division of roles, with their associated norms and values, is a critical factor in the creation of social order has been part and parcel of modern sociological studies since, at least, the seminal work of Emile Durkheim in *The Division of Labour in Society*. For Talcott Parsons, who followed Durkheim, social systems acquire stability because of their adaptation to the underlying distribution of resources, because of their capacity to develop collective goals, because of the integration among the units of the system and because of the latency in creating and transmitting social norms. His focus on adaptation, goal, integration and latency (the so-called AGIL model) made him conclude that the structure of society was a manifestation of the interaction among different types of organizations, starting with the creators of wealth and resources (business) and permeating the rest through the goals identified by governments, the integration achieved by associations and the maintenance of social patterns guaranteed by cultural institutions.[33] These founding social norms are then transmitted from generation to generation through a process known as 'socialization', reinforced through imitation, peer approval and rewards, which generate self-reinforcing feedback loops. This institutional structure is reflected in the sociobiological organization of animal species (including humans), which pass on institutional mechanisms, both vertically, from parents to offspring, as well as horizontally, through interaction with other individuals and groups, including epigenetic information, that is, the transmission of non-genetic institutional artefacts across generations.[34]

As I have argued elsewhere, statistics have an institutional power, especially when they are applied to social conduct and governance.[35] Performance assessments, for instance, influence our behaviour at work, even when we disagree with their underlying principles. Credit ratings constrain obligation-issuing authorities like governments or private companies, even when they are broadly contested by society. Their power derives from the so-called 'logic of appropriateness', which affects a behaviour that is 'intentional but not wilful', given that actions stem from 'a conception of necessity'.[36]

GDP is the most powerful statistic ever invented. It is not just a number, but the ultimate objective of policy and a global benchmark for success. It has not only been essential to generating the current 'rules' of governance, but it also enjoys an ideational power throughout society. As citizens, businesses and policy makers have internalized the conception of 'value' underpinned by GDP, a particular set of ideas, beliefs and expectations have come to acquire legitimacy in society, while others have been delegitimized. When this concept is 'institutionalized', either through formal policies or social norms, it acquires a 'universal' validity. As maintained by Mugge, 'Institutionalizing a particular definition of a macroeconomic concept in an indicator gives that definition power, both because it becomes more consequential and because it elevates this definition to the universal one, obscuring that definitional choices had ever been made.'[37]

Dominant discourses frame logics of appropriateness, establish consequences for (non)compliance and help predict behaviours, thus impacting institutional processes. A discursive institutionalist perspective shows three ways in which ideational power occurs: through persuasion of normative validity of a certain worldview; through the imposition of certain ideas while shaming opponents into conformity; and through the formal institutionalization of certain beliefs.[38] The convergence of historical factors (specifically the Great Depression and the Second World War) as well as the emergence of neoclassical economic theory and economic globalization, have afforded GDP an unprecedented ideational power as the 'lens' through which politics, business and society decide what 'counts' for development and what policy choices are acceptable.

How change can happen

GDP has become part of governance operating systems partly through coercion and partly through persuasion. Laws, regulations, ratings and treaties have incorporated GDP into our formal institutional mechanisms. Performance assessments, advertising, public discourse, the media and a consumption-based culture have embedded it into our informal social relations. Its inherent focus on market transactions, economies of scale, top-down control and clear separation between production and consumption have deeply contributed to designing the type of economy and, by extension, the type of society in which most people live, from North America to Europe, Asia and Africa.

But there are alternatives to this state of affairs. As Elinor Ostrom has shown in her Nobel-fame path-breaking work, hierarchical control over economic processes is not necessarily the most efficient and enduring model of governance.[39] Throughout history, communities of different cultural, ethnic and religious profiles have developed formal and informal institutions that have challenged top-down mechanisms and economies of scale to build effective systems of shared governance, based on co-design and co-management. By studying community-based models created to manage common pool resources (the so-called 'commons'), she demonstrated that the design of institutions is key to understanding the functioning of any system of economic governance. While certain rules, technologies and belief systems can support highly hierarchical models of governance (as GDP does), others can challenge this state of affairs by helping participants shift perceptions and operating logics. Alternative institutions based on the value of sharing, reciprocity and mutual benefits, especially if accompanied by effective systems of rewards and sanctions that discourage free-riding, can allow communities of users to self-manage economic interactions, even in the absence of an external, top-down authority.

By extension, this book's argument is that, if we break the dominance of GDP's logic of appropriateness and perception of value, we can build horizontal institutions of shared governance, with the relevant systems of rewards and sanctions, thus changing incentives and behaviours. External factors can further help this transition. As highlighted in the peer-to-peer literature (which I will discuss in greater detail in chapters 3 and 4), new communication technologies and innovative mechanisms of production and distribution based on network collaboration can support this institutional shift to a post-GDP system of governance, bringing progressive forces in business and civil society on board. In this vein, the socio-economic-political critique of GDP has the potential to erode the current 'institutional' system, resulting in a new system of preferences, behaviours and interests across society and affording political and social actors a new platform to build an alternative 'institutional' trajectory for society.

Institutions guarantee stability and continuity. According to Campbell, they are 'the foundation of social life':

> They consist of formal and informal rules, monitoring and enforcement mechanisms, and systems of meaning that define the context within which individuals, corporations, labor unions, nation-states, and other organizations operate and interact with each other. [. . .] They reflect the resources and power of those who made them and, in turn, affect the distribution of resources and power in society.[40]

Yet, to survive in dynamic environments, they have to adapt: 'Not all rules are necessarily good ones, least of all indefinitely . . . some currently "surviving" rules are in the process of disappearing.'[41] Analysts of institutional change place emphasis on two different logics, namely the evolutionary process of gradual adaptation versus the punctuated equilibrium of disruptive critical junctures. Proponents of the former argue that processes of change usually occur piecemeal and over long periods of time. They maintain that path dependencies and gradualism also drive most episodes that look revolutionary at first glance.[42] The opposite position highlights the significance of ruptures in embedded routines and opportunities for institutional entrepreneurs to radically alter the future course of events. In this regard, change is explained in terms of 'punctuated equilibrium', particularly when the 'deep structure' is fundamentally contested and ultimately replaced by a new configuration, resulting in a new equilibrium.[43] An important role in breaking this inertia is played by newcomers to the field, who are better suited to question commonly accepted routines than the representatives of the orthodoxy. As argued by Kuhn in his classical study on scientific revolutions, crises of meaning and explanatory capacity also matter as they make a system's deep structure obsolete, thus generating disequilibria and opening space for the establishment of a new paradigm.[44] Evolutionary economics indeed postulates that complex exchanges within and across the system 'bring about novel, emergent and unpredictable forms and events' and that there are 'no hermetic analytical boundaries between the social and natural world'.[45]

Systems science confirms the non-linearity of change. Operating systems in nature and society are in a continuous state of non-equilibrium, although they may display order characterized by regular collective behaviours. They may appear static, but they actually never settle down to a steady, unchanging condition. Think of a pile of sand, a metaphor usually employed to describe self-organized criticality, a mechanism by which complexity emerges in nature. With no fresh input or energy, the pile becomes static. But if grains are continually dropped from above, the various slopes keep on reshaping themselves, growing and steepening, only to be eroded by avalanches of grains that might partly affect the contours of the pile or wash it out completely. Each of these events is like a cascade in which rolling grains collide with each other, dislodging the structure they themselves contribute to shaping. Statistical physics, a branch of the natural sciences focusing on macro masses rather than atoms and molecules, also points to the existence of thresholds capable of triggering discontinuous change. Minor drops of temperature below zero are enough to radically change the state of water from liquid to solid, even when the underlying state of its components, atoms and molecules, does not change. What these 'phased transitions' show is the incredible power of interactions and relations within systems that can lead to radical transformation.

According to the former editor of *Nature*, Philip Ball, complex systems are typically affected by threshold effects whereby a sudden change in institutional rules can affect the overall behaviour of the system 'by only small change in the governing parameters'. Moreover, these changes are non-linear, 'meaning that the magnitude of an effect doesn't necessarily follow in proportion to its cause'.[46] They can only be 'guided [. . .] by tweaking the conditions or the rules of interaction'.[47] Institutional processes, no matter how sophisticated, are always incomplete. Exploiting the incompleteness of stable processes is essential to promote change. A first element in this regard has to do with 'attention'. According to March and Olsen, existing rules make us selective as to which aspects of the political, economic and social process we pay attention to: 'What happens depends on which rule is evoked, which action is imitated, which value is considered, which competitors are mobilized, which opportunities are seen, which problems and solutions are connected, or which worldview is considered.'[48] So, one important step in shifting attention is to *make the invisible visible*. This is what 'post-GDP' scholars and activists are trying to achieve. By building alternative indicators and using them to affect public discourse and institutional processes, they are shifting the attention of policy makers, opinion leaders and citizens to hitherto invisible sectors and processes in the economy. At the same time, their objective is to erode the credibility of GDP as the chief governance benchmark by showing its inconsistencies, flawed assumptions and inherent weaknesses.

After several decades of being limited to expert circles, the critique of GDP has now reached a level of institutional maturity, triggering the establishment of high-level commissions and informing the work of various UN agencies, the World Bank and numerous national governments. Since 2015, with the ratification of the SDGs, the need to move beyond GDP has become a fundamental requirement for the international community, finally opening a window of opportunity to promote radical change. With the convergence of economic, social and environmental crises, the threshold has been reached.

But how can change happen? The political economy approach of this book can be described as the 'sandwich' represented in Figure 1.1. At the top level, the institutionalization of the SDGs, climate change regulations, renewable energy policies and statistical reforms (currently mandated by national governments, the UN statistics division and the OECD, as well as regional groupings like the European Union) is expected to influence policy-making processes in at least two ways: firstly, by providing alternative benchmarks for the assessment of economic policy; secondly, by stimulating different reputational mechanisms, both for politicians and for nations. This process will influence (and will be further reinforced by) the introduction of post-GDP indicators, thus shifting policy focus away from the maximization of output with a view to questioning certain forms of production and consumption, as well as their impacts on equity, social well-being and sustainable development. For instance, all indicators presently discussed within the SDG institutional processes require policy makers to

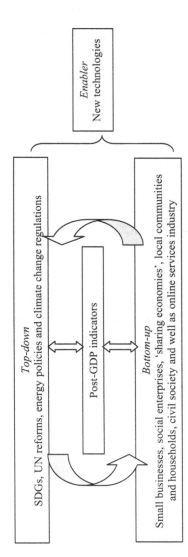

Figure 1.1 How post-GDP indicators connect top-down trends and bottom-up pressures

Source: author own.

seriously reconsider their investment in fossil fuels, while all aggregate measures for assessment of natural capital demonstrate the uneconomic nature of extractive industries. The alternative indices that I will discuss in chapter 2, such as the genuine progress indicator or the social progress index, also boost the economic relevance of household activities, community work and social capital, while the UN-backed Inclusive Wealth Index downplays the importance of the produced output measured by GDP, highlighting the essential contribution to development made by human and natural capital. As international rankings based on these new indicators begin to boost the reputation of certain countries traditionally marginalized by GDP, we may see the formation of innovative alliances and forums, which could complement or challenge traditional GDP-based groupings such as the G7 or the G20,[49] given that benchmarking has a powerful impact on international politics too.[50]

Similarly, business leaders may find themselves under increasing pressure to embark on sustainable development trajectories, as current trends in integrated reporting already show. As I will discuss in chapter 3, the introduction of total cost accounting (which measures both social and environmental costs, thereby 'internalizing externalities') will demonstrate how many large industries (especially the big polluters) take away wealth from society, rather than adding to it as is conventionally portrayed by the GDP accounts.

The introduction of new indicators will thus be a consequence of and, at the same time, a booster for policy reforms. By giving visibility to hitherto invisible practices, it may not only promote change at the top but may also reinforce innovation at the bottom, supporting social innovators, alternative business practices and civil society movements. Strengthened by 'numbers' that depict a very different type of economic growth, small businesses, cooperatives and socially minded enterprises will be more likely to demand a central role in value creation through society. Civil society groups will also challenge the conventional GDP-based classification of for-profit versus non-profit, which has traditionally relegated the so-called 'voluntary sector' to a marginal role. Moreover, as post-GDP indicators reveal the hidden costs in conventional production processes, many arguments traditionally put forward by civil society may start becoming mainstream. Some of these would include the environmental costs of coal mining and oil drilling (thus making the economic argument for a ban on fossil fuels), as well as the social costs of large distribution processes, whether for food, energy, consumer goods or other large-scale commercial activities. The traditional justice-based arguments put forward by many social movements will therefore be reinvigorated by the new metrics which will add evidence-based econometric arguments too. A new system of accounting and financial reporting may have an effect on the media as well, starting with business newspapers, which will be expected to report on how companies fare according to alternative indicators, thus contributing to depicting the economy and society in a different light.

As mentioned earlier, the connection between the top and the bottom of the 'sandwich' made possible by post-GDP indicators can be further facilitated by new technological advancements. In the past decade, we have witnessed an explosion of technological processes, from digital communication to 3D printing as well as open-source software and hardware, which have challenged conventional vertical structures of production, turned consumers into producers and generated synergies across sectors.[51] Thanks to this technological revolution, collaborative systems organized horizontally and distributed across society can outsmart conventional proprietary systems of production. Communication systems and data-sharing platforms would allow small businesses to compete with large companies while reducing social and environmental costs. As I will discuss in subsequent chapters, one of the crucial flaws of GDP is its inability to capture the dynamic value embedded in all sorts of innovations, especially when they reduce costs, distribute access and increase what economists call 'consumer surplus'. Whether it is Silicon Valley giants like Google and Facebook, 'sharing economy' rising stars like Airbnb and Uber, the millions of small businesses operating in communities across the world or any household interested in a system of rules that respects the multifaceted ways in which human beings can bring value to society, all these actors have a vested interest in questioning the power of GDP and moving to a different, more comprehensive operating system. As the top and the bottom sides of the 'sandwich' press for change, they further reinforce each other, opening space for radical transformation. This is precisely how the civil rights movement succeeded in its demands vis-à-vis the US institutional establishment. When, in 1944, minorities' representatives approached President Roosevelt to embed their rights in the UN consultations that would lead to the ratification of the Universal Declaration of Human Rights, he candidly said: 'Okay, you have convinced me. Now go out and bring pressure on me!'[52] The same strategy was adopted by President Johnson and Martin Luther King in bringing policy reform and civil society pressure together to pass the Civil Rights Act of 1964. It is a circular process of influence: not only are policy openings the outcome of social pressures, but they also trigger additional pressures throughout society, which open up further possibilities for institutional change. Indicators can be crucial tools to connect the dots in this circle of influence.

The window of opportunity we currently face is unprecedented. Because of top-down and bottom-up pressures, which are aided by a technological revolution disrupting conventional processes of production and consumption, governance systems may undergo a non-linear transformation with far-reaching implications. Just as the standardization of GDP during the twentieth century triggered all sorts of institutional consequences, a new system of accounting may very well provide opportunities for radical change from the local level to the global sphere. The non-linearity of the process is further supported by the fact that changes in the economic rules (our 'operating system') are likely to generate a fertile ground for shifts in political rules, which in turn will create positive feedback loops for further evolutions in the underlying economic principles of the social order. The shift to a post-GDP world will thus increase openness and disrupt conventional hierarchies in economic and political institutions, which may contribute to exponential opportunities for transformation by dispersing power throughout society. Leadership itself, a crucial factor in social change, is likely to become increasingly dispersed, generating a constellation of pockets of evolution through which the entire system can learn, evolve and adapt.

As in all complex systems, there is no guarantee that these mutually reinforcing processes will lead in the desired direction. Powerful forces interested in preserving the status quo will invest in derailing or minimizing change. As March and Olsen remind us, an anomaly of adaptive institutions 'is the tendency for innovations to be transformed during the process of adoption'.[53] Some of the post-GDP metrics may be altered, revised, obfuscated and ultimately depleted of their innovative potential: 'By shaping a change to make it more consistent with existing procedures and practices, institutions maintain stability in the face of pressure to change.'[54]

As I will discuss in the Conclusion, this is precisely why we should be hesitant to trade GDP with another almighty benchmark of success.[55] A number of scholars have warned against replacing a myopic institutional performance system with one that is less myopic but equally technocratic and difficult to adapt to different needs. The Stiglitz–Sen–Fitoussi commission, for instance, recommended the introduction of dashboards to avoid the reductionism inherent in the process of aggregating different phenomena and trends into one single index. The OECD has introduced a set of indicators of societal progress that users can weigh according to their views and needs. The social progress index allows for the customization of which dimensions are deemed more important for societal success by any country, region or city. Others have been advocating for the introduction of participatory accounting systems that allow social groups and civil society to collaborate with statisticians in deciding what matters for economic and social progress, as is the case with the Italian official survey *Benessere Equo e Sostenibile* (Equitable and Sustainable Well-Being).[56] From a system science perspective, collective leadership and distributed innovation are not only less amenable to capture by concentrated interests but are also more supportive of continuous change and adaptation, thus increasing resilience and sustainability.

Ultimately, the post-GDP world is just a possibility. Like all institutional processes, both bureaucratic inertia and the risk of co-optation are always present. Understanding how GDP has influenced our governance systems and our societal preferences is therefore an essential first step towards the development of new institutional mechanisms. And outlining the possibilities for transformation that a post-GDP system of accounting can offer is crucial to ensure that current changes will result in a meaningful transition towards a better and happier world for both humans and their ecosystems.

2

The Rise and Fall of GDP Ideology

We live in world dominated by economic decisions. Most of our daily activities, whether we reside in the supposedly wealthy global North or in the emerging or 'underdeveloped' South, are organized around principles of economic interaction. Roles, responsibilities and tasks in society are deeply influenced by economic considerations. It is our operating system, which contributes to generating social order through a series of formal and informal institutional processes.

In this context, it is not surprising that people are increasingly described through economic categories such as consumers, rather than socio-political denominations such as citizens. Consumption and production patterns do indeed contribute enormously to structuring coordination in society. Not all people in the world enjoy most citizenship rights, as many do not have the right to vote. Those who enjoy such freedom only exercise it sporadically, on average every two years, during national or local elections. By contrast, almost everybody around the world is a consumer. Not just sporadically but every day. With few exceptions (e.g. some aboriginal populations in South America, Africa and Oceania), the 'consumer' is today's dominant human characterization. In a society in which participation is mostly realized through consumption, the consumer is today's activist. This frame of reference has become very popular in public discourse, with the mushrooming of movements and civic groups performing activities and promoting goals traditionally associated with active citizenship but calling themselves 'consumer associations'.

In this operating system, the ultimate goal of society is to work collectively and in an orderly fashion towards increasing output, which is what is measured in GDP. As I discussed in the previous chapter, this is not just a number but a powerful institutional framework. It has become a crucial parameter to achieve social order and establish collective goals, thus reinforcing a vision of progress based on economies of scale and centralized governance. As remarked by Dirk Philipsen, author of *The Little Big Number: How GDP Came to Rule the World and What to Do about It*, 'GDP defines what we do and why we do it. And who we are. [. . .] In critical areas of our lives, it is the air we breathe, represents the language we speak.'[1]

Technocracy, a dominating factor in current political systems, has also been reinforced by the institutional influence of GDP as the definition of rules and goals of collective action has largely been taken out of public debate. GDP growth has become the policy goal of virtually all countries around the world, with most political parties and movements accepting it as given. While alternative political forces compete for authority over marginal reforms, the very management of a country's development is in the hands of technocrats, from central bankers to treasury officials and international financial institutions. Finance ministers are often more accountable to private financial actors than they are to their constituencies, and this is largely praised as a sign of good governance. When democratically elected governments challenge the institutional power of macroeconomic benchmarks, as has been the case for Greece in 2015, they are coerced into obedience, despite referenda and public consultations.

GDP was introduced into public governance mechanisms in the early twentieth century and gradually came to dominate political processes around the world. It has played a fundamental role not only in countries characterized by strong market economies (e.g. the United States), but also in command and control economies (e.g. China, but also during the last years of the Soviet Union), in countries inspired by more socio-democratic and solidaristic values (e.g. in Europe, where GDP was given legal power through the Stability and Growth Pact) and in most 'developing' nations. Criticized by some experts throughout the previous century, it has only become the target of institutional critique since the early 2000s, when a number of high-level commissions and corrective initiatives were launched. This chapter charts the history of GDP, discusses the many ways in which this almighty number was integrated into national and global policy processes and analyses how it contributes to defining the contemporary operating system of society.

The rise of GDP ideology

The ambition to measure economic prosperity has been part of human activities since time immemorial, mostly because of its intimate relationship with the perception of power. In ancient civilizations, the display of prosperity took the form of sumptuous infrastructure, religious temples, royal tombs, elite academies and public-gathering spaces, like circuses and forums. It was also evident in the strength of the military apparatus, as well as the scale of arsenals and ammunitions. Empires associated prosperity with land and the revenues therein, hence their continuous drive to expand domination and jurisdiction over the territory. In modern times, after the formation of kingdoms following the collapse of the great empires, royal gold reserves became the key indicators of prosperity: it was the monarch and its personal property to benchmark a country's wealth, an approach aided by the introduction of modern taxation systems and fledgling interstate commerce.[2] For instance, the British economist William Petty developed an early survey of national wealth by measuring the value of land and the properties therein (including housing, cattle, etc.) for Oliver Cromwell after the British invasion of Ireland in the seventeenth century. This approach was then retained by subsequent monarchs as a useful tool to manage the inflow of tax revenues. Petty's survey was clearly designed not only to support the state in its internal control of productive activities, but also to project Britain's external image as an ascending power.[3] The French scientist Antoine Lavoisier, who is commonly considered the father of modern chemistry, developed the first prototype of national accounts in France in the late 1700s to support customs and excise operations for the king. Napoleon Bonaparte used economic surveys to provide specific information on citizens with a view to making military conscription more effective while strengthening the state's capacity to collect taxes, as well as to design better ways to manage the economy in wartime.[4]

With the industrial revolutions of the eighteenth and nineteenth centuries, the concept of prosperity came to be increasingly associated with industrial development. Classical economists such as Adam Smith and David Ricardo challenged the traditional notion of wealth as immobile property, including land and gold, by postulating the idea that productive capacity was the real indicator of economic success. For Smith, the 'wealth of nations' was to be found in the 'industry' of individuals, whether owners of private capital or labourers, whose activities resulted in that national income 'ultimately destined for supplying the consumption of its inhabitants'.[5] All other functions in society, from the bureaucratic system to all types of public institutions, were of no economic value for Smith, as they 'are maintained by a part of the annual produce of the industry of other people'.[6] Labour and capital were also the key indicators of prosperity for Ricardo, an approach endorsed by Karl Marx, according to whom societies 'obtain their share of the annual product of commodities [. . .] primarily only out of the hands of those classes who are the first to handle the product, that is to say, productive laborers, industrial capitalists, and real estate owners'.[7]

In a sense, all major economic transformations in history were preceded or, at least accompanied, by new approaches to measurement, which affected public perceptions as to which sectors of society were actually driving progress and prosperity and which sectors operated at the expense of others. It was the measurement of productivity that changed perceptions, eroded the traditional power of dominating elites (e.g. kings and aristocracies), emboldened the previously marginalized (e.g. the bourgeoisie and the working class), boosted their political and social demands and eventually led to a new institutional order. GDP was no exception.

The contemporary measurement of national income was developed in the 1930s.[8] It was the outcome of pioneering statistical work conducted concomitantly in the United States and in the United Kingdom, first formalized by a young economist by the name of Simon Kuznets, who would later receive a Nobel Prize for his research on economic growth and development. Kuznets presented the first report on the design of national accounts to the US Senate in 1934, building on decades of work conducted in the United Kingdom by economists such as Colin Clark in the late 1920s, and then followed by refinements made by Richard Stone and James Meade in the 1940s. All these scholars were profoundly influenced by John Maynard Keynes's approach to macroeconomic policy, which emphasized the key role played by governments in steering economic policy and demanded some overall statistical capacity to monitor the economy's inputs and outputs, so as to align policy stimuli accordingly. The Great Depression provided a fertile terrain for systemic change because it demonstrated the inefficiencies of a *laissez-faire* approach, with the US government headed by Herbert Hoover failing to weather the financial crash and the prolonged economic contraction of the early 1930s. When Roosevelt ascended to the presidency in 1933, his New Deal took an opposite stance, advocating a strong role for the state in economic governance. To succeed, however, the New Deal needed a system of constant monitoring of production and consumption patterns. By conflating the amount of spending for goods and services into one single number, the GDP – at the time known as national income produced and later Gross National Product – provided the answer. As the economy began to recover some steam, GDP became society's thermometer of success.

It was only in the 1940s, with the outbreak of the Second World War and its massive need for a top-down command over industrial production, that the relationship between GDP and governance was finally sealed. The American government indeed used its new national income accounts to devise a modern approach to war planning, vetting military strategies and munitions targets through a statistical examination of the domestic economy's productive capacity. The president's overarching war-planning initiative, the so-called Victory Program, was closely examined by Kuznets and his team using the GDP accounts. The involvement of economists in war-planning meetings was harshly opposed by the military command, but their statistical information proved essential to successfully converting the civilian economy into a war machine without hampering internal consumption.[9] Thanks to statistical planning, military procurement rose from 1.6 per cent of GDP in 1940 to 48 per cent in 1944 without civilian shortages of consumer goods. By mapping areas of industrial production that were under-exploited, the US economy managed to produce 300,000 planes, 124,000 ships of all types and more than 2.4 million military trucks during the same period.[10]

According to the popular economist John Kenneth Galbraith, GDP statistics were the equivalent of 'several infantry divisions in their contribution to the American war effort'.[11] For Clifford Cobb, Ted Halstead and Jonathan Rowe, leading critics of the national income accounts in the 1990s through their work at the think tank Redefining Progress, the degree to which GDP acquired power 'as a war-planning tool is hard to exaggerate'.[12] Based on its impact on America's comparative advantage in the war, they equate it to the Manhattan Project, which led to the invention of the nuclear bomb. Policy planning through GDP had turned out to be a formidable asset in successful war management. As the conflict wound down, the same accountants became powerful masters of governance decisions, allocating resources and labour to support a thriving consumer market: 'GDP accountants [. . .] seemed to possess the keys to prosperity. Long before the war was over, the logic of GDP growth grew into the central target of post-war planning.'[13]

The Bretton Woods Conference of 1944, which redesigned the world system and instituted international financial institutions such as the International Monetary Fund (IMF) and the International Bank for Reconstruction and Development (later incorporated into the World Bank), sealed GDP's footprint on global politics by elevating it to the global parameter of success.[14] The IMF was designed as a forum for the multilateral management of international monetary exchange, while the Bank was instituted to provide investment funds for infrastructure development in post-war areas in Europe and Asia, as well as in 'underdeveloped' nations, from Latin America to Africa. At Bretton Woods, the United States and the United Kingdom took a leading role through the representation of Harry Dexter White and John Maynard Keynes, who led their countries' delegations. Their leadership was instrumental to the integration of GDP into the operating systems of financial institutions, with the IMF using it as the key parameter to assess the stability of national economies and the World Bank adopting it as a benchmark of development to gauge the scale and interest rates of loans.[15] Similarly, the creation of the Organization for European Economic Cooperation, which helped administer the Marshall Plan, was instrumental in entrenching GDP across European governance systems in the late 1940s.[16] Then, in the 1950s, the UN published the first framework for the international System of National Accounts, which was largely based on a report drafted by Richard Stone, thereby exporting the approach developed in the United States and the United Kingdom to the rest of the world and entrenching GDP even further as the 'gold standard' of economic governance.[17] Moreover, the wave of bilateral and multilateral development aid programmes that followed the end of colonialism in the 1960s also incorporated statistical technical cooperation into its packages with a view to training recipient countries from Africa to Asia and South America in the measurement of GDP as a necessary tool to drive national policy and gauge the attainment of economic development as well as the success of policies.[18]

The influence of GDP on international politics was further reinforced during the Cold War, when the contest between the United States and the Soviet Union revealed the deeply political nature of all measurements of economic performance. More than the arms race, it was the ambition to achieve prosperity that constituted the essence of the struggle between capitalism and socialism. Yet establishing prosperity required some commonly agreed way of measuring it. GDP had been invented to gauge the size and scope of market economies and was calculated in terms of market prices. The Soviet Union, by contrast, rejected the market economy and had developed a different metric, the so-called material product, which reflected the characteristics of a command economy and privileged some economic activities (e.g. production of goods) at the expenses of others (e.g. production of services) because the former were considered to constitute the backbone of the socialist economy. After a prolonged 'stats war', the Soviet Union decided to compile official GDP statistics in the late 1980s with the official purpose of supplementing the Marxist–Leninist-based indicators of industrial production with a view to facilitating international comparisons. At the same time, it may not have been coincidental that the adoption of GDP held the promise of helping 'massage' upward the plummeting numbers of economic output because of the rapid growth of the services sector.[19]

With the end of the Cold War, GDP became the only game in town. The triumph of western capitalism heralded in the 'end of history' also resulted in a set of statistical adjustments to capture the institutional shifts underpinning the global economic expansion of the time. While GDP had been traditionally focused on income produced by national economic actors (it was indeed conventionally referred to as gross national product, GNP), the new version adopted a 'domestic' focus, thus providing an institutional accounting system in support of neo-liberal economic globalization. Traditional GNP referred to all goods and services produced by the residents of a given country, regardless of whether the income had been generated within or outside its borders. It meant that, for instance, the earnings of a multinational corporation were attributed to the country where the firm was owned and where the profits would eventually return. With the introduction of the 'domestic' product, this calculation changed. GDP is indeed territorially defined, which means that the income generated by foreign companies is formally attributed to the country where they operate, although the profits may not remain there. This apparently insignificant reform contributed to reinforcing the dominant perception that globalization was in everybody's interests and that stronger trade ties held the potential to bring development everywhere. The very notion of an 'emerging market', which has become commonplace in today's jargon, should therefore be seen not only as a by-product of shifting production processes away from more industrialized economies towards hitherto 'underdeveloped' countries but also as the result of statistical reforms that suddenly recorded massive growths in output in the new sites of production. For some, this statistical reconfiguration simply hides the fact that 'the nations of the North are walking off with the South's resources, and calling it a gain for the South'.[20]

It was during this period that GDP was 'constitutionalized', that is, institutionally integrated into national and international policy documents. The European Union (EU) championed the policy formalization of GDP through the Stability and Growth Pact of 1992, which tied the member states' capacity to sustain public expenditure to the performance of their GDP (the so-called Maastricht criteria), a principle retained by the new Fiscal Compact, despite widespread criticisms about the cyclical implications of such policies, especially in times of crisis.[21] For the first time in history, a set of fixed ratios to GDP for public deficit (3 per cent) and debt (60 per cent) would acquire legal powers, with coercive measures to be applied in case of non-compliance. The new parameters would also dictate the contribution of member states to the common budget, establish priorities in terms of economic policies and gauge the affordability of social investment. Since 2000, the European common currency (the euro) and its economic area (the eurozone) have been greatly influenced by such parameters, often infringing the democratic accountability of elected governments. First of all, countries need a certain GDP 'profile' to access the common currency system. Secondly, macroeconomic management is deeply constrained by GDP trends, which can easily worsen economic contraction in times of crisis: a plummeting GDP means stricter conditions and less room to invest and stimulate the economy, which in turns undermines the recovery even further. Besides Europe, most countries around the world have implicitly accepted the rule of fixed GDP ratios with debt and deficit, a policy corroborated by the major credit rating agencies, always keen to downgrade countries that exceed such parameters.[22]

At the turn of the millennium, the US Department of Commerce held a major event to celebrate the invention of GDP as 'its achievement of the century'.[23] The Department saluted GDP as a powerful tool that allowed standardization of economic policies around the world and a common approach to macroeconomic success. In his official speech, the former chair of the Federal Reserve, Alan Greenspan, paraphrased Keynes's argument that the ideas of economists are more powerful than commonly understood by stating that 'data systems are more powerful and important than is commonly understood'.[24] Nobel laureates Paul Samuelson and William Nordhaus, also present at the event, argued in their *Economics* textbook that 'much like a satellite in space can survey the weather across an entire continent, so can the GDP give an overall picture of the state of the economy': 'The GDP and related data are like beacons that help policymakers steer the economy toward the key economic objectives.'[25]

GDP has become an extremely popular presence in public discourse. A cursory search on Google conducted in late 2016 gives about 120 million hits for 'gdp'. By contrast, 'human development' reaches 20 million hits, 'honesty' 80 million, 'well-being' 96 million and 'climate change' 111 million. These are all critically important issues for contemporary society, yet less talked about than GDP, at least in cyberspace. A search through the English publications stored in Google Books shows that GDP is a more common topic for intellectual and scientific publications than inequality, economic growth, sustainable development, climate change, well-being, gender equality and many other topics, with a steep curve of upward interest since the 1960s (Figure 2.1).

GDP as a dominant institutional framework

But is it really true that, as Samuelson and Nordhaus argue, GDP provides an overall picture of the state of the economy? Is it really a useful tool for decision making, whether in government, in business or in society at large? To answer these questions, we must analyse what this statistic is and how it has influenced societal perceptions, creating distorted logics of appropriateness and ultimately misleading decision makers and society at large. One of the powers of institutions is, indeed, their influence on 'the structure of meaning'.[26] This can be achieved through technologies that are precise, as is the case with measurements that establish 'success and failure', or through diffuse conceptualizations that define 'worldviews', 'visions of the nature of things' and 'legitimate authority'. The resulting institutional dynamics frame values, set boundaries, establish control and develop coercive mechanisms for compliance.

Framing value

GDP is a sum of market transactions. It uses prices as indicators of value, counting all formal exchanges in goods and services regardless

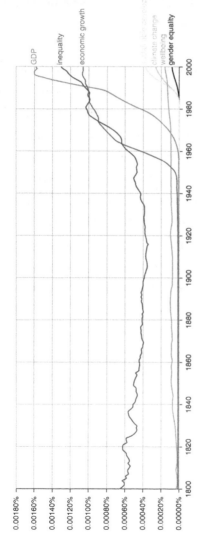

Figure 2.1 Popularity of GDP in books as compared to other key policy issues (percentage of occurrence out of entire Google Books database over the period 1800–2000).

Source: Google Books/Ngram Viever (checked on 30 June 2016)

of whether these are beneficial or detrimental to society. What is not transacted through the market or does not feature a formal price is implicitly considered of no economic value. This apparently technical prerequisite has a number of consequences for public perceptions of prosperity as well as for public policies.

First of all, official decisions tend to privilege a model of development that is biased against free resources and services, such as those provided by informal social interactions and natural ecosystems. In western societies, urban areas are constantly redesigned to suit the needs of the GDP-based economy, taking away space for activities that are free of charge to maximize opportunities for consumption. Incentives are provided for consumers to buy processed food (not to grow their own for free), to solicit external care for family members (rather than spend more time with them directly) and to disregard free natural services, such as fresh air and running water, often by substituting them with manufactured ones.

In his closing speech at the above-mentioned Department of Commerce's celebration, Greenspan dwelled on the risks of equating priced output with economic performance by referring to the everyday distinction between technologically conditioned air, which comes at a price, and a fresh breeze, which is provided free of charge by nature:

> I think we're all acutely aware of the fact that, for example, there are a number of southern states that use a huge amount of air conditioning in the summer and that appears as output in the GDP. The wonderful breeze you get up in northern Vermont during the summer, which eliminates the requirement for air conditioning, doesn't show up in the GDP. And other things equal, the standards of living are the same, but the GDP will be less in Vermont than it will be in the South.[27]

The problem is that GDP does not treat free resources as priceless but, rather, as valueless, despite their important contribution to economic success. This is very problematic, especially when it affects expectations and behaviours in society. To win elections, politicians must boast their capacity to grow GDP, which comes with both political and social rewards. Yet neither fresh air nor free time will do the trick. As a consequence, the state of Vermont may need to encourage its people to start buying air conditioners to cool their homes, even when natural cooling is the most economically (and ecologically) intelligent option. Local administrators faced with a choice between building a shopping centre, which increases the types of profits and expenditures counted by GDP, and a public park, which is for free use and thus not captured in GDP (although it may add enormously to the welfare of users and therefore contribute to society's overall economic performance), will need a lot of public pressure to choose the latter. It is no coincidence that recent decades have seen the spread of shopping centres, toll roads and parking areas, accompanied by the disappearance of public squares and parks which were a traditional characteristic of cities in both Europe and North America.

But the effects of the GDP-based perception of value have not been confined to the West. No other country has come to exemplify massive consumption and the development of costly entertainment areas more than China, where GDP has grown exponentially between the 1990s and the first decade of the 2000s. To achieve that, the Chinese ruling party explicitly institutionalized a specific reward mechanism for party officials, whose chances to be promoted through the party ranks have been directly linked to the GDP growth rates of their localities.[28] In Africa, too, investors, the media and international institutions such as the IMF have welcomed the commercialization of free resources as a sign of development. The new dominant narrative of 'Africa rising', which depicts the continent as the new high-return destination for foreign investment, is entirely based on recent GDP growth rates: the 'lions on the move', a catchy expression used by consulting companies and investment banks to describe African economies in obvious comparison to the Asian 'tigers', have indeed topped the world's GDP growth rankings since the first decade of the new millennium.[29] As reported by the *Economist*: 'Over the past decade, six of the world's ten fastest-growing countries were African. In eight of the past ten years, Africa has grown faster than East Asia.'[30] Nigeria, one of the champions of this new growth wave, has been repeatedly presented as a poster child of success: shops 'stacked six feet high with goods', streets 'jammed with customers and salespeople', 'sweating profusely under the onslaught, in what many consider the world's biggest market'.[31]

As mentioned earlier, the very concept of consumerism is embedded in an economic system that only sees success in the volume of market transactions processed in a given society. In many ways, the consumer has replaced the notion of active citizen in a world in which GDP-based consumption is the ultimate sign of participation. In this context, it is not surprising that continuous consumption has become a main preoccupation of policy makers. In no circumstance was this as evident as in the first reactions of world leaders to the terrorist attacks of 11 September 2001. US President George W. Bush felt compelled to remind a terrified nation that 'the American economy will be open for business' and urged consumers to visit Disney World, instead of inviting them to engage in solidarity, altruism and community work. His British counterpart, Tony Blair, reminded everybody 'to travel and to shop' in order to get the economy back on its feet.[32] Jean Chrétien, the Canadian head of government at the time, maintained that the best way to defeat terrorism was through sustained consumption: 'it is time to go out and get a mortgage, to buy a home, to buy a car. [. . .]

The economy of the world needs people to go back to their lives. [. . .] It is the way to fight back.'[33] In a radio interview after the attacks, New York's mayor Rudy Giuliani put it quite clearly: 'There is a way that everybody can help us, New Yorkers and everybody all over the country. Come here and spend money [. . .]. And go shopping, we're the best shoppers in the world.'[34]

The framing of value through prices triggers a number of additional distortions. First of all, not all things that have a price produce clear 'utility'. Traffic jams come at a price in terms of fuel consumption, stress and pollution, but nobody feels better off after having been involved in one. The same can be said about a variety of expenses, from post-disaster reconstruction, to personal and national security and even health care: rising prices in all these sectors can hardly be associated with increasing marginal utility for consumers. Both Libya and South Sudan topped the world's list of fastest-growing economies in 2012 and 2013 respectively.[35] Far from being a sign of utility maximization, these countries' growth was a direct outcome of their civil wars which produced unwanted expenses, brought about destruction and eventually triggered more expenses for reconstruction, all of which pumped up their GDP.

The focus on prices is also misleading because many purchases calculated in GDP do not happen in the allegedly 'open' conditions of the market economy. This is certainly the case with government outlays which are the result of bargains, negotiations and decisions that are not necessarily a reflection of conventional market prices. Military expenses, for instance, have long been criticized, not only because they are 'at best a necessary evil, but still an evil', as Kuznets famously remarked, but also because their price is influenced by political considerations, limited supply, oligopolies and cartels.[36] And the same can be said about a host of other government outlays, including health care and security. After 2008, with the publication of the new UN System of National Accounts, many statistical offices were compelled to standardize data-gathering procedures. In Europe, this resulted in a decision to include income from sex work and illicit drugs as part of GDP. As official prices for these transactions cannot be found in formal invoices, statisticians adopted ambiguous proxies, including using charges for lap-dancing clubs to estimate the price of sex and assuming that the sex market expands or contracts in line with the male population.[37]

Prices are poor indicators of economic value also because of inflation, which can easily push up the numbers without any real increase in output. This is why statisticians distinguish between nominal and real GDP, the latter being controlled for inflation. Yet each national statistical agency uses different formulas and corrective methods to correct for inflation (the so-called GDP deflators). For instance, European statisticians have been criticized for underestimating inflation, perhaps to support the European Central Bank's institutional mandate to avoid rising prices, while the United States has done the opposite, also encouraged by the Federal Reserve's goal to secure employment. This has resulted in different estimates of GDP growth.[38]

Technological innovation, too, presents problems for a conceptualization of progress based on market prices. Improvements in technology indeed tend to reduce prices while increasing utility: e.g. a car, computer or smartphone today are proportionally cheaper than they were a few years back, even though their performance is higher. In Kenya, for example, the World Bank reports that the cost of sending remittances dropped by up to 90 per cent after the introduction of M-Pesa, a digital payment system.[39] In order to account for the qualitative changes in technology that are not reflected in prices, some countries have adopted methodologies (the so-called hedonic models) designed to help 'correct' the value of high-tech goods and services by considering their quality improvements. Once again, this had introduced a fair degree of subjectivity into the calculation of GDP.

The GDP price-based model of prosperity is also increasingly unfit to capture the economic contribution of digital corporations like Google and Facebook. For GDP, these companies only contribute to the economy in terms of the advertising revenues they collect. Yet it is evident that their impact on the utility of users is incommensurate to their profits because they provide a host of services for free, which are not captured by output statistics. Millions of users now have direct access to free email services, maps, translations, books and much more, thanks to Google. The explosion of free services has made a myriad of creative economic activities possible, yet GDP is unable to capture this ripple effect. The same holds true for Facebook. In 2016, CNBC's data journalist Mark Fahey noted that:

Facebook's users spend an aggregate of 10.5 billion minutes per day on the platform [. . .] that means people all over the world have spent a collective 55 million years on Facebook since the beginning of 2009. Twenty minutes a day is a lot of time – well more than a year over the course of the average life span. If users spent just that time working for minimum wage instead of liking and poking each other, each would pull in about $880 a year. That's almost $900 billion in aggregate hypothetical labor last year.[40]

This citation is a good example of how GDP filters our understanding of value. Time that is not spent producing something that GDP captures as economic value is treated as time wasted. Even the business magazine *Forbes*, which is notoriously 'obsessed' with wealth, recognizes that this understanding of value is a 'fetishisation, a reification, of GDP':

> If we don't spend time on Facebook (or reading Wikipedia, or whatever) then we could be doing something else. Perhaps trimming our toenails, maybe doing some work and earning some money. That's all entirely true too. But then they say that the time we spend on Facebook is a waste, a loss of productivity, because we are doing Facebook rather than working to make money. And that's entirely the wrong way around. That we are on Facebook rather than making money shows that we value the Facebook time more than the money.[41]

By measuring only prices, this statistic has become utterly unable to capture what economists call 'consumer surplus', that is, the utility generated for users above and beyond the cost of a good or service. The extreme case is a tool like WhatsApp, which has replaced conventional telephone and even text messaging for more than a billion users globally. In 2016, the company announced that it had dropped subscription fees and would not run any advertisements.[42] If we exclude a few wages paid by its mother company Facebook for the basic operations, WhatsApp's contribution to GDP is virtually nil. Yet this technology is what most people around the world use every day to communicate, arguably one of the most significant enablers of economic activity and progress in the history of humankind. Old telephones were expensive and grossly inefficient. They were, however, a measurable contribution to a country's GDP. New technologies are extremely efficient for a fraction of the original cost. In some cases, they are free. Yet GDP sees them as having little value for economic growth. Nobel-winning economist Robert Solow once quipped: 'You can see the computer age everywhere except in the productivity sta-tistics.' In the early 1990s, this became known as the 'productivity paradox'. Over two decades later, GDP is still blinding us to new forms of value creation. According to Hal Varian, Google's chief economist, GDP depicts the new economy as less productive than previous forms of production, thus making policy makers unable to fully harness the digital revolution.[43]

Visibility and boundaries

GDP is the lens through which we frame value as market transactions. What is not counted by GDP therefore becomes invisible for policy and, often, for society at large. Reflecting on the paradox that the services rendered by a housewife mean nothing to GDP while paid domestic work is fully accounted in national income, the economist Paul Samuelson jokingly quipped in his early editions of the textbook *Economics* that the economy contracts 'when a widower marries his maid'.

As a consequence of the GDP-inspired logic of appropriateness, governments pursue policies that strengthen the market at the expense of informal economic systems, including all activities performed free of charge within households and communities. Of little relevance is the fact that these activities have a clear impact on economic perfor-mance by strengthening, among other things, the social trust that is a precondition for the functioning of any economy, as political scientists Francis Fukuyama and Robert Putnam have demonstrated in bestsell-ing research books.[44] In particular, the GDP model of governance has traditionally depicted civil society as the unproductive sector because of its non-profit orientation, thus relegating it to the margins of policy relevance.

Although GDP sees economic value only in those activities we perform in exchange for money within the formal (market) economy, the productive economy is much broader than that. Many activities that make economic growth possible and support progress are performed free of charge as part of human beings' natural predisposition to provide for one another. People of all kinds carry out vital unpaid work for relatives and for the wider community. Volunteering, caring for the elderly/disabled, supporting community-based groups, assisting migrants, training sport teams and the like deeply contribute to economic progress.

Households are the cornerstones of this 'care' economy, as Marilyn Waring showed in her pioneering book *If Women Counted*. Despite their essential role in supporting the very architecture of social life, households have been completely neglected by mainstream economic thinking and traditionally ignored by GDP. For economist Nancy Folbre, the care economy has become 'the invisible heart' of contemporary production systems.[45] Ignoring household economies may bias measures not only of inequality and poverty, but also of sustainability.[46] If household production and services were to be included in official estimates, the US economy would be surpassed by a number of European countries, thus shaking traditional stereotypes about America's economic leadership.[47] In China, for example, GDP per capita relative to the United States improves by 50 per cent when all household production of non-market services is included.[48]

Formal or informal care-based activities support the functioning of all other economic processes. No country could ever develop, even in simple GDP terms, without the underlying contribution of households, families and communities. They perform a 'collective' welfare-enhancing role which arguably should position these creators of value at the very core of a modern approach to economic development. This is true also in terms of pure self-interest. For instance, children are the future workers and taxpayers of a country. The level of care that goes into raising them is a public good, benefiting society as a whole. Investing time in them at the family and community level offers a significant payback to all participants in the economy.

Despite the collective benefit that society derives from these core activities, GDP has treated them as irrelevant in the calculation of economic growth. This has resulted in policies that neglect (and often oppress) households, voluntary work and civil society. GDP-inspired policies, for instance, try to limit the amount of time individuals spend in social activities or within the household, as these are considered a loss for economic growth. Governments have an incentive to reduce the number of economic activities performed in households or through collaborative community processes, as these cannot be used as evidence of development and economic progress. Cooking, caring and working for the community are discouraged by the GDP institutional model which, by contrast, provides opportunities and incentives to buy pre-cooked meals and to resort to external child care, while treating voluntary work as having no economic value.

GDP also establishes clear boundaries when separating what counts as productive and what does not. For instance, the value of 'do-it-yourself' repairs and maintenance to vehicles or household durables, the cleaning of dwellings, the care and training of children, or similar domestic or personal services produced for own final consumption are not considered productive.[49] Only the expenditures on goods utilized for these purposes, like cleaning materials and books, are included in the household final consumption calculation. Education itself is not considered productive, as established by the UN statistical rules, because learning and studying 'cannot be undertaken by anyone else on behalf of the student' and therefore is not transaction-based, 'although the instruction conveyed by education services is'.[50] This is clearly at odds with common sense, which suggests that the investment in human capital should receive the same treatment as investment in produced capital and financial capital. Unfortunately, GDP sees the latter as economically valuable because of the formation of gross fixed capital, but it disregards the former as of no economic value, despite the likelihood that 'the acquisition of knowledge, skills and qualifications increases the productive potential of the individuals concerned and is a source of future economic benefit to them', as admitted by UN statisticians.[51]

The so-called informal economy, an imprecise term often used to describe a wide range of activities, from flea markets to street vendors, including the burgeoning 'gig economy', is notoriously neglected by GDP. Recently, the mushrooming of 'sharing economies' around the world has further contributed to challenging the GDP 'lens', taking decision makers and conventional businesses by surprise. These new economic activities are strongly influenced by social and environmental considerations, transforming consumers into participants. They provide opportunities for collaborative financial management, for example through time banks, local exchange trading systems, peer-to-peer and cryptocurrencies. They also incentivize shared use of common resources, from car-pooling, to couch-surfing, ride-sharing and co-housing. VizEat, a global community inspired by the values of social dining, allows visitors to enjoy authentic meals in the homes of locals across the world, challenging the conventional approach of restaurants, which separate hosts and customers. Not only are guests exposed to local cultures and habits, but they can also share in some of the social dimensions of cooking, including preparing meals and washing dishes. The proliferation of online markets for reuse, such as Freecycle, or for sale, such as Etsy but also eBay and Gumtree, has massively reduced intermediary transactions and incentivized customization rather than mass production. According to a 2016 survey, almost 80 per cent of Americans make use of services provided by the sharing economy, with percentages of users rising massively in other countries too.[52]

The British economist Diane Coyle, author of a bestselling book on GDP, believes the strength of this new economy is that 'users and providers save time and costs involved in searching for someone to trade with. The result is a pure gain in economic efficiency benefiting both sides'.[53] By helping match supply and demand, new technologies also reduce waste in terms of production excess as well as time. This increases consumer surplus and overall well-being, especially in so far as more time is available for leisure and less trash has to be disposed of. Yet it deals a blow to GDP. There is also some evidence that new patterns of peer-to-peer collaboration may benefit especially low-income groups by turning some of their assets into income-generating opportunities and by providing goods and services at a relatively affordable price.[54] Through Airbnb, holidaymakers can now enjoy comfortable accommodation at prices that no hotel can match. At the same time, they can rent their homes while on vacation: a double plus for their pockets. The reduction in costs and the increase in disposable income are however not registered in official statistics, affecting conventional measurements of inflation and, ultimately, the size of the economy as measured by GDP.

The classical 'production boundaries' between paid work, leisure and household activities have become much less clear in contemporary societies. For instance, online portals allow users to become travel agents. As a consequence, people's leisure time is spent to perform a productive function (booking a holiday), but formal agency fees are eliminated, thus diminishing GDP. Swapping homes or inviting peer-guests turns household services into income-generating activities, albeit informally: yet GDP will not capture that. Coyle concludes that 'the blurring suggests the need to rethink the definition of the economy in terms of GDP, and develop instead a measure that is not affected by the variety of ways people can choose to share assets and to work, whether paid, unpaid, or a mixture.'[55]

Institutional control

The inability of GDP to capture the multifaceted nature of contemporary economies is also a consequence of its focus on top-down control as well as ownership. The UN Statistics Division, which oversees the measurement of GDP across the world through its guidelines for the system of national accounts, understands production as 'a physical process, carried out under the responsibility, control and management of an institutional unit, in which labour and assets are used to transform inputs of goods and services into outputs of other goods and services'.[56] For outputs to be treated as part of economic production, they 'must be such that they can be sold on markets'.[57]

A necessary condition for an activity to be treated as productive is that it must be carried out 'under the instigation, control and responsibility of some institutional unit that exercises ownership rights over whatever is produced'.[58] By the term 'institutional unit', the UN understands any formal entity, public or private, that can claim control and ownership over what is produced and consumed. Invariably, this approach biases the entire economic system in favour of top-down institutional appropriation at the expense of shared governance of common resources. In turn, this generates evident paradoxes, which routinely affect the way in which regulations are designed. For example, 'the natural growth of stocks of fish in the high seas not subject to international quotas is not counted as production' because the process is not directly controlled or owned by any institutional unit.[59] Yet 'the growth of fish in fish farms is treated as a process of production in much the same way that rearing livestock is a process of production.'[60] Because of the institutional appropriation approach, 'the deliberate felling of trees in wild forests, and the gathering of wild fruit or berries, and also firewood, counts as production,' exactly like 'the cultivation of crop-bearing trees, or trees grown for timber or other uses'.[61] However, what is grown in common and shared by users through open-access systems is of no economic value: 'the natural growth of wild, unculti- vated forests or wild fruits or berries is not counted as production.'[62] According to this centralized approach to economic progress, 'rainfall and the flow of water down natural watercourses are not processes of production, whereas storing water in reservoirs or dams and the piping, or carrying, of water from one location to another all constitute production.'[63] Even if 'rainfall may be vital to the agricultural produc- tion of a country', the lack of institutional control and centralized ownership make it 'not a process of production whose output can be included in GDP'.[64]

The same principle applies to assets. To be considered of economic value, assets must be 'owned by some unit' and must generate some direct economic benefits derived to 'their owner(s) by holding or using them over a period of time'.[65] This may be rather straightfor- ward if we consider fixed assets like machinery and equipment which are themselves outputs of past production processes. Yet it becomes controversial if we consider natural resources, which nobody has produced. For GDP, only when companies or governments have an exclusive right to exploit resources 'such as land, mineral deposits, fuel reserves, uncultivated forests or other vegetation and wild animals' can these be considered as part of the economy. By contrast, resources 'over which no ownership rights can be exercised', as well as 'mineral or fuel deposits that have not been discovered' or that are not exploited will never be included in the economy 'as they are not capable of bringing any benefits to their owners'.[66]

The way in which GDP adopts top-down institutional control as the overarching parameter of economic activity is also evident in the distinction between depletion of natural resources and depreciation of man-made assets. The GDP system makes full provision for measuring depreciation, with detailed guidelines on how to account for the consumption of goods used in the production process. The concept of depreciation is indeed perfectly in line with the price-based framing of value and the institutional control principle: machinery is indeed bought at a price, which is incorporated into the accounts at the moment of purchase. Its depreciation is calculated consistently with the internal principles of GDP. By contrast, the using up of assets generated by nature is of no consequence for national income. These resources become valuable only when appropriated and commercialized but, since they are not purchased from Mother Nature, their depletion cannot be priced and, therefore, will never appear in the balance sheets. Ultimately, the disregard for natural provisions is a consequence of the fact that 'nature is not recognised as a factor of production by economists or national accountants.'[67]

Hiding costs

By not considering the costs of industrial production, GDP depicts polluting companies as profitable for society, even when the detrimental effects of their activities outstrip the financial gains therein, as I will discuss in greater detail in the next chapter. GDP also makes decision makers prone to support economies of scale which are efficient in terms of production targets only because GDP hides the costs associated with waste and overconsumption. The economist Robert Repetto and his team highlighted this problem in a prescient report published in 1989 and titled *Wasting Assets: Natural Resources in the National Income Accounts*: 'A country could exhaust its mineral resources, cut down its forests, erode its soils, pollute its aquifers, and hunt its wildlife and fisheries to extinction, but measured income would not be affected as these assets disappeared.'[68] Their work was pioneering in its attempt to identify ways in which natural resources could be integrated into the calculation of GDP. Their interest was not simply methodological: they were indeed fully aware of the fact that 'misguided economic incentives cost governments huge sums and distort investment decisions while inviting environmental abuse and wasting natural resources'.[69] Their recommendation was to treat natural resources as any other form of financial capital with a view to gauging 'what signals the new results would give to those who make decisions about economic development'.[70]

Over time, the environmental costs of GDP growth have become an issue of major concern for the international community against the backdrop of biodiversity loss, ecological disasters and climate change. The World Bank has confirmed that neglecting the costs of industrial production is a short-sighted approach to development policy, with negative impacts that can easily outstrip any real or apparent financial gains. In a report titled *Where Is the Wealth of Nations? Measuring Capital for the 21st Century*, the Bank confirmed such distortions and concluded that 'in all countries, intangible capital is, by far, the largest share of wealth' and 'in poorer countries, natural capital is more important than produced capital', thus suggesting that properly managing natural resources should become a fundamental component of development strategies, 'particularly since the poorest households in those countries are usually the most dependent on these resources'.[71] Repetto had already warned against the perverse incentives generated by the application of GDP as a macroeconomic policy tool, particularly in the 'developing' world: 'Ironically, low-income countries, which are typically most dependent on natural resources for employment, revenues, and foreign exchange earnings are instructed to use a system for national accounting and macroeconomic analysis that almost completely ignores their principal assets.'[72]

Celebrating the 'rise' of Africa because of its GDP growth rates obscures the fact that most increases in output are the result of massive exploitation of natural resources, often chaotic urbanization and skyrocketing levels of inequality. Nigeria, which in 2014 became Africa's largest economy, was soon thereafter plagued by an escalating civil war with armed groups like Boko Haram, which have taken advantage of the anger and discontent generated by the relentless exploitation of oil fields in the Niger Delta.[73] Fossil fuel reserves have turned Angola into one of the most corrupt countries in the world, with living costs reaching unprecedented levels. Its capital, Luanda, is one of the world's most expensive cities, where a pair of blue jeans sells for more than US$240 and a fizzy drink costs about US$20, vis-à-vis a subsidized litre of oil at US$0.61.[74] All these dynamics have increased GDP, including corruption, which leads to higher prices. Yet the economic dynamism of the country is questionable.

That the integration of ecological costs would have the potential to shift perceptions and trigger different policies was evidenced by the opposition of the coal industry to an early attempt at reforming GDP made by the Council of Economic Advisers to President Bill Clinton in the 1990s. As revealed by Joseph Stiglitz, chairman of the council at the time, their proposal for a 'green GDP' was short-lived: 'the coal industry knew what it would mean – and it used its enormous influence in Congress to threaten to cut off funding for those engaged in this attempt.'[75] As the proposal was ditched, a representative of coal-rich states candidly admitted that, if GDP was to account for the depletion of coal reserves and the effects of air pollution, 'somebody is going to say [. . .] that the coal industry isn't contributing anything to the country.'[76] A similar process unfolded in China in the mid-2000s. In response to concerns about pollution and environmental degradation, the Chinese environmental agency piloted a 'green GDP' project which revealed that environmental damage had cost the country up to 15 per cent of its annual GDP and that the country had lost 'almost everything it has gained since the late 1970s due to pollution'.[77] As these results challenged a long-standing practice in the Communist Party to reward officials that had achieved high growth rates in their localities, the political leadership stepped in to halt the project. To assuage the media, the Chinese Academy of Sciences, a government think tank, published a GDP 'quality' index to allegedly demonstrate an increase in 'true wealth, sustainable development and social harmony'.[78]

A research and policy initiative on 'the economics of ecosystems and biodiversity' (commonly known as TEEB) argues that 'Nature is the source of much value to us every day, and yet it mostly bypasses markets, escapes pricing and defies valuation. This lack of valuation is [. . .] an underlying cause for the observed degradation of ecosystems and the loss of biodiversity.'[79] More recently, a global study conducted by the agency Trucost revealed the massive unaccounted costs generated for society by large businesses, pointing fingers primarily at the extractive industries and commercial farming, and confirming the behavioural and institutional shifts that could be triggered by reformed accounting.[80] But environmental costs are not the only ones hidden by GDP. There is a host of social costs too, including inequality, crime, stress and family breakdown. If we were to deduct all these costs from GDP to identify what many analysts call 'genuine progress', the neoliberal representation of the economic 'miracle' of the 1980s and 1990s would need some serious rethinking, as I will show in chapter 3.

Standardized coercion

In many cases, the institutional power of GDP has been made explicit, like the case of the Stability and Growth Pact and the Fiscal Compact of the European Union. As we have seen throughout the 'Eurocrisis', especially in Greece, institutional parameters and policy choices are dictated by GDP-influenced supranational treaties, with no regard for the outcome of democratic elections and referenda. Outside Europe, the institutional power of GDP is not necessarily enshrined in treaties, but it is invariably evident in how policy makers relate to global investors and credit rating agencies. Governments faced with a contracting GDP are not primarily worried about unemployment, given the numerous cases of 'jobful recessions' and 'jobless recoveries'. They are not even preoccupied by the prospect of shrinking tax revenues, at least not in the short term, as there is a significant lag between contracting consumption and fiscal impacts. Rather, they are concerned about international perceptions, which may influence investors' choices. This is ultimately why credit ratings based on GDP projections are so powerful: not because of the value of their technical judgements, which are based on shady and questionable methodologies, but because of their influence on investors' perceptions.[81] Market participants are not particularly interested in rational moves. They do not care too much about distinguishing between evidence and rumours, between good or bad economic statistics. GDP triggers consequences because of the herd mentality embedded in the type of institutional mechanisms it has itself generated, not differently from self-fulfilling prophecies and regardless of the quality of the measurement.[82] The power of GDP thus holds even in cases where formal legal constraints are absent. As shown by a recent study of the IMF, most countries, especially those classified as poor or 'middle income', strive to keep their ratio between deficit/debt and GDP within internationally accepted limits, despite there being no scientific evidence that these ratios are any good for development.[83] By the same token, a society in which the relationship between production and consumption is informal will most likely be punished by those investors using GDP as their institutional 'lens', regardless of the merits of such assessment. As is the case with many southern European nations, austerity policies predicated on GDP-based parameters are unlikely to be reviewed because these societies have strong informal economies, community work and household production, even when the OECD shows that these activities make a significant contribution to the overall performance of a country and often count more than GDP.[84]

Moving beyond GDP

Since the early days of the GDP accounts, Kuznets himself raised doubts about his 'creature'. For instance, he warned about the risk of using a 'gross' measurement to design policies. He recommended that not only the depreciation of machinery and capital be subtracted from GDP, but also the 'wearing out of people'. Indeed, the system of production takes its toll not only on 'things' but also on 'human beings'. This is what Kuznets called the 'reverse side of income', that is, 'the intensity and unpleasantness of effort going into the earning of income'.[85] Yet, as GDP focuses only on satisfying consumers' demands for commodities and services, he admitted that 'the burdens of work and discomfort are ignored'.[86] Kuznets also acknowledged that GDP focuses exclusively on formalized economic transactions, which make it unsuitable for countries largely dependent on informal economic structures.[87] In industrialized countries, by contrast, growth of GDP might be easily overestimated by counting in goods and services whose sole purpose was to offset the drawbacks of industrialization, such as the increasing cost of traffic, pollution and security, a phenomenon that ecological economists refer to as 'defensive consumption'.

Kuznets was also worried about the way in which GDP growth affects the distribution of income. His famous 'curve' showed how rapid growth is usually associated with rising inequality, which is partly due to the fact that policies aimed at supporting GDP tend to destroy informal economic structures to replace them with formal (often market-based) systems of production. In the process, many people – especially the most marginalized – lose out. This is something that more recent research has confirmed, highlighting the widening gap between rich and poor in times of high growth, especially in countries where inequality trends were not corrected through purposeful redistributive policies.[88] Kuznets also raised doubts about the reliability of the accounts, for which data were often missing, and took great pains to single out the disparate sources of error in international comparisons, including the use of prices. Finally, he pleaded with policy makers to always distinguish between the mere 'quantity' of economic growth and its actual 'quality' in order to clarify what type of growth they want to achieve and 'for what'.[89]

Taking the baton from Kuznets, who had always argued in favour of a welfare-oriented understanding of growth, over the past few years progressive economists, ecologically minded think tanks and NGOs have been criticizing GDP with a view to reducing its influence on policy making. A myriad of alternative indicators have been produced in an effort to dethrone this 'almighty number' and produce more reliable measures of economic well-being.

The first attempt at revising GDP was made by Nobel-prizewinning economists William Nordhaus and James Tobin in the 1970s when they developed an index called the Measure of Economic Welfare, which 'corrected' GDP by adding the economic contribution of households and by excluding 'bad' transactions, such as military expenses and what they called 'the disamenities of urbanization', which included some environmental impacts.[90] The ecological economist Herman Daly and the theologian John Cobb launched the Index of Sustainable Economic Welfare in the late 1980s, later revised into the genuine progress indicator.[91] Their approach rejected the notion that only market-based goods and services were relevant to economic prosperity: they therefore included positive contributions such as leisure, public services, unpaid work (housework, parenting and care giving) and deducted the economic impact of negative factors like income inequality, crime, pollution, insecurity (e.g. car accidents, unemployment and underemployment), family breakdown and the economic losses associated with resource depletion and long-term environmental damage.

During the two decades between the first Earth Summit in 1992 and the Rio+20 in 2012, a variety of official initiatives were launched, with the pace accelerating exponentially after the 2008 global financial crisis. The UN Development Programme mainstreamed the Human Development Index, which complemented GDP with measures of life expectancy and education, more recently corrected for inequality. The UN Environment Programme, in partnership with the UN University International Human Dimension Programme, launched the Inclusive Wealth Index, a new indicator coordinated by welfare economist Partha Dasgupta from the University of Cambridge, which measures stocks rather than flows (as GDP does) and divides them in terms of human, natural and produced capital.[92] The World Bank promoted global initiatives such as the Wealth Accounting and Valuation of Ecosystem Services to mainstream assessments of natural resource flows into policy making and economic planning after having streamlined its adjusted net savings (or genuine savings) as an indicator of sustainability in the 1990s.[93] Commissions like the one chaired by Stiglitz, Sen and Fitoussi in France in 2009 prompted similar initiatives in Europe and the United States, with the OECD setting up well-being and development task forces in other regions of the world with a view to following up on the commission's conclusion that 'what we measure affects what we do; and if our measurements are flawed, decisions may be distorted.'[94] The OECD itself launched a new set of well-being indicators as part of its Better Life initiative, whose slogan is 'There is more to life than the cold numbers of GDP.'[95] Several US states, from Maryland and Vermont to Hawaii, adopted the genuine progress indicator as their macroeconomic policy impact measurement.[96] The small Asian kingdom of Bhutan acquired global notoriety for having promoted gross national 'happiness' (GNH) since the 1970s. In 2008, Bhutan published the result of its first national survey, dividing GNH into four pillars (good governance, sustainable socio-economic development, preservation and promotion of culture and environmental conservation) and nine domains, from living standards to time-use.[97] Since 2012, the UN Sustainable Development Solutions Network has been publishing an annual World Happiness Report, coordinated by economists like Jeffrey Sachs and Richard Layard, and based on subjective well-being surveys conducted by opinion pollster Gallup.[98] In South America, Paraguay has been the first country in the world to adopt a new metric of national performance, the social progress index, a multidimensional measure of well-being, economic opportunity and satisfaction of basic human needs.[99] In 2014, more than 700 municipalities across the Amazon in Brazil launched sub-national indicators of social progress with a view to inspiring other regions, cities and communities of the world.[100] In 2015, the European Union announced its plan to adopt the social progress index as a key tool in deciding how to allocate over €63 billion to deprived regions across the continent, launching a first roll-out in 2016.[101] Other, relatively less known, alternative indicators introduced or experimented with in the past few years include the Happy Planet Index (launched by the New Economics Foundation), the Legatum Prosperity Index (coordinated by the Legatum Institute in London), the Satisfaction with Life Index (developed in 2006 by the University of Leicester), the Life Quality Index (initiated by the Institute for Risk Research in Canada), as well as the Quality-of-Life Index produced by the Economist Intelligence Unit (more recently used as a forecasting tool through the Where-to-be-Born Index). Table 2.1 reports the best-known post-GDP indicators and their main methodological approaches.

The GDP ideology has come under fire in a fast-growing economy like China, too. According to the diplomatic cables released by WikiLeaks, the Chinese premier Li Keqiang had candidly admitted that 'China's GDP figures are "man-made" and therefore unreliable' as far back as 2007.[102] A paper published in the *British Journal of Political Science* also shows severe inconsistencies in Chinese economic data over time. The research demonstrates how 'economic statistics dominate policy analyses, political discussions' and 'central leaders also use them to evaluate local officials', thus generating perverse incentives.[103] The author concludes that there is a need for a more critical approach 'of the messy world of Chinese and cross-national economic data, which are ubiquitous in the political world and the quantitative study

Table 2.1 Most cited post-GDP indicators and their key characteristics

Name	Source	Methodology	Introduced (date)
Measure of Economic Welfare	Nordhaus and Tobin 1973	It corrects GDP by adding household production, excluding military expenses and controlling for some environmental impacts.	1973
Index of Sustainable Economic Welfare (genuine progress indicator)	Daly and Cobb 1989; Redefining Progress	It adds household activities and volunteering and subtracts 'bads' like crime, pollution, social breakdown.	1989
Human Development Index	United Nations Development Programme	It aggregates income, literacy and life expectancy (adjusted for inequality).	1990
Adjusted Net Savings	World Bank	It deducts depreciation of produced capital and depletion of natural capital depletion but adds human capital.	1991
Ecological Footprint	Global Footprint Network	It represents the productive area required to provide the renewable resources humanity is using and to absorb its waste.	1995
Gross National Happiness	Centre for Bhutan Studies	It conceives 'national happiness' as founded on four pillars (good governance, sustainable socio-economic development, preservation and promotion of culture and environmental conservation). The survey is operationalized into nine domains: living standards; education; health; environment; community vitality; time use; psychological well-being; good governance; cultural resilience and promotion.	2008

Name	Source	Methodology	Introduced (date)
Legatum Prosperity Index	Legatum Institute	It operationalizes prosperity along eight dimensions, including economy, entrepreneurship, governance, education, health, safety, personal freedom and social capital. Sources include World Development Indicators, Gallup World Poll, World Values Survey and International Communication Union.	2008
Better Life Index	OECD	It measures 11 dimensions (housing, income, jobs, community, education, environment, civic engagement, health, life satisfaction, safety and work–life balance) and allows users to customize weights.	2011
Happy Planet Index	New Economics Foundation	It multiplies subjective well-being (as measured in Gallup World Poll's 'Ladder of Life') by life expectancy and divides them by ecological footprint as an efficiency measure of how long and happy lives fare in comparison to environmental impacts.	2012
World Happiness Report	UN Sustainable Development Solutions Network	It uses the Ladder of Life evaluations from the Gallup World Poll. The English wording of the question is 'Please imagine a ladder, with steps numbered from 0 at the bottom to 10 at the top. The top of the ladder represents the best possible life for you and the bottom of the ladder represents the worst possible life for you. On which step of the ladder would you say you personally feel you stand at this time?'	2012

(Continued)

Table 2.1 (*Continued*)

Name	Source	Methodology	Introduced (date)
Inclusive Wealth Index	UN Environment Programme and UNU-IHDP	It measures stocks rather than flows and specifically assesses the value of human and natural capital besides produced capital.	2012
Social Progress Index	Social Progress Imperative	It is an outcome index focusing on three dimensions: basic human needs, foundations of well-being and opportunity. It uses data produced by a variety of institutions, including the World Health Organization, World Bank, International Energy Agency, Gallup and the Economist Intelligence Unit. It allows users to customize the set of variables included in the final calculations.	2014

of political economy': 'These statistics drive our assessments of policy and policy makers, of countries on the rise and wane, and of the present and future. Politically sensitive data such as GDP at the national and sub-national levels are likely targets of manipulation.'[104]

In 2015, local officials across the country publicly admitted they had systematically inflated GDP numbers because of political pressures.[105] At the same time, support for a green GDP resurfaced as the costs of environmental clean-up spiralled out of control, while official GDP growth began to slow down.[106] Even President Xi Jinping weighed in with a public statement in which he demanded that GDP no longer be considered a parameter of success for the promotion of public officials in China.[107] So far, more than seventy Chinese cities, including Shanghai, have announced that GDP would cease to be used as their primary economic policy tool.[108] For the first time since Deng Xiaoping's market reforms, the Chinese government is considering abandoning GDP growth targets for the coming years, opening up possibilities for new, alternative indicators to steer official policy.[109]

The SDGs as a window of opportunity

The ratification of the SDGs in September 2015 can be seen as the culmination of over a decade of work in post-GDP 'circles'. Although the SDGs present some inconsistencies, including a problematic Goal 8 that still makes reference to GDP growth targets for developing countries, all other objectives focus on both human and ecological well-being. The selections of indicators, which is presently underway, also suggests that measurements of shared prosperity, ecological footprints, as well as natural, social and human capital will occupy centre stage in future development policy.

The SDGs are far from perfect, but they present a window of opportunity. As I have indicated in an article published in the *Guardian* on the eve of the UN ratification, their focus on human and ecological well-being could lead to a profound governance revolution.[110] To start with, the separation between the economy and 'the rest' will need to be challenged as it undermines holistic development and encourages short-termism. Similar to GDP, the new public management's approach to governance has instilled in policy makers and managers the belief that the separation of offices, portfolios and tasks makes decision making in governments and companies more efficient in terms of sectoral outputs. The reality, however, is that it has made organizations unable to approach problems holistically. In the present condition, officials and managers are rewarded for spending cuts in their area of work, even if that increases costs for their colleagues and for society at large. Some of these costs have a direct monetary impact, such as health conditions, increased insecurity and traffic, while others are socialized in different ways, from ecological degradation and climate change to family breakdowns.

As discussed in this chapter, GDP is the 'lens' through which policy makers, the media and society have framed value in the human economy. What is not counted by GDP becomes invisible and valueless to public policies and social debate. To make it valuable, it must be brought under the institutional control of a proprietor, either public or private. Shared resources are of no use in the GDP economy. No surprise then that the GDP world has been characterized by a relentless privatization of public spaces, commodification of the household (including the ever-decreasing time which family members enjoy 'together') and destruction of natural beauty.

Because GDP has influenced the operating logic of the current economy by incentivizing certain consumption patterns, focusing on market-based activities and providing a 'face lift' to polluting companies, a shift to a new system of accounting has the potential to alter the institutional pillars supporting conventional production systems. In the following chapters, I show how this change may play out by making reference to processes that are already underway and outlining prospective developments that may unfold in the near future.

3

Post-GDP Economics

As a building block of contemporary institutional systems, GDP has contributed to 'regulating' our economic and political choices by establishing institutional logics, setting standards and framing values. As remarked by Dirk Philipsen, 'what we measure matters.' As a matter of fact, 'agreeing on what to measure requires articulating values, defining targets, and making choices. Once in place, measurements establish the ground rules by which we operate.'[1] The fact that GDP establishes the ground rules of contemporary economies is evident in how policies are justified, as well as in the nature of the crises we face. Public subsidies, tax breaks and privatization policies are routinely presented as key tools to support business expansion, consumer demand and ultimately GDP growth. In many respects, the 2008 financial collapse was a result of more than a decade of GDP-fuelling policy choices. Indeed, throughout the 1990s, public and private institutions incentivized a credit bubble which triggered massive GDP growth in the United States through investment in real estate. In turn, this created a housing bubble, eventually sinking the global economy by dragging down banking and insurance markets. Similarly, China has been experiencing a 'triple' bubble for the past decade, whose underlying cause is to be found, once again, in GDP-driven policy reforms. Since the early 2000s, Chinese authorities have been subsidizing consumption and production, investment in real estate and cheap credit. Then, in 2015, the Chinese stock market collapsed, triggering a cascade effect on many emerging markets and industrialized economies. According to Credit Suisse, one of the world's largest banks, what happened in China in 2015 was just the tip of the iceberg, given that the country sits on 'the third-biggest credit bubble of all time, the largest investment bubble [. . .] and the second-biggest real-estate bubble'.[2] All of this against the backdrop of 'near record producer price deflation, near record low growth in bank deposits (the main source of internal liquidity), FX outflows (the main source of external liquidity), and falling house prices (with property accounting for the majority of household wealth)'.[3]

The hesitation that our societies have demonstrated in tackling climate change and inequality is also a by-product of the GDP's rules of the game, which give no value to ecosystems and social cohesion. Of course, there are vested interests not wanting issues of equality and ecological well-being to dominate the public debate. It is logical to assume that such interests would oppose more progressive legislation regardless of the statistical approaches adopted by policy makers and society. At the same time, it is clear that GDP has provided status quo interests with a powerful 'cloak', depicting centralized and polluting corporations as 'efficient', while sidelining economic experiences operating through decentralized structures and circular economies.

Can different indicators and alternative economic analysis help change this state of affairs? Economic sociologist Fred Block agrees that new theories and approaches can help reform social institutions, thus challenging dominant paradigms and triggering change.

There is an ongoing process of institutional selection through which people reshape and reform social institutions along particular lines [. . .]. But the balance of forces among competing groups is itself influenced by ideas of what makes sense in this kind of society, and it is here that social theory plays a major role by helping to shape the way people think about particular institutions.[4]

With a view to levelling the playing field between dominant forms of economic organization and alternatives characterized by decentralization and cooperation, this chapter discusses the inherent structural inefficiencies of the GDP economy and explores the characteristics of post-GDP forms of economic prosperity.

The inefficient economy

Assessing the performance of the GDP economy by accounting for negative environmental externalities is a first step towards recognizing its hidden inefficiencies. According to Trucost, a world-leading agency in sustainability metrics, the value of the main corporate global externalities is at least US$7.3 trillion: that is, our societies forfeit more than 13 per cent of global GDP every year due to the natural capital lost or misused in conventional production processes.[5] Coal power generation, rice and wheat farming, as well as cattle ranching, are among the most impactful sectors globally. These sectors appear in the top ranks because of their total costs from natural resource use, pollution and waste, all effects neglected by the GDP system of accounting. Table 3.1 reports the sectors and the regions with the highest negative impacts on natural capital, including their overall revenues in comparison to the environmental costs generated for society. In all cases, the costs largely outweigh the financial gains.

While coal power generation costs in East Asia are slightly higher than those in North America, the latter exhibits far greater health

Table 3.1 The hidden costs of the GDP economy: top environmental impacts (2009 prices)

Sector	Region	Natural capital cost (US$ billion)	Revenue (US$ billion)
Coal power generation	East Asia	452.8	443.1
Cattle ranching and farming	South America	353.8	16.6
Coal power generation	North America	316.8	246.7
Wheat farming	Southern Asia	266.6	31.8
Rice farming	Southern Asia	235.6	65.8

Source: Trucost (2013), p. 9.

impacts associated with air pollution. Natural gas extraction, a new energy field largely touted as an efficient way to guarantee power independence to the United States, is one of the sectors responsible for the highest projected costs in terms of greenhouse gas emissions. The next highest impacts are caused by agricultural production in areas of significant water scarcity and where the level of production, and therefore land use, is high. As natural ecosystems in South America and Southern Asia are particularly crucial to support human development, it is in these regions that the impacts from cattle ranching and wheat farming are the highest.

The heavy impact of environmental costs is also confirmed by a post-GDP indicator developed by the World Bank, the so-called adjusted net (or genuine) savings, which 'measures the real difference between production and consumption, taking into account investments in human capital, depreciation of fixed capital, depletion of natural resources, and damages caused by pollution'.[6] Figure 3.1 reports the results of a simple accounting operation, in which GDP is corrected for immediate consumption (net national savings) and then education expenditure is added as a measure of human capital development while deducting environmental degradation, namely, energy depletion, mineral

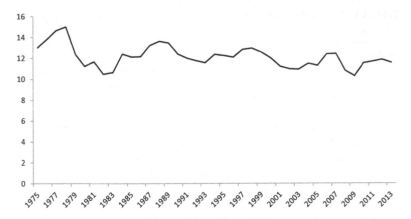

Figure 3.1 Environmental degradation offsets GDP growth since the mid-1970s (adjusted net savings expressed as percentage of GDP).

Source: Author's elaboration on World Bank's data provided through the World Development Indicators 2013 and accessed via Data Market. This data excludes particulate emissions damage.

depletion, net forest depletion and carbon dioxide emissions. The result is self-evident: overall global growth has basically been stationary over the past four decades, despite the conventional perception that describes the 1980s and 1990s as decades of high economic performance. Negative environmental impacts have, indeed, offset whatever additional value may have been generated by industrial output and investment in human capital, with a sharp fall in the late 1970s.

While the so-called 'developing' countries experience significant production costs, it is ultimately the 'developed' world that is responsible for most of this consumption. Consuming companies in North America and Europe often take advantage of more lax environmental regulations and standards in other countries, which come with a relatively 'higher' negative natural capital impact. Because of global supply chain mechanisms, 'even a company that buys a product from a low-impact producer, but where global impacts for that product are high, is at risk from pass through of costs' to the rest of society.[7]

While GDP's focus on market prices and formal transactions regards all production processes as profitable, even a basic approach to natural capital impacts shows the economic magnitude of the losses involved in such sectors, painting a completely different picture. As reported by Trucost, the overall global results merging all regions together indicate that no industry 'would be profitable, let alone cover its cost of capital after environmental impacts are taken into account'.

> Average pre-tax profit margins for companies listed in the MSCI World Index before natural capital costs are included were found to range from 7% for iron and steel manufacturing, to 19% for crude petroleum and natural gas extraction. After natural capital costs are included, the range is –67% for cement manufacturing to –1% for crude oil petroleum and natural gas extraction.[8]

As recently explained by Trucost's chief operating officer, 'we have created an irrational market that incentivizes business profit at the expense of planet and society.'[9] Some analysts have described the modern corporation as an 'externalizing machine', appropriating profits while benefiting from an institutional system that neglects overall costs which are ultimately socialized through additional taxation, climate change adaptation and rising inequalities.[10] In the words of Pavan Sukhdev, a former executive at Deutsche Bank turned environmental adviser to the UN, the basic assumption of today's corporations is 'more is better', a creed that 'feeds that other mantra of today's dominant economic model, "GDP growth"'.[11] Firstly, businesses are institutionally encouraged to pursue 'size and scale in order to achieve market dominance'. Secondly, they resort 'to lobbying for regulatory and competitive advantages'. Thirdly, advertising has become a strategic priority 'to influence consumer demand and, often, to create entirely new demand by playing on human insecurities and "turning wants into needs" which can only be satisfied by new products'. Finally, shareholders' investments are leveraged to support the growth of the company even further, which in turn attracts additional funds for incremental expansion. These various processes trigger additional feedback loops which are assumed to create 'cost efficiencies and economies of scale which can deliver competitive pricing that, in turn, leads to more sales'. Sukhdev's conclusion is: 'In the corporate quest for growth, even without the excess, misuse, or abuse that so often attends lobbying, advertising, and leverage, the collateral damage inflicted on society is not small.'[12]

According to Sukhdev, the GDP economy has institutionalized an 'enabling environment' for this externalizing system of production and consumption.[13] For instance, fossil fuel subsidies reached at least US$1.9 trillion globally in 2013, that is, over 2½ per cent of global GDP and more than 8 per cent of total government revenues.[14] The 'developed' world was responsible for the bulk of subsidies, while oil exporters accounted for about one-third. As remarked by the IMF, 'Removing these subsidies could lead to a 13 per cent decline in CO_2 emissions and generate positive spillover effects by reducing global energy demand.'[15] The Global Ocean Commission reports that fisheries subsidies exceed US$35 billion per year, about half the landed catch value worldwide.[16] After a decline during the first decade of the new millennium, agricultural subsidies have reached new heights. In the twenty top food-producing countries, farmers received about US$486 billion in 2012.[17] The Worldwatch Institute maintains that subsidies urge farmers to grow a few particularly widely used commodities, exacerbating agriculture-related environmental problems: 'By predominantly funding a few staple crops for the largest farms, subsidies support industrial-scale operations. [. . .] These factory farms tend to lack crop diversity, which over time saps the soil of nutrients and in turn requires substantial use of artificial chemical inputs like fertilizers and pesticides.'[18]

As a leading cause of global environmental change, the production of food is a critical example of the institutionalized inefficiencies of the GDP economy. In all high-GDP countries, there is a worrying disconnection between the retail price of food and the true cost of its production. The natural capital costs associated with crop production exceed US$1.15 trillion, that is, over 170 per cent of its global production value, whereas livestock production is responsible for natural capital costs of more than US$1.18 trillion, the equivalent of 134 per cent of its production value, as reported by the Food and Agriculture Organization.[19]

As a consequence of GDP's selective accounting, food produced at great environmental cost, in the form of greenhouse gas emissions, water contamination, air pollution and habitat destruction, can appear to be cheaper than more sustainable alternatives. The focus on size and economies of scale has not only produced costs that have often exceeded the marginal profit made by the companies themselves, but it has also led to unfair competition (and often exclusion) vis-à-vis alternative forms of production (including those generated by small- and medium-sized businesses) and consumption (especially those focused on self-production).

In the food sector, a number of alternative practices can not only achieve better results at a lower cost for society, but can do so in a more socially integrated fashion. Environmental cost-accounting experiments conducted in Brazil, for instance, have shown that the use of holistic grazing management can result in the regeneration of grassland, thus supporting carbon sequestration and the reduction of greenhouse gas emissions (to the tune of US$1232 per tonne of beef produced), as well as lowering natural capital impacts by 11 per cent (resulting in at least US$68 of financial benefits to the farmer for each cow).[20] Similar post-GDP measurements carried out in India have shown that significant reductions in soil, air and water pollutants can be achieved by adopting modern techniques for rice intensification, with a reduction in natural capital impact of up to 97 per cent, 78 per cent and 16 per cent respectively. Gross margins increase by 18 per cent per hectare, whilst operating costs decrease by 13 per cent. Farmers that adopt organic practices, including crop rotation, organic manure and the use of cover crops (which reduce the need for fertilizers), can achieve significant reductions in air pollution as well as water overconsumption and contamination, saving on average US$20 for each tonne of soybeans. In these farms, gross margins increase up to 219 per cent per hectare. The same holds true for wheat, with cost savings as great as US$43 per tonne of wheat produced and gross margins increasing by 111 per cent per hectare, whilst operating costs decrease by 32 per cent.

The problem is that none of the crucial costs saved by these forms of production, nor their capacity to generate positive externalities, appears in official economic statistics. As GDP only looks at formal profit, alternative farming practices are systematically regarded as inferior. As subsidies are then developed according to GDP-framed profit margins, our institutional decisions reward practices that are highly inefficient while excluding those that support innovation and decentralization. According to food activist Raj Patel,

If products do generate costs and benefits, then those need to be reflected in the price in order for the economic logic of markets to work properly. Otherwise, this is corporate subsidy on a massive scale, and there's nothing free marketers claim to like less than a subsidy. [. . .] [D]espite its protests, corporate capitalism has yet to prove that it can operate without these kinds of subsidies.[21]

In response to this state of affairs, the goal of alternative measurements focusing on natural capital is to 'make visible the value of ecosystems and biodiversity services for business, as well as the costs of business impacts on biodiversity and ecosystems'. For as long as 'these values and costs are invisible to business decision makers, business dependencies and impacts on nature also become invisible', resulting in the simple reality that crucial and expensive externalities are 'not factored into decision making'.[22]

Environmental costs are just one type of losses that are systematically disregarded by GDP. Social costs are equally important. All forms of centralized production, indeed, tend to increase negative social effects, including repetitive routines, long-distance commuting and fragmentation of the workforce: important factors that lead to alienation. Top-down structures are also more likely to trigger inequalities, with economies of scale separating managerial and operational roles and salary gaps widening accordingly. When these 'hidden' negative externalities are taken into account, the overall picture of the state of the economy changes dramatically. Figure 3.2 reports the results of a study comparing trends in GDP growth globally, with trends in the genuine progress indicator (GPI), an alternative measurement that also considers positive and negative environmental, as well as social, externalities. The results show that, since the late 1970s, the social and environmental costs generated by GDP growth have largely exceeded the gains in terms of national income, thus reducing the level of progress and making societies poorer overall.

To change this state of affairs, internal voluntary corporate social responsibility mechanisms will not be enough. Sukhdev contends that 'exogenous changes with the collaboration of governments, businesses, media and civil society will be required to make a new design arise from the old'.

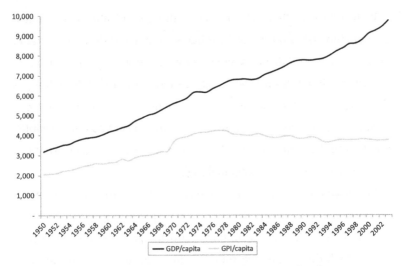

Figure 3.2 Global genuine progress contracts due to social and environmental costs since the late 1970s (per capita figures in 2005 US$). *Source:* Author's own based on data provided by Kubiszewski et al. (2013).

[S]uch activities will make the corporation of the future a veritable 'capital factory' – not just creating one line of category of capital (financial profit) but a whole array of capitals (physical, social, human and natural), and not just for itself, but also (in the form of positive externalities) for society at large. This behavior at the 'micro' level will make way for a very different world at the 'macro' level.[23]

Challenging the supremacy of GDP opens up new possibilities to show the economic value of a shared and cooperative economic system: 'Public ownership of the commons and community ownership of common-pool resources would be understood as economic *reality*, and not disparaged as "market failure".' Ultimately, '[g]rowth in complexity – rather than just size – would be an underpinning principle of the emerging green economy.'[24]

From *homo economicus* to *homo socialis*

As discussed in the previous chapter, GDP possesses a specific anthropological dimension. The GDP 'man' only exists in so far as he works and spends. He dislikes pure leisure, unless it is priced and commercialized. For the GDP man, time spent in the family or in the local community is wasted because it does not count for development and growth. The GDP man buys new stuff and throws it away once it breaks: fixing goods for long duration is indeed of no value in this dominant framework because GDP only counts the price of goods and services at the moment of purchase, giving no recognition to the intrinsic value of repairing.

This anthropological perspective on utility maximization is an extreme version of a dominant concept in economic sciences, that is, *homo economicus*. As famously declared by Adam Smith, 'it is not from the benevolence of the butcher, the brewer, or the baker that we expect our dinner, but from their regard to their own interest.'[25] *Homo economicus* is driven by personal returns and motivated by self-interest, an assumption that allows economists to predict behaviours and choices thanks to a strict utility-based rationality.

In the approach of *homo economicus*, it becomes clear that competition is more likely to achieve efficiency and results, as collaboration and collective action are marred by all sorts of problems. This is particularly true when property and institutional boundaries are not clearly defined. In a landmark paper published in *Science* in 1968, the ecologist Garrett Hardin discussed the inherent problems of cooperation in social settings through the metaphor of the 'tragedy of the commons'. Building on an 1833 essay by the economist William Forster Lloyd, who had studied grazing patterns in the villages of the British Isles, Hardin developed a hypothetical scenario of utility-maximizing herders sharing a common land. His conclusion was that rational behaviour would inevitably lead to over-grazing and depletion of the common resource because of a natural incentive to maximize individual pay-offs. The social dilemma underpinning the 'tragedy' is the unresolvable contradiction between personal and collective interests, ultimately leading to sub-optimal outcomes for all. Indeed, while collective welfare would require herders to limit their levels of consumption so as to share in the limited resource sustaining their economic activities, self-interest would push them to do the exact opposite. In the absence of top-down control over the common land, self-interest takes priority because of the uncertainty of collective behaviour: by limiting consumption, a herder may indeed find himself at a disadvantage compared to others who maximize individual returns. As a consequence, self-interest maximization becomes the dominant strategy, resulting in the depletion of the resource: the worst outcome for all. As Hardin recognized, this tragedy appears in a number of social organization and governance dynamics, from environmental preservation and water management to virtually all sorts of production and consumption processes: 'The rational man finds that his share of the cost of the wastes he discharges into the commons is less than the cost of purifying his wastes before releasing them. Since this is true for everyone, we are locked into a system of "fouling our own nest," so long as we behave only as independent, rational, free-enterprisers.'[26]

Hardin's thesis points to the inherent complexities of cooperation among individuals in the absence of a pre-existing system of institutional control exerted either by the state or the market. Successive economic research has reinforced this argument, showing that coordination across peers is particularly arduous to achieve.[27] In this light, the always-present temptation of free-riding on other individuals' efforts is a powerful social deterrent to collective action, resulting in poor coordination among large groups and the dominance of a few individuals over the rest, often through centralized top-down institutional command.

The alleged inevitability of this 'tragedy' has justified the introduction of coercive mechanisms through state regulation and/or market privatization as the only ways to deal with the depletion of common resources. From a GDP perspective, this makes perfect sense as it ensures institutional control, clear ownership boundaries and a system of formal payments for access and use. Yet this system of control and coercion can be counterproductive. In particular, the top-down control and boundary specifications achieved through the privatization of common resources not only provides an institutional reinforcement to self-interested behaviour but can easily trigger perverse incentives. Hardin himself admitted that:

> our particular concept of private property [. . .] favors pollution. The owner of a factory on the bank of a stream – whose property extends to the middle of the stream – often has difficulty seeing why it is not his natural right to muddy the waters flowing past his door. The law, always behind the times, requires elaborate stitching and fitting to adapt it to this newly perceived aspect of the commons.[28]

Top-down management may limit abuse by those not entitled to access or use the resource, but it may very well open opportunities for over-exploitation by those enjoying institutional command. By selling rights of access, those in control would naturally be driven to increase profits, thus leading to overuse. The natural sense of restrain that is associated with accessing a 'public' domain gives way to a sense of entitlement by what are now 'private' owners, which may very well lead to a second-order tragedy. As a matter of fact, the hypothetical scenario proposed by Hardin is inherently biased by the assumption that the participating herders view grazing as a private business rather than a shared activity. It can therefore be argued that the tragedy is not inherent in the common access to the land but rather in the discrepancy between a drive for profits through private property (that is, the individual ownership of cows and the need to maximize profit) and the limited resources available (that is, the commonly shared land). Would the outcome be the same if the cows, not just the land, were held in common?

Similar perverse incentives may also arise in the case of public property, whereby the institutional control is not exerted by a private legal personality (individual or company) but by the state. As is the case with market-based prices and purchases, the imposition of public tolls and fees for access may easily lead to overuse because of the need to maximize revenue collection by the state administration. Corruption is, of course, another evident problem, which is however fully coherent with the GDP framework in so far as bribes increase expenses and, therefore, national income. Moreover, state-driven institutional control requires a system of top-down management, monitoring and enforcement that comes at a cost. Yet this cost counts positively towards GDP, leading – once again – to all sorts of perverse incentives.

An alternative to this form of top-down control via market or state is what Carol Rose calls 'inherently public property'. In a classic 1986 essay published in the *University of Chicago Law Review* and aptly titled 'The Comedy of the Commons', she argues:

> there lies outside purely private property and government-controlled 'public property' a distinct class of 'inherently public

property' which is fully controlled by neither government nor private agents. Since the Middle Ages this category of 'inherently public property' has provided each member of some 'public' with a bundle of rights, neither entirely alienable by state or other collective action, nor necessarily 'managed' in any explicitly organized manner.[29]

Known in the legal field as 'public trust doctrine', the focus on horizontal forms of management has become central to both political and economic research since the pivotal empirical work conducted by the Nobel prizewinner Elinor Ostrom in the field of shared resource management. As Ostrom demonstrated, there are no valid reasons to believe that 'individuals are incompetent, evil, or irrational' when it comes to coordination and cooperation in the presence of common property.[30] In her view, conventional theories of collective action have postulated coordination problems and tragedies of the commons because they have failed to realize the inherent complexity of systems of social organizations. By forcing one-sided approaches onto the variability of governance mechanisms, conventional theories have triggered policy choices that reinforce top-down control and access boundaries: 'until a theoretical explanation [. . .] for self-organized and self-governed enterprises is fully developed and accepted, major policy decisions will continue to be undertaken with a presumption that individuals cannot organize themselves and always need to be organized by external authorities.'[31] Ostrom applied an institutionalist approach to highlight the effects that rules have on social logics, behaviours and preferences. She then complemented that with a specific interest in the evolution of complex systems, especially in the natural sciences. Her research points to a myriad of successful community-based management initiatives, which are not only efficient in terms of sustainable use of resources but also enduring and resilient, having purposefully adapted and evolved over hundreds of years. What makes these integrated systems for the management of 'common pool resources' effective over time is their particular governance arrangements, which are designed to avoid free riding, ensure collective monitoring and provide a set of monetary as well as reputational incentives that guarantee compliance. These results question various tenets of the GDP economy. First of all, they call into question the assumption that top-down institutional control, whether via the state or the market, is a precondition for economic activity. Secondly, they show that a standardized system of performance assessment can be highly inappropriate to steer economic processes and gauge their impacts, given that rules and indicators of success must be tailored to specific local conditions. By contrast, GDP implies a homogenization of economic processes around the world, which makes it blind to the inherent diversity of human activities. Finally, Ostrom's findings disprove the assumption that economies of scale and large corporations are necessarily more efficient and resilient than a horizontal system of cooperation, in which scale is achieved through modular organization and 'nested' forms of enterprise.

Applications of this new way of thinking are growing globally. In the United States, where community economies and collaborative systems have been weakened by a dominant culture of competition and top-down market control, the Business Alliance for Local Living Economies has been working with more than a hundred thousand local businesses to support the localization of economic systems, following Ostrom's research tenets with a view to creating 'a global system of human-scale', that is, a series of 'interconnected local economies that function in harmony with local ecosystems to meet the basic needs of all people, support just and democratic societies, and foster joyful community life'.[32] They constitute an example of bottom-up pressure for systemic change, supporting local economic innovation, the emergence of local leaders inspired by collaborative values and the creation of small businesses rejecting the GDP economy. Their theory of change connects institutionalist approaches with system thinking by maintaining that 'once corrupted, a complex system has an almost impossible time fixing itself'. 'The only real path to wholesale transformation is to find or create safe spaces outside the dominant system where something wholly new can emerge from the ground up.'[33]

In 2016, the Alliance published a report focusing on the most effective approaches to integrated health, rejecting the alleged efficiency of the top-down institutionalization of public and private systems. These approaches focus on the 'social determinants of health', that is, what the World Health Organization defines as 'the conditions in which people are born, grow, live, work, and age, and the wider set of forces and systems shaping the conditions of daily life', including 'economic policies and systems, development agendas, social norms, social policies and political systems'.[34] The report shows how the primary factors shaping health outcomes are access to education, income, civic participation, housing quality and neighbourhood safety, as well as access to transportation and healthy foods. In a similar fashion, research conducted by the Greater Good Science Center at the University of California in Berkeley demonstrates that people tend to be healthier and more resilient when they are connected to each other through local social systems, have opportunities to express generosity and live in proximity to the natural world.[35] As the County Health Rankings and Roadmaps project shows, more than 80 per cent of health outcomes are determined by factors such as the physical environment, social connections, economic participation and collective behaviours, rather than the availability of clinical care and medical treatment.[36]

In this context, America's largest integrated health system, Kaiser Permanente, has been advancing the concept of 'total health', an innovative framework aimed at capturing, measuring and delivering on a number of health-related dimensions, which breaks away from the traditional unidimensional focus on clinical output. This strategy is driving local economic development, especially in communities that have been marginalized by the GDP economy, and it is prioritizing supplier diversity, with purchases of more than US$1.5 billion made from cooperatives managed by women and minority groups.[37] Other health-care providers have adopted similar approaches, using their resources to support small businesses, local jobs, community development and assisted housing. Dignity Health, the fifth-largest health system in the United States, has created a US$100 million loan fund to support economic emancipation in underserved communities.[38]

Understanding health as a social good rather than an output that can be individually 'consumed' challenges the foundations of the GDP economy. Moreover, the very concept of 'total' health runs counter to the dominating logic of GDP, which postulates that high levels of consumption are good for the economy. This new approach, indeed, aims to reduce transactions by approaching social health from a multidimensional perspective, resorting to clinical care only as a marginal measure. Much to the contrary, GDP equates good health with high levels of expenditure, which usually reward costly, inefficient and highly unequal health-care systems. In the United States, where millions of citizens have limited assistance in a system notoriously skewed towards the well-off, the overall costs of health care are unparalleled in the world: it is the second-highest contributor to national GDP after financial services.[39] By contrast, in Cuba, health care is mostly preventative and delivered at a very low cost as doctors receive salaries that are commensurate with the local living standards and the rest of the labour market. Although Cuba's health-care system is globally renowned as one of the best, the national economy is penalized by the GDP approach, which is why the statistical office has been correcting the overall contribution of health-care services to the economy by estimating their impact on social welfare rather than the mere number of monetary transactions.[40] As the Business Alliance for Local Living Economies' report concludes, 'When ownership is rooted in community and held broadly, the economy benefits the many rather than the few. Worker, producer, and consumer cooperative ownership models are increasingly recognized as a strategy for building security in low income communities.'[41]

Competition triggers a number of social effects, including conflict, resentment and exclusion, which can be more easily neglected in the context of top-down approaches designed to separate corporations from the rest of society. According to the GDP framework, indeed, an organization can prosper through competition because the negative social effects are absorbed externally. But when activities are localized, competitive tendencies become inefficient, at the very least because those excluded will continue operating within the same system, potentially threatening its sustainability: in the real world of local-level economic processes, 'losers' do not leave the game; they cannot be assumed away. Moreover, the perceived costs of competition may be increased by social norms and reward mechanisms in a given community, for which exclusion may be viewed as a socially unacceptable outcome, regardless of its alleged economic benefits. As Amartya Sen famously remarked, the *homo economicus* conventionally described by mainstream economics 'is close to being a social moron'.[42]

That small-scale localized interaction supports cooperation is also confirmed by computer models applied to real-life situations. Researchers have indeed found that, while free riding and competitive attitudes dominate large-scale interactions among individuals, the opposite is true in interactions that are locally clustered.[43] Random, disorganized interactions may cause a tragedy of the commons leading to non-cooperation and systemic failure, but not when appropriate systems of decentralized governance are introduced in interactions confined to specific geographical spaces or in social networks, where compatible behaviours cluster together and reinforce each other.

According to my colleague Dirk Helbing, a highly cited physicist holding the chair of computational social sciences at ETH Zurich, 'locality is very important in our universe'.

> Most physical forces are extremely short-range. Locality is also crucial to self-organizing processes in socio-economic systems. For example, niches that support diversity and innovation can only exist locally. Moreover local interactions foster cooperation. [. . .] One might even say that the most interesting socio-economic phenomena are based on co-evolutionary processes that happen on the meso-level, which is a layer between individual system components and the entire system.[44]

Whether it is schools of fish in the ocean or flocks of birds in the sky, complex systems operate through a decentralized system of rules that are interacted upon through local exchanges. In these adaptive systems, it would be extremely inefficient to generate order through top-down, competitive, utility-maximizing processes. The secret of success is horizontal coordination through micro-exchanges shaped by clear rules. Ostrom's intuition was correct: social organization processes can learn a lot from the complex adaptive equilibria found in natural ecosystems.

Not only does the inherent complexity of social systems defy the anthropological dimensions of the GDP man, for whom top-down appropriation of common resources and continuous consumption are preconditions for development, but they also call into question the academically mainstream notion of *homo economicus*, paving the way for the definition of a complementary, if not alternative, paradigm: *homo socialis*. Psychological studies have demonstrated that, even in institutional environments that promote material self-interest, individuals are affected by norms of fairness and reciprocity.[45] For instance, recent experiments dealing with consumer elective pricing have confirmed the deep social nature of human behaviour.[46] Consumer elective pricing refers to any commercial transaction in which the buyer can pay any price for a good or service: maximizing immediate self-interest would move people to pay zero, whereas considering the welfare of those responsible for the production would push them to pay more. Since the music band Radiohead released their 2007 album *In Rainbows* through a pay-what-you-want licence, gaining a windfall in revenues, consumer elective price has become a burgeoning economic phenomenon. Panera Bread, a large restaurant chain, has opened flexible-price cafés selling soups and sandwiches. The online network Humble Bundle offers a pay-what-you-want scheme to millions of customers purchasing video games, music, e-books and other digital goods. What makes these apparently paradoxically business models successful is the realization that social dynamics have a considerable weight in directing people's purchasing choices. This is even more evident in cases where customers not only set the price, but they pay it forward to benefit future clients. A practical example of a pay-it-forward scheme is the 'suspended coffee' movement in Europe, which went viral after 2013 with thousands of businesses having joined the initiative. Its origin can be traced to the working-class cafés of Naples, Italy, where owners would run a tab with coffees pre-paid by other customers as a gesture of generosity vis-à-vis less privileged future clients. A pay-it-forward framing transforms the buyer–seller binomial dynamic of consumer elective pricing into a social relationship between the giver and society at large, represented by the anonymous receiver of the gift. Contrary to the tenets of self-interest economic theories, experimental research has demonstrated that people elect higher prices when paying forward than when they can benefit individually from electing their own price.[47] It appears as if generosity plays a crucial role in altering the individual parameters of utility, producing additional pleasure for the customer when the payment is beneficial to the rest of society.

The reverse also appears to be true: monetary compensations can crowd out generosity considerations. In his 1970 book *The Gift Relationship*, the sociologist Richard Titmuss argued that voluntary actions, like donating blood, would be undermined by the introduction of economic incentives. A more recent study, conducted in Sweden, confirmed that payments decreased blood donations among female volunteers, generally more susceptible to issues of social care. Similar to the pay-it-forward dynamic, donations only resumed when volunteers were given an option to donate the money to a foundation working on children's health issues.[48] A series of studies in behavioural economics has also demonstrated the crowding-out effect of monetary transactions in a number of fields.[49]

Different logics of appropriateness, framing processes and institutional conditions can be decisive factors in shifting people from self-interested competitiveness to more cooperative and generous behaviour. For instance, in a 2004 study conducted at Stanford, social psychologists tested the predisposition towards competition vis-à-vis cooperation in two groups of students playing the same game but with different names: the first was called Community Game, while the second had the label Wall Street Game. Despite similar approaches, the 'name of the game' mattered a great deal: cooperation levels turned out to be much higher in the first game (over 70 per cent) than in the second (about 30 per cent).[50]

The existence of *homo socialis* is also confirmed by discoveries in neuroscience. Neuroimaging studies, which monitor brain activity in the presence of specific stimuli, have confirmed that material resources, including money, are often less important than the social context in which these resources are allocated. In particular, fairness and cooperation provide positive reward mechanisms that disprove the assumption of pure self-interest.[51] Social studies had already found substantial increases in self-reported utility and positive emotions when performance was associated with fair and cooperative treatment, while controlling for material outputs.[52] In some cases, it was found that monetary compensations were perceived as reducing personal well-being and utility if achieved in unfair conditions.[53] Modern functional magnetic resonance imaging has further confirmed these findings by showing unequivocally the activation of areas of the human brain associated with pleasure in the presence of outcomes that are based on fairness and cooperation, even at the expense of monetary rewards.[54] Specifically, cooperation leads to more activity in the orbito-frontal cortex as compared to competition, indicating higher levels of satisfaction.[55]

In his 1976 classic book *The Selfish Gene*, acclaimed biologist Richard Dawkins argued that those passionate about building cooperative and common-good societies 'can expect little help from biological nature [. . .] because we are born selfish'.[56] But a few decades later, this approach is now being challenged in arguably all fields of scientific progress from economics to anthropology, biology and neurology. In a 2006 issue of *Science,* Harvard mathematical biologist Martin Nowak remarked: '[W]e observe cooperation on many levels of biological organization. Genes cooperate in genomes. Chromosomes cooperate in eukaryotic cells. Cells cooperate in multicellular organisms. There are many examples of cooperation among animals. Humans are the champions of cooperation: from hunter-gatherer societies to nation-states, cooperation is the decisive organizing principle of human society.'[57]

Novak pointed out the crucial role played by rules of engagement and logics of appropriateness in the context of natural selection. In an environment in which institutional rules favour competitive individuals and defectors, who benefit at the expense of cooperators, natural selection leads to the demise of cooperation as its champions perish due to lower fitness. But in a society in which cooperation is reinforced by the appropriate rules and logics, natural selection works the other way around: cooperative groups have a higher level of fitness and resilience, thus outnumbering defectors. For Novak, 'natural cooperation' completed the classical triad of fundamental principles of evolution, alongside mutation and natural selection. Sociobiologist Herbert Gintis has developed a series of models to study the complex interaction between norms, genes and institutional systems in the creation of social tendencies among human beings. In partnership with Helbing, he has concluded that 'extra-familial socialization institutions are necessary to support altruistic forms of prosociality' and that 'cooperation is robustly stable when antisocial behavior is punished by the voluntary, and largely decentralized, initiative of group members.'[58]

Adam Smith himself was probably not as convinced that self-interest leads to better outcomes as is often proclaimed by mainstream economists. His *Wealth of Nations* became a manifesto for classical economic thinking, but another book of his, *The Theory of Moral Sentiments,* presented a very different view. Here, Smith openly addressed the complexities of human behaviour and the intersection between utilitarian dynamics and deeper social norms. And his conclusion was that 'How selfish soever man may be supposed, there are evidently some principles in his nature, which interest him in the fortune of others, and render their happiness necessary to him, though he derives nothing from it except the pleasure of seeing it.'[59]

A horizontal economy

In *Postindustrial Possibilities,* economic sociologist Fred Block identified a set of trends characterizing the shift in economic systems at the end of the twentieth century. One of these was 'the growing importance of the services in the economy, and the declining weight of goods productions'.[60] Another trend was 'the arrival of computer-based automation', which disrupted conventional patterns of work organization, namely the repetitive linear process of production.

Less than two decades into the twenty-first century, the growth of a distributed economy appears to have continued eroding the conventional industrial model, with top-down production processes being outcompeted by efficient and often high-tech aided systems of co-production. As Ostrom notes, co-production is 'the process through which inputs used to produce a good or service are contributed by individuals who are not "in" the same organization'.[61] The phenomenon has become quite evident in the software industry. In the late 1990s, the technology giant IBM, which had historically promoted a top-down proprietary approach to research and development, endorsed the 'open-source initiative' and adopted Linux, the world's best known co-produced operating system.[62] It has ever since invested hundreds of millions of dollars in open-source technologies, leveraging the collaborative inputs of thousands of developers around the world, which use and improve IBM's software. It is also well known that one of the world's most popular web browsers, Firefox, is an open-source software developed by a non-profit organization, the Mozilla Foundation, and co-produced by users around the globe. In less than a decade, Firefox has managed to erode the market advantage of proprietary software like Microsoft's Internet Explorer, and it is likely to become the most common software worldwide in the next few years. A digital repository like Wikipedia, which is co-produced by hundreds of thousands of volunteers with a passion for knowledge, has become the go-to platform for students and scholars worldwide, making traditional encyclopedias like Britannica largely obsolete. Stack Overflow provides opportunities for computer experts to exchange information and opinions, challenging conventional handbooks and manuals. The website has over four million members and more than ten million answered technical queries. Open Street Map, a co-produced alternative to Google Maps, is supported by more than 1.5 million volunteers. The platform Zooniverse allows over a million citizen scientists to share data and participate in crowdsourced scientific research, which is routinely used by the world's leading universities. Initiatives like PatientsLikeMe and Cure Together allow millions of patients to share experiences, data, health information and ratings of treatments, complementing the traditional top-down authority in the medical industry and providing valuable information for patient-driven research.[63] The car manufacturer Tesla, a pioneer in electric vehicles, made its inventions open source in 2014 to allow the electric car industry to step up the game.[64]

Most of these initiatives operate through general public licences, refusing intellectual proprietary control and allowing end users the freedom to run, study, share and modify the invention. They are just examples of a groundswell of peer-to-peer co-production, which some have termed 'wikinomics': a collaborative economy that is challenging conventional proprietary forms of top-down control even in the current GDP-dominated market economy.[65] From car sharing to couch surfing, the peer-to-peer industry is on the rise all over the globe, with crucial impacts also on livelihoods, especially among those marginalized by the mainstream economic system. In the United States, the annual cost of car ownership is estimated at US$9,000, eating up – on average – a quarter of household income, making it the second most expensive cost after housing.[66] On the contrary, car-sharing or ride-sharing schemes provide access to transport for tens of dollars, allowing less-privileged families to enjoy modern mobility without any upfront investment.[67] A 2013 survey by Airbnb in the United Kingdom showed that 80 per cent of their hosts rent out the home they live in with a view to topping up income. Over 60 per cent of their respondents maintained peer-to-peer renting was essential to pay bills, with 45 per cent indicating they would probably lose their homes without it. Overall, the study found that 42 per cent of hosts were self-employed, freelancers or part-time workers.[68]

Besides their co-production approach, most of these new businesses scale horizontally rather than vertically. For instance, GitHub, the world's leading service provider for peer-to-peer software development, which boasts more than 10 million active users and contributors, follows the managerial philosophy of a 'flat organization' in so far as workers operate with a high degree of autonomy and are closely involved in decision making.[69] In horizontal businesses, employees tend to be more adaptable in changing circumstances, thanks to flat hierarchies and lack of bureaucracy. Work groups assigned to specific projects, for example, can craft their own unique operational processes without seeking the approval of higher levels of management.

Since employees operate on a level playing field, more responsibility is placed upon each individual, creating a situation where innovative, collaborative self-starters excel while passive followers lag behind.

Computer scientists have confirmed that co-production can achieve higher levels of performance, with less input than the conventional producer–consumer relationship.[70] By collaborating, two people can generate open-source software that would have required at least two and a half developers. 'Superlinearity', that is, the mathematical concept used to describe relations that grow above pure linear increments, is found to hold for group sizes ranging from five to a few hundred developers. This is because collaborative groups 'function at or close to criticality, or in a "superradiance" mode', that is, in a developed modality 'defined by the build-up of correlation between the contributions of developers'.[71] The inherent diversity and integration of social systems is becoming key for the emergence of a new form of business, with terms such as 'ecosystem' replacing that of 'scale' or 'network' in the jargon of new business ventures.[72]

Having originated in the software and communication industries, the ecosystemic revolution appears to be spreading to other areas of production and consumption. In particular, additive production methods, more commonly known as 3D printing, can support highly dispersed systems of production, where the boundaries with conventional consumption are increasingly blurred. 3D printing indeed allows consumers to produce their own artefacts while downloading, modifying and sharing highly sophisticated designs. While home-based 3D printing is still in its infancy, small businesses are now using these technologies to co-produce with conventional 'clients', achieving customization at a fraction of traditional costs. For less than US$3,000, a popular 3D printer such as MakerBot Replicator allows hobbyists to create a wide variety of objects, from glasses to plates, utensils, lamps, sculptures and hammers. Its upgraded version Z18 was used to 'print' the suits of the alien invaders in the American TV series *Colony* in 2016, a new frontier in low-cost high-results special effects.[73] Larger 3D printers have been successfully employed to manufacture a virtually endless variety of objects, from prosthetic limbs to violins, aircraft components, tractors for small farmers and even apartment blocks. The European Space Agency has been exploring using additive technologies to build a permanent base on the moon, using local materials and avoiding the logistical costs of shipping components from earth.[74]

Additive technologies efficiently complement the peer-to-peer digital revolution by providing the post-GDP economy with a hitherto missing link, that is, the capacity to blur production boundaries in the field of hardware. Through these innovations, households can cease to be the 'passive' locus of consumption depicted by GDP to become more involved in self-production and co-production. Through the mushrooming of high-tech small-scale manufacturing, community-level businesses can finally compete with large corporations in the co-production of manufactured goods, a sector in which they have been traditionally at a disadvantage. Moreover, small businesses will be able to customize, reuse and adapt with a higher degree of efficiency. With digital designs that can be shared across the world, modified and customized for a fraction of the original costs, small workshops that allow customers to personalize their gadgets are likely to become increasingly popular. From a total cost-accounting perspective, this mode of co-production is enormously more efficient than the vertical economy, at least in so far as it minimizes waste through customization, reduces mileage and transportation costs through localization, empowers customers by rejecting the passive notion of consumers, creates economic opportunities in previously marginalized communities and replaces standardization with creativity and diversity.

As argued by management scholar Jerry Davis, '[t]he traditional large corporation that dominated the twentieth-century US economy has reached its twilight': 'It is no longer suited to fulfilling the functions that it did for much of the past century – producing goods and services, providing stable employment, insuring health care, and creating returns for savers.'[75]

A 'third industrial revolution', a term popularized by Jeremy Rifkin and the *Economist*, which blurs production boundaries, turns consumers into producers, scales horizontally rather than vertically and reduces social and environmental costs, is currently underway.[76] The energy sector, especially in Europe, is another typical example of this transition. In Germany, where sustainable energy technologies have proliferated faster than in many other countries, large private conglomerates have been outcompeted by peer-to-peer producers, with more than 40 per cent of the production managed directly by households.[77] In the United States, almost one thousand rural electric cooperatives provide energy to 42 million customers in all but four states, with transmission lines covering three-quarters of the nation's landmass.[78] The island of Samso, in Denmark, has become completely energy independent thanks to a mix of renewable energy systems managed directly by its inhabitants.[79]

This new horizontal economy is also more likely to adapt to changing needs, thus achieving higher degrees of resilience. On average, 40 per cent of the Standard & Poor's 500 companies disappear within a 10-year time period.[80] Publicly listed companies in the United States went from about nine thousand in the early 1990s to less than half that number in 2010. Only seven of the Dow Jones Industrial Index companies in 1973 are still listed today.[81] Through modular design, co-production with customers and collaborative relationships with suppliers, the post-GDP economy is more likely to build robust value chains.[82] Moreover, its distributed control can adapt 'real time' and adjust more flexibly to changing local conditions. Cooperatives, for instance, have demonstrated a higher degree of adaptability and resilience in the face of the global economic crisis, vis-à-vis their corporate alternatives, especially in the banking sector.[83] On the contrary, top-down institutional control suffers from high organizational costs, crystallized routines that stifle innovation and 'flashlight effects' which bring attention only to a limited set of variables in a context of complex multifaceted data.

Blurring the boundaries of work

In an essay dedicated to the 'economic possibilities for our grandchildren', penned in 1932, John Maynard Keynes predicted that within a century there would be a time when people would only dedicate a few hours to the formal earning of an income, spending most of their time pursuing activities that would be much more rewarding, such as family and community life.[84] Others after him have foreseen 'the end of work' generated by increasing labour productivity and the introduction of robotics into traditional top-down assembly lines.[85] Silicon Valley analysts have also predicted a near future in which robots and artificial intelligence will make most jobs redundant, leading to massive unemployment.[86] McKinsey reports that almost half of firms that reduced their workforce since the 2008 financial crisis have done so by replacing people with automation.[87] In 2013, a study conducted by researchers at Oxford University estimated that about 47 per cent of all jobs in the United States will be at risk in the near future due to the rise of automation in conventional production processes, especially in areas where repetition and routines are critical. Moreover, a survey covering the period 1950 to 2006 shows that there is strong link between an economy's vertical concentration of jobs, that is, the share of the labour force employed by the largest corporations, and its overall level of inequality.[88]

This is perhaps not particularly surprising against the backdrop of what we have already argued with respect to the GDP economy. Top-down control, clear separation between production and consumption and economies of scale are more likely to lead to inequalities and unemployment, especially if more 'efficient' production alternatives are found, namely through the use of automation systems. In many ways, the 'productivity trap' is a driving force behind the GDP economy's focus on continuous growth in production and consumption: unless the economy expands infinitely, jobs are lost through incremental labour productivity, as fewer people manage to achieve more output with less input. With less growth, inequality rises too. But what about the post-GDP economy we have been describing in this chapter? Will it also lead to structural inequality and unemployment?

To address this question, it is crucial to ask: what is work? The value frame provided by GDP understands work as the formal transaction-based earning of a monetary income. The gross national income (which is the equivalent of GDP measured in terms of income paid out rather than production or expenditure) only measures activities that are institutionally controlled, performed in exchange of monetary compensation and happen within the formal boundaries of the GDP economy. In this vein, all activities that are carried out informally or without a monetary exchange are, by the definition, not work. Yet research published by the International Monetary Fund indicates that more than 40 per cent of economic activities in so-called 'developing countries' are informal by nature and thus not captured by official statistics, with Nigeria and Egypt boasting the highest figures, equivalent to 77 per cent and 69 per cent respectively.[89] In post-communist societies, informal work accounts for about a third of all economically valuable activities, while in the world's richest countries about 15 per cent of all transactions belong to the 'shadow' economy, with countries such as Greece and Italy showing the largest informal working sectors, with 30 and 27 per cent respectively.[90] In a high-income country like Denmark, which routinely tops a variety of global prosperity ranks, the informal economy's share of total labour doubled during the 1980s and 1990s, from about 8 per cent to more than 15 per cent. Similar trends have been registered in other high-income countries such as Germany and France. Moreover, the informal economy is not just a 'parallel' economy: it performs critical functions, from repairing and reusing to customized production, personalized services and craftwork, which the GDP economy does not produce because it is inconsistent with the underlying model of growth. In Germany and Austria, for instance, two-thirds of all value produced informally would not be produced at all if the parallel economy did not exist.[91]

The GDP-induced categorization of work also hides the fact that only a fraction of people's time is spent on formal jobs. As studies conducted by the OECD have shown, an average human being in the world's richest nations spends no more than 20 per cent of his/her time on paid work, a category including also the non-working population's time spent studying. Besides personal care and leisure, which account for about 60 per cent, a significant portion of time (on average 14 per cent) is spent performing 'unpaid work', that is, household-based care activities and voluntary community involvement, all productive activities neglected by GDP.[92] European countries top the world rankings in terms of time spent on unpaid work, with Denmark being the country with the highest level of unpaid work performed by men.

Household-based activities challenge the GDP economy in at least two regards: they are provided for free and they are mostly based on self-production. As the writer Katrine Marçal quips in her book *Who Cooked Adam Smith's Dinner?*, the conventional focus of *homo economicus* on the self-interest of 'the butcher, the brewer or the baker' has overshadowed a hard reality: it is the unaccounted selflessness of families (mostly through the unpaid work of women, including Smith's mother) that provides the essential services and goods that make any formal economy able to operate.[93] Even though it is not directly monetized, unpaid work represents implicit income.[94] As countries strive to modernize according to the GDP approach to prosperity, however, a substantial part of household-based production and services (e.g. food, clothing and caring activities) is transferred to the market and formally purchased by families. In turn, household external consumption pushes up volumes of transported goods, centralizes systems of production and generates economies of scale, which contribute to overproduction and waste, ultimately taking a toll on the environment.

GDP treats such a shift from the household to mass production as progress, which gives a false impression of improving living standards. As discussed earlier in this chapter, economies of scale may make goods and services cheaper but only because the pricing mechanisms embedded in GDP do not take into account the cost of negative externalities, from waste disposal to transportation and pollution. This is also true at the micro-level of family life. Parents with enough 'free' time to take care of their children and perform other household-based functions often enjoy a higher disposable income than families with slightly higher gross income but where both parents work full time and must purchase all these services from the market.[95]

In line with its anthropological dimension, the perfect 'GDP society' is that in which parents spend all of their waking time at work and pay their entire take-home salary to a domestic worker and nanny to produce the services they are no longer able or willing to provide. As full-time workers and simultaneously employers, they would contribute twice to GDP growth. The reality, however, is that our economies would arguably grind to a halt if the innumerable free-of-charge functions rendered at the household level (from child and elderly care to education) were to be exchanged for a fee. In the United States, household services accounted for about one-third of the national economic output since the mid-1960s.[96] Such figures would be much higher if applied to 'developing countries' where households are larger and economies less formalized. By imputing the opportunity cost at the average market rates for each country, the OECD's estimates of the economic value of household production and community work are astounding, ranging from a bit less than 40 per cent of GDP in Hungary to almost 80 per cent in the United Kingdom, as reported in Figure 3.3.

As we have seen, the post-GDP economy blurs the boundaries of production, giving households and communities a pivotal and productive role in the economy. As manufacturing becomes increasingly

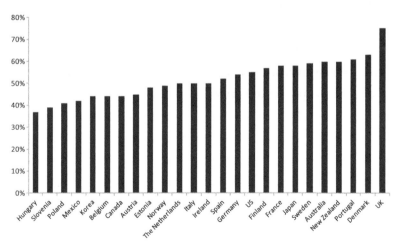

Figure 3.3 Economic value of household work in terms of opportunity cost (percentage of GDP).

Source: Author's elaboration of OECD data published in Miranda (2011).

localized, the rise of small businesses benefits community-based activities through a horizontal distribution of professional opportunities. In this economy, work is no longer associated exclusively with a formal job, but it encompasses a variety of socially productive activities, including peer-to-peer care and volunteering. Self-employment opportunities and cooperative schemes would therefore become even more popular than they are already because the institutional system would support rather than suffocate them. Through the mainstreaming of additive technology, economies of scale and large distribution may be gradually replaced by a new form of 'post-industrial artisanship', in which small workshops of co-producers customize manufacturing and engage in recycling and upcycling, that is, the constant upgrade of used goods into new, higher-quality versions. As total cost accounting shows, a 'circular' economy driven by highly skilled artisans would enjoy a considerable level of performance, potentially eliminating negative externalities. In terms of employment capacity, hybrid forms of business hold the potential for being much more labour intensive than vertically structured corporations. For instance, cooperatives employ more than 100 million people globally, with one person in every seven being affiliated with a cooperative. In the United States, about 80 per cent of the people are directly or indirectly involved in the activities of cooperatives. In Canada, it is one in every ten. In India and China, 400 million people belong to cooperatives. In Kenya, 63 per cent of the population derive their livelihoods from cooperatives. In Denmark, consumer cooperatives control more than a third of the retail market. In Norway, every second person is a member of a cooperative.[97] Across the European Union, 10 per cent of people live in cooperative housing schemes.[98] Because GDP has traditionally relegated cooperatives to the margins of the productive economy, experts of co-production have publicly called for the cooperative sector to stop 'fighting against old windmills' and push for the demise of the GDP system of accounting as strategy to acquire more visibility in the new economy.[99]

According to the Inclusive Wealth Index – a post-GDP measurement developed by the United Nations – the real wealth driving progress across the world is not produced capital (which is what GDP measures) but human and natural capital (which GDP ignores).[100] I have covered the importance of natural capital earlier in this chapter. Here, the central question is how to develop an economic system in which human capital acquires the centrality it deserves. In a word, can the post-GDP economy become a people-centred system of social organization? As a new strand of research in economics has shown, the inefficiencies of the GDP economy can only be addressed by developing forms of work that are based on people-to-people services, in which businesses are no longer controllers of production but facilitators of peer-to-peer collaboration and co-production.[101] Such a shift from a conventional, top-down manufacturing basis to a co-production service economy is likely to re-invent the concept of productivity, thus creating new opportunities for meaningful employment and sustainability.[102] For instance, if households and communities were to become more energy independent through the use of micro-grids or off-the-grid technologies, a post-GDP business would shift from the direct supply of energy (as is the case with most conventional utilities these days) to selling 'energy services' such as maintenance and smart distribution. Instead of producing more and more cars, post-GDP businesses would provide mobility services, including apps for car sharing, traffic updates, mechanical repairs and upcycling. Instead of building ever larger supermarket chains, post-GDP alternatives would look into 'smart retailing', optimizing local value chains, bringing co-producers together and supporting small farmers to interact more effectively with a host of active customers.

Environmentalist Bill McKibben identifies the emergence of what he calls the 'deep economy' in the myriad peer-to-peer energy projects, local farmers' markets, slow food cooperatives, community gardening projects, maintenance and refurbishment services, craft workshops, people-to-people care initiatives, integrated health, parent-driven schools and participatory conservation practices that are mushrooming in contemporary societies.[103] These enterprises are almost completely neglected by the GDP system of accounting and, as a consequence, they are seen as unproductive and backward by the rest of society, treated as the 'Cinderella economy'.[104] The crucial point missed by the GDP economic structure is that this service industry relies on exchanges that involve personal interactions between people so that they produce high value without the conventional approach to productivity, opening unprecedented possibilities for full employment in an age of constant innovation. The classical work carried out by the economist William Baumol in the performing arts (also known by the problematic label of 'cost disease') shows that productivity is less likely to increase in sectors where personal performance is at the centre of value creation.[105] Teachers, doctors and hairdressers are, by and large, as productive today as they were hundreds of years ago. Asking teachers to teach more students or doctors to visit more patients may count as a plus for the GDP economy, but it would certainly be disastrous for society. Data confirm this: for instance, between 1995 and 2005, labour productivity in the personal and social service sectors declined by 3 per cent across the European Union, the only economic sector to show negative productivity growth.[106]

In an article published in the *New York Times*, economist Tim Jackson openly advocates for society to shift towards a completely different approach to productivity. He points out how the future economy should focus on tasks that 'rely inherently on the allocation of people's time and attention' because 'the time spent by these professions directly improves the quality of our lives'. For Jackson, this does not only apply to the care sector but also to manufactured goods. 'It is the accuracy and detail inherent in crafted goods that endows them with lasting value. It is the time and attention paid by the carpenter, the seamstress and the tailor that makes this detail possible':

> The endemic modern tendency to streamline or phase out such professions highlights the lunacy at the heart of the growth-obsessed, resource-intensive consumer economy. Low productivity is seen as a disease. A whole set of activities that could provide meaningful work and contribute valuable services to the community are denigrated because they involve employing people to work with devotion, patience and attention. But people often achieve a greater sense of well-being and fulfillment, both as producers and consumers of such activities, than they ever do in the time-poor, materialistic supermarket economy in which most of our lives are spent.[107]

Redesigning money

In chapter 1, I introduced this book's conceptualization of the economy as a complex system of social organization whose rules establish logics of appropriateness, help predictability and thus frame interaction. Economic rules are not neutral vis-à-vis the kind of society they contribute to creating, which is why changing the underlying economic operating system has the potential to trigger a cascade effect or, at least, to generate a powerful spillover onto the political and social realm.

How does money fit into this framework? Although monetary theory generally describes money as a unit of account, a currency and a store of value, money is primarily a tool of social organization. Money coordinates economic activity, making transactions predictable while lowering their coordination costs, especially in societies where there is limited interpersonal trust and reciprocity. As Georg Simmel described in *The Philosophy of Money*, currencies are markers of the underlying values held by a community, shaping human social interaction. The reason why people often equate money with power is because money is a substitute for other 'tools' when it comes to affecting behaviours. Reputation, love, sympathy and force, for instance, are also forms of power, at least in so far as they can be used to influence other people's choices and actions. Money is, however, the most generic of all: unlike the others, it has a wide range of applications, from anonymous purchases to the coordination of the employee–employer relationship and the taxation system. To paraphrase Adam Smith, the exchange of money makes the reaction of the baker, the butcher and the brewer extremely predictable. A simple exchange of currency guarantees that our dinner will be served, even in the absence of a personal relationship with those providing it and without the use of force (provided we conveniently forget that Smith's loving mother was ultimately responsible for cooking his dinner, for free!). Of course, there are many things that money cannot buy, from friendship to respect, including a wide range of non-monetary goods that most people cherish. In all other cases, however, money works quite reliably in shaping social coordination processes. I therefore agree with Charles Eisenstein's depiction of money as 'a system of social agreements, meanings, and symbols that develops over time': 'It is, in a word, a story, existing in social reality along with such things as laws, nations, institutions, calendar and clock time, religion, and science. Stories bear tremendous creative power. Through them we coordinate human activity, focus attention and intention, define roles, and identify what is important and even what is real.'[108]

Like the underlying economic rules, money systems are not neutral. The fiat money, which refers to the monetary production managed by public institutions, as is the case with most state currencies issued by central banks, is highly centralized and narrowly controlled. Moreover, it affords banks widespread control over the supply of money through the issuance of credit/debt, thanks to a vertical process of lending from central authorities.[109] The link between contemporary interest-bearing money and credit/debt is particularly important from the perspective of GDP. As money is created through interest-based lending, it sets the economy on a continuous process of vertical growth (that is, increasing conventional production and consumption), which becomes essential to generate the additional resources needed to clear the original debt. The very nature of interest-bearing money, which has allowed the expansion of credit in modern societies, thus inherently requires the economy to function according to the rules of GDP growth. Moreover, it allows for concentration and hoarding, thus favouring a 'transactional economy' in which the pure flow of money is associated with increasing wealth, regardless of its utility for society.[110] Quite importantly, the current money system provides an institutional framework for short-termism, favouring exchanges that bring immediate returns over those with a more long-term horizon. Since interest-bearing money creates more money (for instance, by simply sitting in a bank account and generating the credit–debt cycle that is at the basis of money creation), spending in the present has an inherent advantage vis-à-vis investing in the future. In this framework, future returns are naturally discounted in comparison to immediate gains, very much in line with the GDP approach discussed in chapter 2. As a consequence, exploiting natural, social and human resources as fast as possible and accumulating the revenues therein even in simple savings accounts (let alone high-return investment schemes) has a bigger impact on GDP than managing them responsibly.

Against this backdrop, monetary analyst Bernard Laetier argues that only through a different money system can a new economy emerge. In particular, he points out how the vertical control of fiat monies and their interest-bearing nature make horizontal cooperation in the economy very hard to achieve by forging institutional rules that lead to scarcity and competition. In the book *Rethinking Money: How New Currencies Turn Scarcity into Prosperity*, Laetier and his co-author argue:

money is assumed to be value neutral, not affecting the type of exchanges made, the kind of relationship among its users, or the time horizon of investments. [. . .] Our monetary system generates scarcity and competition. The rivalry and contest are so pervasive that we have become inured to its impact in our daily lives in all levels of society.[111]

In the past few years, partly because of the global financial crisis and partly because of technological innovations, new forms of horizontal money have emerged. Similar to the processes described in the previous sections, these currencies challenge top-down institutional control. Alternative money systems are by no means a complete novelty in the global political economy. The Great Depression, too, prompted the emergence of complementary currencies across most of the countries affected by the economic contraction. Early twentieth-century anarchists like Silvio Gesell theorized and applied the ideas of interest-free currencies in local communities, from Germany to Argentina. The novelty about the current trend is the scope of distribution as well as the convergence of social and technological innovation, which are turning horizontal currency systems into a potentially game-changing phenomenon.

It is hard to establish how many alternative and complementary currencies exist in the world, as many have been in existence for some time while others have had a relative short lifespan. The Complementary Currency Research Group provides details of more than three hundred networks engaged in innovative systems of exchange, while Laetier puts the overall tally at about six thousand worldwide.[112] Most of these systems are not alternative to fiat money: they aim to complement the dominant framework by supporting horizontal exchange and creating opportunities for different values and principles to be factored into economic interactions. Many of them are community based, a generic definition to describe local exchange trading systems (LETS) and local currencies.[113] Some of them use time units as currency, providing participants with a horizontal coordination system that incentivizes social interaction. In this framework, centralization is impossible because only users can generate credits by availing their time. Accumulation is possible, but counterproductive, given that the value of the currency is in its circulation. As time units do not grow in value, hoarding is self-defeating. Credits expand in relation to the degree of mutual involvement within the community of users, providing an incentive for peer-to-peer support and social cohesion. Moreover, time is valued at the same rate regardless of the type of service offered, which instils a sense of democratic equality and also a perception that no skill is superior to others. Laetier argues that this type of horizontal money helps people cooperate by overcoming scarcity and putting users in the driver seat: 'As soon as you have an agreement between two people about a transaction using Time Dollars, they literally create the necessary "money" in the process.'[114] According to this perspective, the drive for competition we see in the world economy is not a result of the nature of things but rather an artificial consequence of the fiat money system and its top-down distribution: 'The scarcity is in our national currencies. In fact, the job of central banks is to create and maintain that currency scarcity. The direct consequence is that we have to fight with each other in order to survive.'[115]

Some LETS use time as the unit of exchange, while others have introduced complementary banknotes. Goods and services are horizontally exchanged among participants, with one account debited and the other credited, resulting in the sum of all participant accounts equalling zero. As these communities operate parallel to the mainstream economy, their units are usually not convertible to fiat money, resulting in a closed circuit between consumption and production.[116] This is paramount to guaranteeing local circulation, thus providing an incentive for wealth to remain within the boundaries of a given spatial area, increasing support for small businesses and local labour. Moreover, such complementary systems are purposefully interest free, institutionally designed to avoid short-term hoarding. Some of them even apply a negative interest, known as 'demurrage', to avoid accumulation and centralization, based on the principle that money is a public good designed to circulate. Illustrious examples of complementary currencies include the WIR Franc, in Switzerland, arguably one of the most long-standing experiments, having been established in 1934. In the United States, there are hundreds of local currencies, among which Ithaca HOURs and BerkShares are possibly the best known. In Germany, a network of local currencies called *Regiogeld* (regional money) connects more than seventy non-profit local currency projects, emitting the equivalent of 800,000 euros in value.[117] In 'developing countries', too, community currencies have grown over the past few years as demonstrated by the Community Exchange System in South Africa and the Bangla-Pesa in Kenya.

At the global level, the past decade has seen a massive proliferation of cryptocurrencies.[118] Bitcoin, a peer-to-peer currency managed by a network of user-owned computers known as the blockchain, has taken the world by storm since it was launched in 2009. Its network basis makes it possible to perform global transactions in a few minutes without any institutional control, guaranteeing higher speed and lower transaction costs than conventional credit card services. In the blockchain, crypto-coins are 'mined' by users through solving complex mathematical equations called 'hashes'. Bitcoin has quickly become a worldwide phenomenon with hundreds of thousands of businesses and users across the globe trading it. As of April 2016, there were more than 15,250 million 'coins' in circulation, with each unit valued at over US$400, making it the most valuable currency in the world. Interestingly, Bitcoin is only the tip of a growing iceberg. Dozens of similar digital currencies have emerged since the global financial crisis, some characterized by specific goals, values and objectives. Litecoin, with a total value of US$331 million, differs from Bitcoin in so far as its mining procedures do not require ever-growing computer power, thus rendering the process of money creation and exchange more democratic. QuarkCoin implements nine rounds of hashing, choosing from six different methods, resulting in a higher level of security. Other innovative examples include Peercoin, Namecoin, Primecoin, Novacoin and Feathercoin, with an average circulation value of US$10 million each. Some cryptocurrencies have also been designed to achieve social goals. FairCoin, for instance, aims to become the leading system of global exchange for those operating in the fair-trade sector. It does not require users to buy coins through mining or exchanges but distributes them equally to all participants, regardless of financial status. In March 2014, approximately 49,750 users were logged for the first giveaway, each able to claim 1,000 coins per hour. Automated airdrop claiming methods had no effect, as each user could only register once per hour, with sophisticated 'captchas' systems to guarantee that only real-life users would participate (as opposed to computer-based participants). Eventually, this distribution method allowed each participant in the cryptocurrency community to claim a little bit of the 50 million coins issued thus far.[119]

My colleague John Boik has published simulations of a complementary local economic system, using an agent-based, stock-flow consistent model.[120] He proposes introducing a local electronic currency that works like a 'democratic voting tool', rather than a mere medium of exchange. Supported by a collectively managed crowdfunding system and a new business model, Boik's democratic money simulations illustrate the potential for radical outcomes: in less than three decades, the typical US county under study eliminates poverty and achieves full employment. Mean take-home annual family income rises to the equivalent of about US$110,000, more than double the value at the onset of the simulation. Income inequality, even for non-working families, is nearly eliminated.

The horizontal peer-to-peer distribution of complementary currencies shows how complex social systems are poorly managed through the adoption of a single money system. Because of the inherent institutional bias in any type of currency, there is an obvious need for different systems to provide a wide range of incentives and framing inputs. Like the economy at large, different types of money can serve different purposes, building flexibility and resilience throughout the system. Some currencies may be designed to perform social roles, while others may focus on local economic development. Some may have a cooperative character, while others may carry no particular value and lend themselves to generic functions. Some may target community exchange, while others would be global in nature, allowing for digital transactions to occur across borders. There is no reason why, in the near future, the average person should not be able to perform exchanges in a multitude of currencies, each performing a specific role and carrying a particular value. Most of us already do that through a portfolio made up of fiat money, various coupons and vouchers, air miles and reward points offered by most retailers: these are all different types of currencies with specific characteristics. As maintained by Helbing, 'the use of a single feedback mechanism (such as money) is usually too restricted to let a complex socio-economic system self-organize successfully, and therefore we need a multi-dimensional incentive and value exchange system.'[121]

Converging dynamics

The type of economy shaped by GDP's institutional logic has generated evident (yet statistically hidden) human, social and environmental cost, which have – in most cases – outweighed the pure financial gains of conventional systems of production and consumption. This logic has influenced our society's organizational philosophy, incentivizing economies of scale and hierarchical systems of control. Post-GDP indicators of economic performance are useful tools to show the many inconsistencies of such an approach, as well as the inherent weaknesses. At the macro-level, the debate on new conceptualizations of economic performance, including the reform agenda triggered by the SDGs, are opening possibilities for change. By revealing the 'dark' face of the GDP economy, new systems of accounting contribute to eroding its institutional power. Yet this influence would achieve little in terms of tangible outcomes without an equally powerful pressure from the bottom up.

What we have seen in this chapter is that innovative research and business practices, as well as alternative community projects, are signalling the emergence of a new paradigm based on horizontal organization, the fusion of production and consumption boundaries as well as complementary forms of exchange. Local currencies have been growing across the globe since the 2008 financial crisis, connecting networks and involving hundreds of thousands of users. Technologies are breaking down industrial monopolies at an accelerating rate, especially across the internet where collaborative initiatives have outcompeted traditional centralized forms of production. This technological revolution is moving from software to hardware, with production value chains being shortened and localized while maintaining high efficiency levels and low costs.[122] Centralized business is increasingly under attack, not only because of high social and environmental costs but also because its model pits productivity against employment, leading inevitably to joblessness. The very notion of 'corporation' is increasingly questioned by the convergence of regulatory systems, accounting methods and new technologies that provide space for co-production, collaboration across boundaries and shared management of common resources. In the words of Eisenstein, 'headlong growth and all-out competition are features of immature ecosystems, followed by complex interdependency, symbiosis, cooperation, and the cycling of resources.'[123] Jeremy Rifkin, too, agrees that 'the steady decline in GDP in the coming years and decades is going to be increasingly attributable to the changeover to a vibrant new economy that measures economic value in totally new ways.'[124]

As summed up by Joe Kraus, one of the leaders of the dot.com boom of the late 1990s, the availability of new manufacturing technologies which diversify production and generate multiple markets for local producers, makes the shift from the vertical to the horizontal economy easier than ever: 'the twentieth century was about dozens of markets of millions of consumers. The twenty-first century is about millions of markets of dozens of consumers.'[125] With the blurring of boundaries, the GDP-influenced distinction between producer and consumer (and the transactional, profit-driven activities that seek to separate them) are beginning to fade. The emergence of the new phenomenon of 'prosumer' is changing the very meaning of work: quite opportunely, post-GDP accounting shows how human beings can be productive in ways that transcend the traditional framework of paid employment. Building on the very value of human capital as a critical resource for progress, the post-GDP economy may move beyond 'jobs' to focus on a variety of productive human activities, including self-production and peer-to-peer co-production, as well as parenting, caring and volunteering.

In a post-GDP system of accounting, economic gains are measured more holistically, which means that a set of regulatory mechanisms such as subsidies and limited liability, which have been essential to support the economies of scale of the GDP economy, will need to be revised according to principles of equity and sustainability. Patterns of ownership may need to change accordingly, with social enterprises and hybrid organizations that connect for-profit with non-profit activities becoming increasingly common, as is the case with the introduction of L3Cs (low-profit limited liability companies) in the United States, which allow organizations to draw on foundation and non-profit funding to operate as socially oriented businesses.

This horizontal distribution would provide a more fertile ground for households to be fully integrated in the social economy. As post-GDP accounting shows, the time spent at home is anything but valueless: it represents indirect income and contributes to the public good, with a double positive effect on a society's economic dynamism. Moreover, the blurring of professional and socially productive activities holds the potential of liberating both women and men from their traditional social roles, transforming the household into a locus of collaboration rather than segregation. As I will discuss in the next chapter, this institutional transition is likely to influence the nature of politics, too, rendering the arbitrary divisions between state, market and civil society increasingly obsolete.

4

Post-GDP Politics

This book's theoretical approach holds that the economy should be understood as a system of social organization. Its rules contribute to shaping behaviours and preferences through a complex interplay of formal and informal norms (institutions), thus structuring collective coordination at different levels. In this approach, the framing of development adopted by a given society matters a great deal for the type of political order it will choose. For instance, ancient republics believed that the ultimate goal of development was the achievement of virtue, *arête* in Greek and *virtus* in Latin. The very concept of economics, *oikonomia*, was an extrapolation of 'household' management, putting families and their structures at the centre of productive life. The political rules of the game were defined accordingly, granting authority and power to a selected public, made up mostly of educated adult males, in which fathers (*pater familias* in Latin) represented the households in public deliberations. As classical republics gave way to empires, the objective of development shifted from the pursuit of moral enhancement to territorial expansion. Politically, this led to the replacement of distributed elite systems with a centralized command. In some cases, this allowed for a federated system of government characterized by a certain degree of internal diversity, yet under a single overarching administration. During the Middle Ages, the accumulation of material wealth was mostly viewed as an aberration and a sin, as religious principles accompanied or even replaced conventional political authority. Society was organized by layers of influence, reinforcing hierarchical structures: status was given by the order of things, with wealth being a consequence of it rather than a cause. Territorial conquest remained central to the political order of modern states but no longer as a primary objective: rather, it became a means for the accumulation of exchangeable wealth, namely gold reserves under the control of the monarch.[1] This required a reinforcement of vertical control structures which resulted in the development of professionalized bureaucracies, taxation systems and security apparatuses. The emergence of modern capitalism and the Industrial Revolution brought about profound political shifts by challenging predefined hierarchies in line with a new idea of economic prosperity founded on capital, paving the way for the establishment of constitutional rule. As the new economy rested on the inalienable right to private property, it automatically led to forms of government by 'owners', with the right to vote and run for office limited to holders of movable and fixed assets, and the emergence of the modern bourgeoisie as the leading political class. On the other hand, socialist and communist systems emphasized labour as the source of value and consequently developed institutional rules that put workers – normally via a single-party state – in the political driving seat. Finally, the evolution of mass consumption as the ultimate objective of development in the twentieth century led to the establishment of representative democracies and universal suffrage, with the concept of the citizen consumer at the core of the political order.

Against this backdrop, the emergence of a post-GDP economy driven by top-down reforms and bottom-up pressures, as well as supported by innovation through distributed business and civil society, presents an opportunity to change the current political rules of the game once again. As I have discussed in the preceding chapters, the mainstream economic approach based on GDP regards all the activities we perform in our households, in our local communities, in voluntary work and in the vast informal economy as of no value to development. When we care for another, when we collectively look after our common resources and when we participate in the public sphere, we are not acting as consumers and, therefore, we are of no or little consequence for the GDP paradigm. Yet new indicators of prosperity show that the social unpaid activities we perform every day occupy not only most of our waking time, but they are the essential 'invisible hand' supporting the formal economy. No transactions would be possible without the trust, social connections, care and human development achieved through voluntary, largely non-monetary work. The same holds true for the innumerable services and resources provided by nature free of charge, which the GDP economy considers of no value even though they are essential to support life systems, including transactional relations. By making these 'hidden' realities visible, post-GDP indicators open up possibilities for the restructuring of contemporary political systems. Just as distributed networks challenge the centralized institutional control of the GDP economy, a post-GDP politics is likely to call into question the sustainability and efficiency of traditional forms of representation, paving the way for participatory governance. The decentralization of production and consumption puts small businesses, households and communities at the core of development, thus empowering them politically, too. With the localization of the economy, forms of direct deliberation and self-governance are likely to achieve a higher degree of efficiency than hierarchical policy-making structures. As *homo socialis* challenges the supremacy of *homo economicus*, the resulting distribution of economic influence will not only empower local communities, small businesses and households, but it will also challenge the conventional distinction between economically productive activities and socio-political activism. By restructuring the concept of work, the post-GDP social order will integrate economic and political participation in one single process, thus removing traditional barriers to the direct involvement of citizens in decision making in areas from financial resources to time availability. This chapter discusses current trends and future possibilities by highlighting how the intersection between the horizontal economy and emerging governance innovations is likely to lead to a different form of politics. I begin by discussing how the evolution of such a complex system will require different types of data.

Data revolution: from vertical control to horizontal distribution

The 'beyond GDP' debate is providing a crucial opening for the reorganization of data systems globally and, as a consequence, for the innovation of governance processes. As argued in this book, statistics are powerful shapers of social institutions, providing frameworks to understand the world, attributing value, defining logics of appropriateness and consequence, as well as supporting policy coordination throughout society. In the words of a recent report published by the UN on the 'data revolution', 'data are the lifeblood of decision-making'.[2] Traditionally, data have been gathered and produced by statistical offices, with a high level of centralization and control. While this vertical structure may have been necessary to ensure quality control, it has invariably resulted in limited access and time lags, making data very selective, not amenable to timely policy planning and, above all, restrictive in terms of user base. GDP itself exemplifies a traditional data system based on boundaries, hierarchical methods of collection and highly exclusionary parameters for selection, largely due to limited gathering and aggregation capacity. As many critics and I have discussed at length, the calculation of GDP is highly inefficient and contradictory, despite being routinely presented as straightforward and uncontroversial.[3] Prices have to be adjusted by statisticians – following different methods depending on each statistical agency – for inflation and quality improvements. As a measure of input/output rather than outcome, it assesses the performance of education and health-care systems in terms of how much they spend, rather than in terms of the literacy and well-being they achieve. Data are often incomplete, leading to numerous imputations, which explain why the 'product' and the 'income' side of the equation often yield different results. Estimates have to be revised on a regular basis, with definite data only being confirmed years after their first publication. Policy decisions, however, are taken immediately after each quarterly update. This is a particularly serious problem when a decimal change in GDP can mean either a 'recovery' or a 'recession', thus leading to opposite sets of decisions and consequences. Small variations can make or break entire societies. For instance, the United Kingdom faced a recession in the 1970s which put the then Labour government through the humiliating experience of seeking assistance from the IMF. The political repercussions were enormous, paving the way for Margaret Thatcher's decade-long Conservative grip on power and ushering Britain and most of Europe into the neoliberal era. As successive corrections on the early estimates revealed later on, however, the alleged recession never was: by a small margin, GDP growth had actually turned positive. As Coyle rhetorically asks, 'who knows whether Mrs Thatcher would have won the same kind of election victory if her predecessors in power had not had to bring in the IMF?'[4]

The production of GDP is also highly secretive, reinforcing a vertical governance system through its mechanical proceedings. In the United

States, the crunching of quarterly estimates happens in a way that is reminiscent of classical religious ceremonies and fortune-telling rites. Statisticians are housed inside a secret 'locked-up' room for days on end, with no access to the media and explicit permission to be granted for toilet breaks.[5] Once produced, the results are sent in a sealed envelope to the chairperson of the presidential Council of Economic Advisers and then to the president. Only after that is a special press conference with selected invitees held for the rest of the world to know what 'the numbers reveal'. With perhaps less theatrical features, other statistical agencies follow very similar hierarchical and secretive procedures.

Basing decisions on a few measurable outputs is extremely dysfunctional in contemporary societies. Like an iceberg, a small minority of partial (mostly) quantitative data enjoy excessive visibility at the expense of a massive wealth of information that is too dispersed and qualitative to be captured by conventional statisticians. In contemporary societies, this state of affairs is inadequate at the very least, especially due to the interconnected and fast-changing nature of the social world. The volume of information is increasing exponentially, with each year producing more data than all the previous years combined, yet escaping statistical collection.[6] Much of the new data are collected passively from the 'digital footprints' that people leave behind (such as sensor-enabled objects) or are inferred via algorithms. Examples abound of innovative applications of what is conventionally referred to as 'big data'. For instance, in Uganda health-care professionals and humanitarian agencies use SMS alerts to inform public health officials about outbreaks so that they can more effectively distribute medicines and avoid shortages. In the past, the Ministry of Health relied on patchy paper questionnaires alone, which resulted in incomplete information and delays. By 2014, about 1,200 district health officials, 18,700 health facility workers and 7,400 village health-team workers were using the new system. The immediate avail-ability of fire data provided by the World Resources Institute through its Global Forest Watch website has enabled paper companies to coor-dinate their response to wild fires more effectively. In Singapore and Indonesia, governments have combined this data with high-resolution GIS maps to crack down on illegal burning.[7]

The UN Expert Group on the 'data revolution' maintains that better integrated and multifaceted data is indispensable in contemporary governance, especially because '[a]chieving the SDGs will require an unprecedented joint effort on the part of governments at every level, civil society and the private sector, and millions of individual choices and actions.'[8] The new data must avoid the bottlenecks of the past, including replicating the biases implicit in the traditional structure of the national income accounts. This is particularly significant for all those functions that GDP neglects from natural ecosystems to the productive role of households and communities. As recognized by the UN report, social and economic inequalities are reflected in verti-cal data structures, which have traditionally disregarded phenomena and issues relevant to minorities and the poor, including undervalu-ing women's activities and priorities: 'Many of the issues of most concern to women are poorly served by existing data,' with only half of countries reporting information on domestic violence and limited information being available on the distribution of money or the divi-sion of labour within households: 'Much more data are needed on the economic roles of women of all ages as caregivers to children, older persons and the disabled in the household and in the labour force.'[9]

Needless to say, the exponential growth in passive data poses a number of problems. As more is known about people and the environ-ment, there is a correspondingly greater risk that data could be used to harm individuals both physically and psychologically. This could ultimately undermine social trust and lead in the opposite direction, that is, towards inward-looking, less collaborative societies. Individuals and ecosystems could also be harmed inadvertently if poor-quality data were used for policy decisions. Inequality of access is also a risk, as new frontiers could be erected between those who have access to information (and can use it to pursue their interests) and those who do not. This is why a genuine 'data revolution' cannot be just about creating more information: it should be about fundamentally altering hierarchies and institutional control systems with a view to granting access. Open data is essential to achieve this goal, with McKinsey estimating the global value of better and more open data at US$3 trillion per year: a massive new economy.[10] The revolution is also about aligning the needs and aspirations of complex societies with the statistical tools used to design policies. This means identifying the most efficient ways to integrate timely data into, among others, policy planning, early warning systems, service delivery, impact evaluation and emergency response. In this regard, the 'data revolution can be a revolution for equality': 'More, and more open, data can help ensure that knowledge is shared, creating a world of informed and empowered citizens, capable of holding decision-makers accountable for their actions.'[11]

The data revolution can help us erode the vertical structure of contemporary policy-making processes through a horizontal distribution of information supporting collective action. The Flu Near You initiative in the United States harnesses 'the power of the crowd' to map the spread of influenza across the country through self-compiled reports by more than 60,000 'flu-trackers', that is, member users in the online community.[12] In Europe, a similar initiative called Influenzanet is operational in eleven countries. In contrast to the vertical system of sentinel networks constituted by primary care physicians, Influenzanet obtains data directly from the population, generating a fast and flexible monitoring system whose uniformity allows for direct comparison of influenza rates across countries. MySociety, an online community in the United Kingdom, allows citizens to report data on government services and infrastructure problems, from potholes to lack of services in the community. The open-source Ushahidi platform, launched in Kenya to allow users to share data on post-electoral violent clashes in 2007, is globally used to crowdsource data gathering in cases of natural and man-made disasters. The U-report social monitoring platform pioneered by United Nations Children's Emergency Fund in Africa has more than a million active users. It is a text-message system allowing young people to share information about a wide range of issues from economic opportunities and service delivery to the spread of infectious diseases. To simplify policy application, data are instantly mapped and analysed, yielding vital information to development agencies and public institutions, as well as increasingly accountability. The Land Matrix, an international collaborative project managed by my research centre in South Africa and listed among the top ten sources of data for international development by the *Guardian*, is a pioneering effort of global data collection and open data that relies on contributions by networks of informed stakeholders, the scientific community and citizens.[13] Through collecting data on large-scale land transactions in developing countries, it increases transparency and supports civic advocacy against the growing phenomenon of 'land grabbing'. Indeed, the secrecy surrounding land investments often allows powerful actors (private investors, host country governments or local authorities) to enrich themselves at the expense of local populations, who are normally not consulted and do not benefit from compensations or lease fees, while paying the consequences in terms of lost livelihoods and restricted access to common resources.

A horizontal distributed-data system must be designed in ways that counter the linear, short-term vertical structure of GDP accounting not only by informing policy making about the present but also by modelling the impact of current decisions on future development trajectories: 'Data that can be re-used at different scales, and combined with other data, can better reflect the complex and dynamic interactions between people and the planet.'[14] With this goal in mind, the computational science team at the Federal Institute of Technology in Zurich, Switzerland, is working on a 'planetary nervous system', that is, a citizen-controlled global data repository of human actions and their interplay with nature, which could be used to aggregate and disaggregate data at different levels and provide real-time information on a virtually endless range of issues, from traffic to social tensions and pollution, while guaranteeing anonymity and open access.[15]

Challenging vertical power through governance innovation

It has become increasingly fashionable to talk about political authority in terms of governance. Unlike government, the term 'governance' indicates the complexity of decision-making processes in contemporary political and economic affairs: in many ways the concept of governance acknowledges the increasing fragmentation and distribution of authority through society away from centralized institutional control. Due to economic, social and political complexity, no government nowadays can simply govern alone: it is bound to share authority with other entities, from non-governmental organizations to regional institutions and private corporations, including social movements and citizens.[16] Governance may take many forms along a continuum spanning a multi-level architecture of decision making to a horizontal structure of diffused networks. As pointed out by Manuel Castells, governance is the result of a 'network society' in which public and private authorities are increasingly intertwined.[17] The traditional vertical institutional system 'now coexists with an equally powerful, though more decentralised, multi-centric system'.[18] Compliance and legitimacy, too, are affected by this distribution of authority, resulting in a non-linear and non-automatic acceptance of traditional sources of power. Vertical influence is only perceived as legitimate when exercised with inclusivity and transparency, recognizing that the economic, social and political resources necessary to govern effectively are distributed among a wide range of actors.[19]

'Governance' can been used as a descriptive term, referring to specific institutional problem-solving arrangements. Some of these arrangements may be formal, involving a wide variety of actors such as state departments, international organizations, regional bodies, non-governmental groups and even individuals. Other arrangements may be informal and even temporary, as is the case with social campaigns and civil society coalitions.[20] In all cases, technological innovation has lowered the transaction costs of direct participation by individuals and organized groups, thus intensifying the structural diversification of authority relations.

Ostrom's work on the 'commons', which I discussed in the previous chapter, shows various ways in which collaborative governance plays out in a variety of contexts.[21] In particular, she has pointed out how top-down systems of control, such as those exerted by the state or by market actors, are not necessarily the most effective to create order and compliance. Local communities and civil society groups can, indeed, develop shared institutions that are often more adaptive, accountable and resilient than those developed by states and markets. Governance is more hybrid than we often think, especially at the local level where the distinction between public and private authority is blurred by overlapping roles, fuzzy memberships and a variety of ways in which individuals can participate directly without any sectoral intermediation. Indeed, associations, public offices and a myriad of private agents continuously interact to shape collective choices and behaviours at the community level.

Like any other social coordination process, governance systems are not static: they evolve and innovate through a complex interaction with the underlying economic rules of the game and the associated conceptualizations of development. But what does innovation in governance mean? Organizational theorists define innovation in rather broad terms as 'the adoption of an idea or behaviour that is new to the organization's industry, market or general environment'.[22] Although innovation is often framed in purely technological terms, the concept spans all areas of social coordination and social theory:

The term 'innovation' makes most people think first about technology: new products and new methods for making them. Typically the word 'innovation' creates an image of an invention, a new piece of technical apparatus, or perhaps something of conventional scientific character. If some people were asked to list some of the major innovations of the last few years, microprocessors and computer-related devices would be mentioned frequently. Fewer people would mention new tax laws or the creation of enterprise zones, even though these are innovations too. Fewer still, if any, would be likely to mention such innovations as quality circles and problem-solving task forces.[23]

Whether one looks at innovation in technology or in organizational theory, all these conceptualizations share an implicit element: innovation is intimately connected with the underlying concepts of adaptation, resilience and efficiency at dealing with contextual dynamics. From the standpoint of technology management, for example, innovation is 'a new idea, method, process, or device that creates a higher level of performance for the adopting user'.[24] From a socio-economic angle, innovation is 'the development and adoption of new and improved ways of addressing social and economic needs and wants'.[25]

It must be noted that the very definition of innovation harbours a degree of uncertainty: 'Innovation means taking risks – and sometimes the risks may be very obvious and the destination unclear.'[26] As actors face context-related uncertainty, their innovation capacity is constrained by path dependencies, inertia, power structures and vested interests. The relationship with the environment (as the overall context of an actor's action) is therefore rather important, as innovation tends to become more likely when structural continuity is challenged by new problems and 'crises'. In this regard, the evolutionary turn in organization theory helps conceptualize institutions as 'open systems' due to their 'dependence on and conditional interaction with [their] environment', which evolve contingent on internal as well as external causes.[27] As I have already mentioned in chapter 2, such systems may rest comfortably in a state of equilibrium (or deep structure) punctuated by strategic reorientations.[28] However, when conventional paradigms are increasingly questioned and become unable to deal efficiently with changing dynamics, the status quo is more likely to be challenged by 'newcomers', that is, tools, ideas as well as individuals and groups that are keen to break down the structural inertia of embedded routines. Some of these innovations are proactive in the sense that they are driven from within organizations due to shifting preferences among key role players, while others are reactive, that is, driven from the outside through external shocks, performance crises and/or regulatory shifts. Following chapter 3, we have seen that a different approach to externalities is demanded by a changing environment characterized by a convergence of crises. Post-GDP indicators are showing a path for a different approach to economic performance and prosperity at a time when bottom-up practices are questioning the vertical structure of the mainstream economy. In this context, innovation is emerging proactively from within the system but significantly reinforced from the outside through alternative models that are now reaching a critical mass.

Traditionally, the innovation process in the business field has been a negative-sum game: innovation rewards some at the expense of others in so far as the drive to acquire competitive advantage results in winners and losers. As already suggested in the previous chapter, it is more complicated to argue in favour of competition-based innovation in public governance. Losers do not leave the governance game: they cannot be externalized, but they are bound to operate within it as stakeholders. Decision processes that outmanoeuvre certain segments within society are more likely to generate conflicts. Encouraging competition-based innovation could be disastrous as it would ultimately result in more exclusions and divisions. Indeed, the rules of the game have to be designed by a variety of stakeholders if the significance of governance as an inclusive and increasingly distributed process of decision making is to be taken seriously. When the level of analysis moves from the individual organization (e.g. a company) to the macro-level of decision processes, it is even more evident that the negative externalities produced by competition would become internalities for society. This reduces the appeal of competitive strategies as underpinning governance innovation. In contrast, it is out of cooperative patterns of interaction that governance, as a multi-actor decision process, can innovate effectively and sustainably.

Civil society at the core of governance

Public institutions have a limited inclination to produce governance innovation on their own. The sheer scale of public bureaucracies, the vertical structure of their operations, the limited capacity to 'listen' to external changes and the separation between internal processes and society at large are among the key factors hampering innovation.[29] Business, too, has an inherent drive towards maintaining status quo conditions, as change is risky and potentially costly. Moreover, companies' operating systems tend to replicate models inherited from the past, thus making them particularly unlikely to promote change unless the ecosystemic conditions are altered. As argued by business guru Peter Drucker, the traditional factors capable of disturbing such path dependency include regulatory shifts operated by public authorities, industry and market changes, new perceptions by citizens and consumer groups, as well as the discovery of new knowledge.[30] All these factors can be divided into demand and supply. Demand-side sources of innovation lie in the shift of consumer (or citizens) preferences due to changes in the social, technological or regulatory environments. Supply-side sources reflect core capabilities of an organization (be it a company or a government) and its overall strategy.[31] A minority of companies do not merely react to change, they 'proactively initiate innovations that reshape their markets'.[32] The best example is provided by the so-called 'ambidextrous organizations' which host 'multiple, internally inconsistent architectures, competencies and cultures, with built-in capabilities for efficiency, consistency, and reliability on the one hand and experimentation, improvisation, and luck on the other'.[33] Here, too, the fact that companies are increasingly connected with entities and groups operating outside the market through governance channels increases their capacity to change. Some suggest that intra-organizational social capital, especially in the form of participation and relational assets, increases the likelihood for organizations not only to innovate but also to innovate radically. Indeed, this capacity to change is 'embodied in networks and communities' and thus 'social capital becomes an essential ingredient to understand innovation'.[34]

In the main, research on organizational structures shows that innovations in governance follow, by and large, the 'sandwich' model described in chapter 1. They are triggered by a combination of factors, which include changes in dominant perspectives, publicly visible crises or failures, demands put forth by citizens and opportunities created by new technologies. As they tend to be more adaptive, horizontal governance systems are more likely to continue innovating, given that different stakeholders have multiple entry points to stimulate change processes. In particular, it is the diversity of participation that challenges the crystallized institutional framing of GDP politics, resulting in a variety of values and perspectives 'being heard' in the policy process. It is mainly thanks to such openness that the problem stream (e.g. the relevance of a particular issue in society), the policy stream (e.g. the availability of new policy tools) and the politics stream (e.g. the emergence of new alliances) come together to open windows of opportunity.[35]

As I have mentioned earlier, the network-based nature of governance is strengthened by forms of open innovation, that is, approaches that leverage 'one another's (even competitors') innovation assets – products, intellectual property, and people'.[36] Through open innovation models, organizations can gather promising ideas throughout the world and participate in an ongoing process of knowledge sharing. For instance, crowdsourcing companies such as InnoCentive and Yet2. com have been able to exploit the soft reputational links of horizontal scientific communities to build a global network of innovators, which not only generates profits but also supports the sharing of knowledge in a collaborative economy. Both companies have fundamentally re-invented the governance structure of modern business by adopting non-proprietary methods, flexible approaches to intellectual property and open-ended systems of collaboration across sectors. Their organizational structure resembles more that of a social movement, with innovations developed through various nodes and by external contributors, rather than through a traditional system of vertical control, industrial secrecy and competition.

Indeed, because of its inherent uncertainty, governance innovation rarely originates in the centre of political systems. Rather, it tends to emerge in the periphery and, even more likely, at the intersections across different systems and fields.[37] The most innovative actors are frequently perceived as 'deviants' and are 'accorded a status of low credibility by the average members of the system'.[38] It is not coincidence that GDP metrics have relegated civil society to a marginal role in society, the unproductive sphere, even if social actors have historically been crucial in initiating and supporting governance innovation. The role of social movements and advocacy organizations in promoting change-oriented initiatives and radical innovation has long been highlighted in national and international contexts.[39] The change potential of civil society stems from its structural location: close to the grassroots and the local level, civil society actors are usually the first to become aware of shifting needs and can become powerful initiators of alternative framing processes. Their ability is also based on the lower transaction costs required to capture popular sentiments. What is more, advances in communication technologies make it much easier for groups to mobilize and organize, not only at the local level but also globally. Finally, not beholden to the ballot box and market expectations, civil society actors enjoy a degree of independence that neither public agencies nor corporations have.

The GDP framework has traditionally treated civil society as performing a lesser function in society, described in opposition to vertical production processes (the 'non-profit') or as a residual category (the 'third sector'). When research has focused on civil society's impact and contribution to society, it has almost invariably adopted the GDP framework of evaluation, measuring the 'quantity' of results in terms of workforce formally employed and financial resources mustered, rather than looking at the broader societal outcomes.[40] Post-GDP indicators turn this approach around: as the locus of social capital, interpersonal care and social cohesion, civil society should be regarded as the 'core' of the productive economy. In a world in which human capital is increasingly considered the key driver of development, surpassing by various orders of magnitude the contribution of produced capital, it becomes self-evident that civil society should play a pivotal role in policy making, too. For instance, some scholars attribute to citizen movements the role of 'social innovators' and credit them with the lead role in overcoming the unsustainable consumerism of the GDP model of growth by 'offering attractive new values and lifestyles'.[41] Others show how the 'joint hands' of 'rebels' in forming social movements transform politics every single day, often below the statistical radar screen, by exerting pressure on companies and governments. 'Market rebels', defined as 'activists who challenge the status quo' by engaging in social and cultural mobilization, are indeed transforming governance at an accelerated rate.[42] The exponential application of distributed intelligence, often spearheaded by civil society groups, is making horizontal collaboration and open-access key tenets of new policy approaches. For instance, initiatives such as Kiva, a website which allows millions of users to make donations to a universe of international development projects globally, have contributed to reshaping a sector traditionally dominated by government agencies and international donor organizations. Similarly, cryptocurrencies like Bitcoin have challenged the traditional authority of central banks, triggering a variety of horizontal monetary experiments that keep growing around the world.

Civil society's self-organization is also challenging the vertical structures of traditional political parties. In Italy, a new political organization, the Five Star Movement, was founded in 2009 by using the online social network MeetUp as an organizing tool. Through flexible horizontal participatory structures, open consultations, online primaries for the selection of all candidates and various web-based communication systems, the movement quickly gained massive popular support.[43] It operates through the voluntary support of thousands of self-organized 'meet-ups' across the country and relies on crowdfunding, having officially rejected institutional public funding and corporate donations. It is currently vying with the traditional, professionalized and vertically structured Democratic Party for the position of largest political formation in the country, having already won the seat of mayor of Rome, the country's capital city, in 2016. Citizen-driven 'pirate parties', which are mostly managed through online forums and inspired by values such as open access and direct democracy, have mushroomed across Europe over the past decade, with strongholds in Sweden, Germany, Iceland and Czech Republic. In the 2009 EU elections, the Swedish 'pirates' won more than 7 per cent of the votes, electing their first-ever member to the European parliament.[44] In 2011, their German equivalents got more than 8 per cent of popular support in Berlin's state elections, winning 15 seats. In Iceland, the party has enjoyed massive popular sympathy since 2015, topping the country's rankings in terms of opinion polls.[45] After the 2016 political crisis, which saw the resignation of the Icelandic government after the 'Panama Papers' revealed suspicious investments made by political leaders in tax havens, the 'pirates' stood at an historic 43 per cent in the polls, enjoying a widening margin from the ruling Independence Party, which sat at 21 per cent.[46] In Spain, the social movement *Indignados*, which mobilized in the wake of the global financial crisis, gave birth to a political formation called *Podemos* (We Can), which is currently the second-largest party in the country after the traditional right-wing *Partido Popular* and ahead of the Socialist Party.[47] At the latest municipal elections, *Podemos* supported citizen movements that won the elections in Spain's two largest cities, Madrid and Barcelona. Another civic movement, *Ciudadanos* (Citizens), won more than 13 per cent of the votes at the 2015 general election. Similar experiences have emerged in many other countries in Europe and beyond. Albeit they are not all at the same level of popular recognition, these movements attest to an unprecedented possibility to erode the vertical nature of representative democracy through direct collective action. At the local level, innovations look even more promising. For instance, thousands of cities have institutionalized participatory budgeting, a process of collective deliberation through which ordinary citizens decide how to allocate parts of the municipal funds.[48] New York City is home to the largest participatory budgeting experiment in the United States. First introduced in only a handful of districts in 2011, the process currently involves more than twenty districts, with tens of thousands of people involved in deciding how to spend more than US$25 million in discretionary funds. Since 2001, Toronto's public housing authority has engaged tenants in allocating up to US$9 million of capital funding per year. The city of Porto Alegre in Brazil pioneered participatory budgeting in the late 1980s, providing inspiration for the rest of the world. Its state Rio Grande do Sul has implemented participatory budgeting to identify priorities for public works and services for a population of over 10 million, a tenth of which directly participated in the deliberations and negotiations involved in the process.

Local power and collective leadership

In many different ways, the Indian political and spiritual leader Mahatma Gandhi was a champion of the post-GDP world. In the context of economic development, he favoured the decentralization and distribution of production. The *khadi* movement he inspired, which draws its name from India's most typical hand-woven cloth, aimed to make communities economically sustainable by supporting self-employment in both the industrial and the agricultural sectors. This approach formed part of Gandhi's concept of *swadeshi*, that is, shared economic systems aimed at local self-reliance.[49] Rather than an ever-increasing system of vertical production with consumers at the bottom, Gandhi envisaged a balanced society in which human needs are in tune with natural conditions:

> I wholeheartedly detest this mad desire to destroy distance and time, to increase animal appetites and go to the ends of the earth in search of their satisfaction. If modern civilization stands for all this, and I have understood it to do so, I call it satanic. It is a theft for me to take any fruit that I do not need, or to take it in a larger quantity than necessary. We are not always aware of our real needs, and most of us improperly multiply our wants and thus unconsciously make thieves of ourselves.[50]

In such a system, he saw an organic relationship between economic and political rules, through the concept of *swaraj* or self-governance. The most appropriate political unit for the institutional application of self-governance was the village, a participatory 'self-contained and self-supporting structure' with the right level of localization, yet in a complex horizontal network of collaboration with other similar units.[51] Gandhi further outlined his vision of *swaraj* by introducing the concept of oceanic circles in opposition to the pyramidal structure of society, placing the individual at the centre of society.

> My idea of the village *swaraj* is that it is a complete republic, independent of its neighbours for its vital wants and yet inter-dependent for many others in which dependency is a necessity [. . .]. In a structure composed of innumerable villages [. . .] life will not be a pyramid with the apex sustained by the bottom, but it will be an oceanic cycle whose centre will be the individual [. . .]. The outmost circumsphere will not wield power to crush the inner circle but will give strength to all within and drive its own strength from it.[52]

Gandhi's vision of the village had little to do with the place of personal and collective deprivation he saw around himself: 'The village of my dream is still in my mind.' He envisioned polities in which 'there will be neither plague, nor cholera, nor smallpox; no one will be idle, no one will wallow in luxury'. A society of 'intelligent human beings', who 'will not live in dirt and darkness as animals', and in which 'men and women will be free and able to hold their own against anyone in the world.' Similar to the post-GDP economy described in chapter 3, Ghandi's vision was that of a strong service sector, with labour intensive functions taking centre stage: 'What I object to is the craze for machinery, not machinery as such. The craze is for what they call labour-saving machinery. Men go on saving labour till thousands are without work and thrown on the open streets to die of starvations. [. . .] Centralization as a system is inconsistent with a non-violent structure of society.'[53]

It is perhaps not surprising that India, the world's largest democracy, has become a champion of self-governance in recent times.[54]

First of all, electoral studies have shown that, while voters' turn-out at general elections has been decreasing, local elections enjoy a steady and, at times, growing participation by citizens. In rural India, the turn-out at neighbourhood elections is close to 100 per cent.[55] After the reintroduction of local self-governance units, the so-called *panchayats*, through a constitutional reform in 1992, various governments have continued pushing for further decentralization. Across the country, there are now more than 250 thousand *panchayats*. Moreover, 'modern' rural communities are mushrooming, with Prime Minister Narendra Modi having publicly committed to inaugurating a hundred new self-governing villages by 2016.[56] This is part of the government's Saansad Adarsh Gram Yojana initiative for rural development through the intersection of three critical factors: social cohesion; direct participation; and modern technology. The governance structures as well as the technical infrastructure of these model villages (*adarsh gram*) are co-designed with citizens to achieve 'holistic development' through human, economic, social and personal emancipation. Figure 4.1 describes the programme's main components.

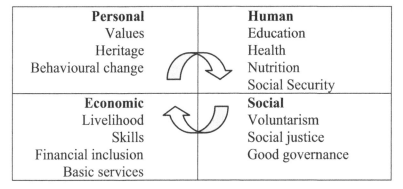

Figure 4.1 Holistic development strategy to self-governance in rural villages. *Source:* Author's elaboration of information provided in Ministry of Rural Development (2015).

These integrated forms of participatory governance highlight the importance of public health approaches as well as the need to tackle marginalization and social exclusion. They also emphasize the importance of human development through universal access to basic health care and education, improving nutrition and providing a thriving environment for people with special needs and disabilities. They promote voluntary work, including the Bharat Nirman Volunteers, who operate as transmission belts between local community and government, and celebrate the crucial social roles played by elders, women, men and the youth in strengthening cohesion and resolving conflicts. For them, good governance is about strengthening citizen committees' participation in local development while institutionalizing regular open platforms for 'airing grievances and their redressal, coordinated by the Gram Panchayat', that is, the formal village administration. Local funds must be allocated through public participatory decision making, including disclosing all information 'in the public domain and through wall-writing, notice boards in the local language'.[57] The economic system must support decentralization and empowerment, mostly through a focus on organic farming, crop intensification through low-water labour-intensive practices, seed banks, micro-enterprises rather than large-scale industrial development, micro-irrigation and the establishment of subsidies for farmers using manure rather than chemical fertilizers. For instance, *Gobar* (dung) banks now support the generation of bio-gas at the local level.

All these development streams are then connected at the environmental level through modern eco-friendly solid and liquid waste management, roadside veggie gardens and tree plantations, the revival of traditional water bodies, rainwater harvesting as well as social forestry, a concept developed in 1976 by India's National Commission on Agriculture to better integrate human settlements and ecological systems through the reforestation and afforestation of unused land.

Unlike other villages and towns, these new formations are 'smart' in so far as they integrate traditional culture and labour-intensive economic development with modern technologies. For instance, the schools are equipped with modern IT systems allowing web-based teaching, and each village/town has an e-library. Electricity is locally generated through renewable energy, mostly solar but also hydro-power and wind, servicing households, common areas and public buildings. Citizens are provided with internet access through comput-ers or mobile phones. The criteria for the successful governance of smart villages also include access to multi-facility hospitals within an area of 10 kilometres, home production systems for grains, vegetable, fruits and *khadi*, Wi-Fi and broadband connectivity, recreation areas for adults and playgrounds for children (e.g. by converting existing *Anganwadi* – 'courtyard shelters' – already available in many villages), a village theatre and a public hall, as well as several outlets for coopera-tive work, including workshops, stands and meeting rooms that can be used by the public.[58]

The intersection between self-governance and distributed technol-ogy systems is providing an ever more efficient response to service delivery, especially in areas marginalized by the vertical centralization of the mainstream economy. This is true not only in India but across the world. For instance, off-grid electricity systems do not require the same expensive supporting distribution infrastructure as traditional forms of centralized power generation. The classic utility model of a one-way flow of energy from power plant to consumer is now rapidly changing, thanks to 'a combination of low-cost solar, micro-hydro and other generation technologies coupled with the electronics needed to manage small-scale power and to communicate with control devices and remote billing systems'.[59] The nexus between local governance and distributed energy opens innumerable applications, from blending production and consumption in manufacturing to challenging top-down control approaches to agriculture and food. For instance, by combining traditional knowledge and scientific discoveries, smart villagers have found that leguminous crops like *Sesbania rostrata* have stem nodules that can enrich the soil by about 80 kilograms of nitrogen per hectare, competing with conventional chemical fertilizers but without negative externalities.[60] The African tree *Faidherbia albida* is ideal to fix nitrogen in its leaves, which are subsequently incorporated into the soil. Uniquely, these 'fertiliser factories in the field' do not compete with the crops for light, water and various soil nutrients other than nitrogen.[61] Chinese and Japanese agricultural scientists have developed strategies to harness the organic matter in the soil, which contains microorganisms rich in phosphorus, potassium and several micronutrients, to enhance the productivity of crops without the waste and pollution (let alone the impacts on human health) generated by energy-consuming industrial chemicals. In Japan, a country whose GDP has been flat or decreasing for the past two decades, the government introduced a so-called 'Sixth Sector Act' in 2010 with the aim of creating a new collaborative economy in which the traditional sectors (agriculture, industry and services) are blended into forms of partnership that support horizontal cooperation. The new legislation has created a framework and funding mechanism to help the agricultural community and entrepreneurs to venture into labour-intensive high-value-added businesses like organic food processing and ecotourism, incentivizing cross-sectoral cooperation and supporting innovative self-governance initiatives across the country, especially in marginalized rural areas.[62] The village of Inakadate, in the country's north, has responded to a widespread economic depression and the departure of commercial farmers since the mid-1990s by turning its traditional work with paddy cultivation into a world-renowned tourist attraction. Every year, over a quarter of a million tourists visit the astounding art murals created by using hectares of live crop.[63] Today, the villagers use the pointillist painting technique and a computer to map out where to plant stalks, so the final pictures would have proper proportions when viewed from the sky through satellite and aero-photography. In another smart village, Nambu, the citizens' charter says: 'We shall love people and nature and create a beautiful town, and help create a warm-hearted town by continuing to practice kindness.' The charter further demands that citizens shall respect the town's history and culture in order to contribute 'mental richness' and to realize a healthy village. According to the mayor, 'With our motto of relaxing, slowing down and feeling nature, we want to create a village where everybody can live healthy and happy.'[64] Through horizontal collaborations between households, local farmers and small businesses, the town turned its traditional rural landscape, as well as its local history and culture, into a sought-after destination for ecotourists, who routinely attend *shiki matsuri*, the village's 'four-season festival', that includes a variety of fruit-picking opportunities in orchards, from cherries to peaches, grapes and strawberries.

In many African countries, centralized energy systems are increasingly being called into question because of their structural inefficiencies at powering the continent. Indeed, they require massive top-down investments, often breeding corruption, and demand high-maintenance costs. Moreover, they take years to deliver results. In South Africa, new coal stations were planned in the early 2000s and expected to come on line in 2012. Yet the first electricity was only produced in 2015, with intermittent operability and blackouts across the nation. Full-scale production is not expected until 2020 or later.

Meanwhile, the planned costs more than tripled over this period.[65] As is always the case with centralized systems, network failures can easily trigger cascade effects and block distribution, as has happened in various instances since the launch of the new stations. A 2016 report on electricity access across Africa shows the inefficiencies of vertical power infrastructure across the continent.[66] On average, only 40 per cent of citizens enjoy a reliable power supply, although those connected to national grids exceed two-thirds of the population. Only 69 per cent of connected households 'actually have electricity that works', with peaks of inefficiencies in Nigeria, where '96 percent of households are connected, but only 18 percent of these connections function more than about half the time'. In Ghana, the term *dumsor* (Akan for 'off–on') has become a commonplace word, as '87 percent of households are connected, but only 42 percent of those connections provide reliable power.' Against this backdrop, the Africa Progress Panel – which includes a number of African political and civil leaders, as well as international experts, under the chairmanship of former UN chief Kofi Annan – underlines two distinct advantages of renewable energy sources: 'speed and decentralization'. Unlike vertical systems such as fossil fuel stations and nuclear plants, 'they can be deployed far more rapidly' and 'can operate both on-grid and off-grid'.[67] In Kenya, Uganda and Tanzania, for instance, the company M-KOPA has combined solar and mobile technology to bring affordable solar technologies to off-grid villages. It has connected more than 330,000 households, with over 500 new homes being added every day.[68] Customers pay a small deposit for a solar home system that would be unaffordable to many villagers through normal retail markets. The balance is then repaid on a pay-as-you-use basis through M-Pesa, one of the world's fastest-growing mobile-payment platforms launched in Kenya in 2007. The Ignite Power project in Rwanda brings together several private companies, the government and philanthropic agencies in a partnership to instal off-grid technology through a pre-paid system that can power four lights, radios and televisions, and can charge cell phones.[69] In Kenya, researchers involved in smart villages found that the introduction of solar-charged lanterns 'essentially eliminated the use of kerosene lanterns, resulting in much lower levels of pulmonary health problems'.[70] In the Laikipia district, they partnered with local movements to develop a solar-powered refrigeration system that was mounted onto a bamboo frame on a camel, enabling nomadic people to transport refrigerated vaccines and medicines to more than 200,000 rural households. All over the world, distributed energy experiments matched with organic small-scale farming provide opportunities for employment and livelihoods for hundreds of thousands of women and men made landless and jobless by the increasing centralization of the GDP economy. As indicated by the Smart Villages Initiative, a global partnership to promote local self-governance around the world, 'The vision for smart villages is that modern energy access can act as a catalyst for development – in education, health, food security, productive enterprise, clean water and sanitation, environmental sustainability and participatory democracy.'[71]

These integrated governance systems allow villagers to become 'both designers and consumers of localised power'.[72] Successful development indeed resides not only in the availability of modern technology but also in the development of governance structures that support decentralization of production and consumption in the long term. This is true even when services are provided from the outside, as has been the case with a pilot programme in Nicaragua, where villagers have co-designed their energy system in partnership with a local commercial plant. Community energy solutions also have the potential to liberate women entrepreneurs and disadvantaged ethnic minorities by tailoring user materials and energy plans to meet the cultural and linguistic needs of these communities. By contrast, centralized programmes 'often ignore business skills, culturally appropriate cooking requirements and other home energy needs'.[73]

A myriad of similar local self-governance initiatives have been growing around the world, largely in opposition to the vertical control structure imposed by the GDP economy. The so-called transition towns, a network of citizen-driven projects supporting energy democracy and off-the-grid solutions, 'prosumerism' (that is, the fusion of production and consumption), post-carbon development, agroecology, food sovereignty and family farming, as well as direct participation in public governance, have become a global phenomenon: from the United Kingdom, where the phenomenon originated in the mid-2000s, they have proliferated to the rest of Europe and to North America, Australasia and Southern Africa. There are more than 470 transition towns around the world, as well as thousands of 'transition'-inspired initiatives.[74] More traditional forms of direct democracy have existed for a long time in many countries and are still implemented on a national scale in Switzerland, where citizens are called to vote several times a year, including public collective deliberations (*Landsgemeinde*), as is the case with the Appenzell Innerrhoden and Glarus cantons. Citizens can also propose changes to the constitution (through a process known as federal popular initiative) or hold referenda to confirm or dismiss any law voted by parliament from budgetary decisions to infrastructure development and foreign policy.

Scholars have long praised the virtues of participatory governance, particularly because it helps strengthen social cohesion and resolve ideological conflict and polarization. Modern political thinkers like John Stuart Mill and G. D. H. Cole, for instance, argued that direct participation fosters an active, 'non-servile' predisposition in citizens.[75] At the same time, however, deliberation systems can reinforce inequalities if the underlying social and economic conditions are not altered. For instance, Switzerland granted women the right to vote only in the 1970s, being one of the last countries in the world to embrace universal suffrage. In Appenzell Innerrhoden, women have only been allowed to participate in public deliberations since 1991. As argued by the feminist political theorist Carol Pateman, if participants are socialized in structures that are 'oligarchical and hierarchical', then the resulting participation would easily replicate the same degree of exclusivity and domination. Pateman's concern was not necessarily with political organizations but rather with the underlying principles dominating economic systems. She explicitly called for 'participation at the workplace' as an essential step towards building meaningful and inclusive public deliberation across society.[76] Similarly, the philosopher Iris Marion Young highlighted how deliberation processes are systematically hampered and depleted of their innovative character because of the limited time that people have to focus on public interest issues.[77] The 'overworked' person has become intrinsically unable to participate, even more so when economically 'disintegrated' households require most of the extra time left after 'outside' work. For Young, conventional economic structures provide an institutional block to effective participation, especially when it comes to the working class, women and minorities. Against this backdrop, she asks: 'Don't ideals of deliberative democracy require shortening the working day? Why should we have to think of deliberation as something that happens after work?'[78] Harvard political scientist Jane Mansbridge agrees that the current economic system, with its top-down institutional control and separation between formal work and the rest, 'has a large effect on people's lives'. She concludes that 'a truly democratic society would give workers control as well as ownership in their workplace'.[79]

This is why the emergence of a distributed economy in which production and consumption boundaries are increasingly blurred, calling into question the conventional conceptualization of work as separate from public life, provides an historic opportunity to build efficient and sustainable participatory governance systems across society. In this respect, rejecting the boundaries and values enshrined in the GDP paradigm will allow communities to reaffirm the inherent productivity of time dedicated to public interest deliberations. It will also contribute to integrating economic, political and social activities in a productivity continuum, in which functions as varied as interpersonal care, farming and manufacturing will happen in sync, further reinforcing the holistic development of self-governed communities. Such a focus on localized governance need not imply an implosion of national representative democracy. In fact, the horizontal distribution of post-GDP politics will provide institutional conditions for integration across communities, thus transforming the current vertical structure of democracy into a networked horizontal system. While deliberation would be driving local self-governance, a multi-level system of decision making would be possible throughout society, including mixed methods of representation and participation, in line with current thinking about deliberative democracy at the national level. In the words of Mansbridge,

> I can imagine a polity in which every citizen is called at least once in his or her life to serve on such a citizen assembly, drawn by lot, just as one is called for jury duty today. [. . .] I believe that such an experience would draw citizens into a fuller sense of responsibility for the whole, lead them to scrutinize more carefully other facts and insights that come their way in their subsequent lives as citizens, make them better watchdogs over their elected

representatives, and give them a more subtle understanding of the kinds of decisions elected representatives have to make.[80]

A civic approach to collective leadership

If the etymology of economics is 'household management', then it is quite a paradox that families and communities have been largely marginalized by the current rules of economic governance. While GDP favours mere transactions, the purpose of the economy has traditionally been that of 'provisioning goods and services to meet our material needs', as argued by Julie Nelson in her book *Economics for Humans*.[81] As discussed in the previous chapters, the economy is really not different from a role play in which we participate to efficiently allocate resources and tasks. In word, it is the decision-making core of 'how societies organize themselves for their provisioning'.[82] With this concept in mind, the philosopher Marvin T. Brown has proposed the idea of the 'civic' as the core of the economy and, by extension, of politics. 'The economics of provision', he writes, 'calls for a deepening of democratic attitudes that would encourage citizens, at different levels of involvement, to participate in organizing the economic system.'[83] But a civic economy like this requires a different understanding of value, new norms of reciprocity and an entirely new approach to prosperity. In a word, it requires the post-GDP political framework described in this chapter.

The recognition that GDP is a misleading indicator of success and a very myopic institutional parameter for policy making has prompted important reforms in the past few years. Besides those already described in the previous chapters, it is worth mentioning current efforts by the UN Statistics Division to revise the traditional approach to national

accounting by integrating economic objectives into long-term considerations of social and environmental sustainability. The new System of
Environmental-Economic Accounting provides governments around
the world with a standard approach to development planning that is
expected to take into account the complex interactions between economic policies and environmental systems.[84] It has also developed a
series of experimental methods to assist governments in the management of natural ecosystems, providing a platform to further integrate
policy making with the complexity of the biosphere.[85] Besides a host
of important reforms at the global level, which – as I have discussed
earlier – include the new SDGs, various public–private partnerships
to integrate economic and ecosystem accounting and natural capital
declarations, macro-level political reforms at the national level have
also covered some important ground. For instance, Latin American
and Caribbean countries have included sustainability as a cross-
cutting principle for policy making through the Quito Declaration of
2012. In 2008, Ecuador became the first country in the world to recognize the rights of nature in its constitution. In 2010, Bolivia passed a law
dedicated to 'the rights of Mother Earth', stating that: 'Mother Earth is
a living dynamic system made up of the undivided community of all
living beings, who are all interconnected, interdependent and complementary, sharing a common destiny.'[86]

In a similar fashion, New Zealand has attributed personal rights to
ecosystems such as the Whanganui River, and courts in various countries have upheld the public trust doctrine by granting citizens the
capacity to use legal avenues to defend the atmosphere as a common
good.[87] Costa Rica has committed to preserving at least 25 per cent of
its territory for wild forests and, together with Paraguay, has adopted
alternative metrics of social progress for policy planning purposes.[88]
In the United States, a number of states have institutionalized genuine

progress indicators to gauge their overall economic performance, while 're-wilding' initiatives aimed at expanding wilderness areas in industrialized societies are mushrooming around the world, especially in Europe.[89] In 2015, France adopted a new law requiring its government to publish annual reports on inequalities, quality of life and sustainable development for current or planned legislation, while in the Netherlands the Central Planning Bureau for Economic Policy Analysis and the Environmental Assessment Agency map out the effects of electoral programmes on both the economy and the environment.[90] The Himalayan country of Bhutan is widely known for having publicly rejected the concept of GDP growth since the early 1970s. As mentioned in chapter 2, its culture of 'gross national happiness' (GNH) has been operationalized into a set of post-GDP indicators, which are routinely used by a governmental GNH commission to vet policies and grant businesses the licence to operate. The country's constitution also demands that an unparalleled 60 per cent of the national territory be left to nature reserves.[91]

These political reforms open an unprecedented opportunity for institutional change but, for them to result in radical transformation, there is a need for a new type of leadership: a leadership able to connect the dots between macro-political openings, new developments in the economy and the potential for the localization of governance. As discussed in chapter 1, institutional dynamics generate social routines that are hard to change. In conditions where competition is supported by a powerful system of incentives and rewards and vertical governance is reinforced by an economic structure that pursues development through top-down industrialization, the transaction costs of collective action are particularly high. The rules of the game favour concentration at the expense of distribution. To challenge the inertia of the current system, there is a need for alternative rules not only to trigger change, but also to sustain it over time. Yet rules-making requires time and effort, resulting in additional transaction costs. Following Ostrom, we can depict collective action dilemmas as nested into one another. Not only does challenging the status quo require resources, but also managing the new equilibrium results in a significant governance investment. As free riders will be able to enjoy the benefits of a new system without having contributed to the effort of creating and maintaining it, the risk is that inaction may prevail. For Ostrom, the only way out of these nested dilemmas is through shared monitoring systems designed to guarantee that individuals affected by the new rules can participate in modifying them in line with local needs and conditions. Local participatory governance is, indeed, more efficient at reducing the risks of short-term thinking and narrow self-interest because of peer pressure, reputational mechanisms and, above all, the very basic principle that those taking decisions are ultimately reaping the benefits or paying the price for their actions. While individual leadership may be indispensable to challenge the initial routines, only collective leadership can lead and sustain the change. As Solomon Asch's conformity experiments have long revealed, it is hard for individuals to question power, traditional dynamics and groupthink, even in the face of absurdity. Yet, when at least another member of society questions the system's overall assumptions, then the personal transaction costs of 'speaking one's mind' become much more tolerable, triggering a positive cascade effect through society.[92] In the following chapters, I will investigate how the convergence of top-down reforms and bottom-up pressures in the nascent economic and political order can affect global dynamics and open space for a new type of collective leadership.

5

Post-GDP World

The power of GDP is not limited to national borders: it profoundly shapes global governance processes too. Since the Industrial Revolution and, even more so, since the birth of the consumerist society in the twentieth century, economic growth has been intimately connected with a country's international status. In his influential book *The Rise and Fall of the Great Powers*, Paul Kennedy concludes that the size of a country's economy is arguably more significant than military strength when it comes to determining its global status. As we have seen, the definitions of 'superpower', 'middle-power' or 'emerging power', which dominate international debates and have become part and parcel of the global political discourse, are all determined by GDP.[1] The commonplace distinction between 'developed' and 'developing' world, which has defined international aid, finance and trade policies in the twentieth century, is also a result of GDP.[2] When allegedly 'poor' nations reach a certain level of GDP, they undergo a process of policy transformation. Normally, foreign-aid funds are terminated or reduced and trade agreements are revised. GDP can push a country from 'least developed' to a 'middle-income' level, often resulting in a growing inflow of foreign direct investment accompanied or preceded by the discontinuation of preferential trade conditions, such as those devised to protect vulnerable industries against the competition of more advanced industrial economies. When this happens, there are winners and losers: often, small producers are wiped out by the competition from multinational corporations, while local elites capture the rents generated by foreign capital.

Positive shifts in GDP growth can result in countries being invited to join exclusive international clubs, with the accordance of status and power that comes with such a membership. For instance, the promotion of South Korea and Mexico from middle-income countries to developed nations opened the door for their inclusion in the Organization for Economic Cooperation and Development (OECD) in the mid-1990s, the first two hitherto 'developing' nations to do so. Because of their reputation as fast-growing economies, Brazil, China, India, Mexico and South Africa were invited to join the G8 meetings in 2007 through the so-called Outreach 5 arrangement, an informal channel for the world's largest economies to interact with their emerging counterparts. The same principle largely applies to the composition of the G20, the world's leading forum for the coordination of global economic policy. The prestige associated with aggregate GDP and/or its growth rates applies not only to traditional governance institutions but also to new 'clubs'. The acronym BRIC (later expanded to BRICS) was introduced in the international political debate by a 2001 report published by Goldman Sachs to describe the then fastest-growing economies, Brazil, Russia, India and China (and now also South Africa).[3] Goldman's analysis was based on estimates of GDP growth, according to which the economic output of these economies would surpass that of the G7 by 2050 and thus create a new planetary leadership. More recently, the same logic was applied to another group of emerging economies, once again through a GDP-based acronym, MINT, alerting the investment community that the real leaders of the future may very well be Mexico, Indonesia, Nigeria and Turkey.[4]

As I have mentioned in chapter 2, global economic policies are also driven by GDP, predominantly through the intermediation of institutions such as the IMF and the World Bank, which assess the world economy through the lens afforded by this statistic. These international financial institutions have specifically been mandated to enforce a form of GDP-based governance, so much so that when GDP growth rates in a country are in distress (what is conventionally known as a 'recession'), they are sent in to advise and often coerce national policy makers, with crucial impacts on democratic governance. Among other things, they use aggregate GDP and growth forecasts to establish interest rates on loans and enforce policies through external pressure and direct coercion on domestic sovereignty, as has been the case with the wave of structural adjustments programmes in the 1980s, as well as post-crisis interventions in Latin America and East Asia in the 1990s and across the rest of the world, especially in Europe, since the eruption of the more recent global economic downturn.

Against this backdrop, this chapter asks: if GDP has been so crucial in shaping the formal and informal operating principles of contemporary global governance, what changes can be envisaged at the international level as a result of a shift to a post-GDP economic and political system? As I will discuss in the following sections, GDP's inherent logics have not only been promoted by powerful organizations like those mentioned above, but they have also contributed to shaping conventional approaches to trade and market integration, depicting globalization as an efficient process of value creation. On the contrary, post-GDP indicators reveal the hidden costs of many processes that the GDP world has taken for granted, thus exerting a potential delegitimizing effect on the current structures of global trade. In a post-GDP world, new forms of leadership may emerge, as well as a restructuring of globalization through innovative forms of regional cooperation and integration.

Global leadership after GDP

GDP contributed in many different ways to designing the system of international governance of the twentieth century. In particular, it did so by establishing the parameters for economic success and providing ordering principles for the distribution of power in global institutions. As such, GDP was instrumental in creating the world's pecking order. But what would global leadership look like in a post-GDP world? If we take into account some of the alternative indicators discussed in chapter 2, we can identify a clear pattern: the new leaders would be countries inspired by socio-democratic ideals and deeply conscious of environmental governance. The best performing nations according to these alternative indicators are also some of the least unequal societies in the world, those with the best social security systems for their citizens and a long tradition of strong social ties and vibrant civil society. Table 5.1 presents a selection of alternative G7 groups, based on post-GDP indicators.

With the exception of Canada, no other G7 member appears in any of the post-GDP rankings listed above. Interestingly, the world's largest economies in GDP terms, the United States and China, often described by the media as 'the G2', have completely disappeared from all these lists. The US ranks 11th in economic prosperity, especially because of its poor track record in safety and security, and 16th in overall social progress. Its performance drops even further, to the 37th position, when well-being variables are considered, including access to basic knowledge and health, and plummets to the very bottom of the global rankings in sustainable development, due to its massive ecological footprint. China is the 52nd country in terms of overall prosperity, held back by governance issues and a poor democratic record. It is also the 92nd country in social progress and among the worst performers in terms of environmental policy (109th).

Table 5.1 Possible 'G7 clubs' according to alternative indicators

G7 of sustainable development*	G7 of social progress**	G7 of environmental performance***	G7 of economic prosperity****	G7 of happiness*****
Costa Rica	Norway	Finland	Norway	Denmark
Colombia	Switzerland	Iceland	Switzerland	Switzerland
Panama	Sweden	Sweden	Canada	Iceland
Ireland	Iceland	Slovenia	Sweden	Norway
South Korea	New Zealand	Spain	New Zealand	Finland
Chile	Canada	Portugal	Denmark	Canada
New Zealand	Finland	Estonia	Australia	Netherlands

* *Source:* Happy Planet Index (data 2012) and Human Development Index (data 2014), adjusted by Ecological Footprint (data 2010) per capita.
** *Source:* Social Progress Index (data 2015)
*** *Source:* Yale Environmental Performance Index (data 2016).
**** *Source:* Legatum Prosperity Index (data 2015)
***** *Source:* World Happiness Report (data 2016)

Indicators focusing on social progress, economic prosperity and self-reported happiness highlight the leadership role of nations with a strong social-democratic tradition, especially in Europe and in the South Pacific (e.g. New Zealand and Australia). Switzerland and Norway are the best performing countries in Europe, followed by Iceland. EU member states such as Sweden, Ireland, Denmark, Finland and Slovenia, as well as austerity targets like Spain and Portugal, would be part of the lead, at least in some areas. To an extent, this demonstrates that the EU would continue showing significant leadership in a post-GDP world and attests to the fact that Europe, despite its internal crises, is still a region of human, social and environmental well-being. The combination of 'footprint' indicators with estimates of human development underlines the important role played by Latin American nations, especially in so far as they have been able to marry longevity, good health and education with limited impacts on the environment. In particular, a country like

Costa Rica stands out as a regional overachiever. According to the Social Progress Index, 'Costa Rica has had strong education, health and welfare systems for a long time, as well as a long democratic tradition,' demonstrating that 'building social progress takes persistence'.[5] The results of the Happy Planet Index also reward Costa Rica for having championed sustainability in its national policies: the country produces most of its electricity from renewable sources, has reversed deforestation trends and has committed to becoming carbon neutral by 2021. At the social level, Costa Rica 'has the second highest life expectancy in the Americas', above the United States. The self-reported well-being among citizens is higher than in many richer nations and their ecological footprint per capita is a third that of America.[6] In 2015, Costa Rica officially reported having achieved an historic target: running for 285 days only on renewable energy. Overall, this meant almost 99 per cent of complete reliance on alternative sources of electricity.[7]

Post-GDP indicators of economic performance make Asia largely disappear from the global leadership map, especially its regional powerhouses. Neither Japan (a G7 member) nor China or India (members of the G20 and the BRICS) makes it to the top seven. The same applies to Russia, another leading emerging economy and an historic 'superpower'. None of these GDP powers would even qualify for membership of a hypothetical G20, with the exception of Japan, which is 16th in the global ranking of social progress and 19th in that of prosperity. It is interesting to note that Japan outperforms other Asian economies despite its prolonged stagnation and plummeting GDP growth rates. The continental leader is undoubtedly South Korea, which has enshrined sustainable development in its national policy strategy. During the global financial crisis in 2008, the country dedicated 80 per cent of its fiscal stimulus to clean energies and sustainable development projects, particularly in infrastructure and transportation. The World Bank credits the country's early recovery from the crisis to its emphasis on environmental sustainability.[8] For the future, the country has also committed to developing the world's first nationwide 'smart grid' system by 2030, to increasing the country's renewable energy to 11 per cent of supplies by 2030 and to reducing greenhouse gas emissions by 30 per cent before 2020.

Although Africa does not appear in any of these indicators' top rankings, there are regional overachievers in this continent too. For instance, Mauritius performs better than emerging powers like Brazil, Russia and India, as well as Indonesia and Turkey, in social progress. It is among those countries enjoying 'high human development', ahead of Mexico, Brazil and China. Botswana leads the 'medium human development' group, ahead of most other African countries, including the much GDP-richer South Africa. It also fares better than a global leader like India, which it surpasses in terms of economic prosperity, as it does China and Russia. Mauritius and Botswana are also regional leaders in environmental governance, followed by Namibia. Such a comparatively prominent role is also confirmed by other governance indicators not included in this list, which routinely position Botswana and Mauritius as the continent's best-performing countries in governance and the fight against corruption.[9] While GDP attributed leading status to heavy-polluting, highly unequal and deeply corrupt countries such as South Africa and Nigeria, alternative indicators help identify better governed, more sustainable and more accountable nations in a hitherto relatively 'underdeveloped' continent.

Overall, it appears that post-GDP indicators highlight the economic performance of countries that have achieved a comparatively higher level of efficiency, producing good outcomes in terms of human and social development, but with a limited impact on the environment. The traditional link between GDP and global authority has relegated some of these countries to the margins of global governance, neglecting their achievements and disregarding some of the policies and ideals they have championed. The 'beyond GDP' policy discourse, institutionalized through the adoption of the SDGs, provides a critical opportunity for some of these countries to reclaim more of a voice within the global governance arena. As has been the case in the past, a first step would be the creation of an informal alliance, similar to the G7 or the BRICS, to pursue a joint strategy in international politics. Some of these countries are members of the EU, while most of them belong to the OECD, two organizations that have spearheaded, at least rhetorically, the objective of moving beyond GDP. The best-performing countries could use their relative influence within these two forums to put post-GDP governance reforms squarely onto the global agenda. By profiling themselves as champions of a new development model, they would gain in terms both of soft power and reputation, potentially inspiring many other nations to follow suit. They would also have much to gain from reinforcing bilateral and multilateral cooperation between themselves. Some of these countries are leaders in clean technologies and renewable energy systems, whose transfer across the alliance would also have important financial returns. Others are regional leaders in their respective continents, a privileged position that could be exploited to trigger ripple effects at the continental level. As we have seen since 2015 with the emergence of the V20, a network of climate-vulnerable nations, the climate change negotiations offer a privileged arena for an alliance of economies inspired by a post-GDP development model to speak with a common voice and provide a different style of leadership.

The inefficiencies of global trade

Governments, international organizations, economic advisers and most media routinely maintain that international trade agreements are crucial for economic progress because they boost GDP. According to the World Trade Organization (WTO), international trade after the Second World War entered a long period of record expansion with world merchandise exports rising by more than 8 per cent per annum in real terms during the 1950–1973 period. Growth slowed a bit in the aftermath of 'the oil price shocks, a burst of inflation caused by monetary expansion and inadequate macroeconomic adjustment policies'.[10] Then, throughout the 1990s, global trade expanded with renewed acceleration, also driven by innovations in communication and information technology. On average, world trade grew by 6.2 per cent per annum between 1950 and the 2007–2008 global financial crisis when, for the first time since 1975, it actually declined. Since 2010, expansion has begun again, with a more modest average of 2.5 per cent annual growth.[11]

In 1999, a widely cited paper published in *The American Economic Review* argued that the geographic distance between countries has an impact on their levels of national income, suggesting that trade (the only economic variable influenced by geography) has a quantifiable and positive impact on GDP: 'The results of the experiment are consistent across the samples and specifications we consider: trade raises income. The relation between the geographic component of trade and income suggests that a rise of one percentage point in the ratio of trade to GDP increases income per person by at least one-half percent.'[12]

In a 2007 speech, the former governor of the Federal Reserve, Ben Bernanke, cited a number of financial reasons in support of more global trade, concluding that 'Our willingness to trade freely with the world is indeed an essential source of our prosperity – and I think it is safe to say that the importance of trade for us will continue to grow.'[13] His data came from a series of studies published a few years earlier which showed a large GDP pay-off from global trade, including an increase of roughly US$1 trillion a year 'or about 10 percent of gross domestic product' annually, resulting 'in annual income of about US$10,000 per household'. The studies concluded that, with further liberalizations and excluding the benefits from potential better communication and transportation systems in the future, a move to complete 'global free trade and investment could produce an additional $500 billion in US income annually, or roughly $5,000 per household each year'.[14] Building on this research, a 2015 paper published by the White House made additional extrapolations about the positive impacts on global trade on GDP, concluding that 'the reduction in US tariffs since World War II contributed an additional 7.3 percent to US GDP, or approximately $1.3 trillion in 2014'.[15] The paper also claimed that 'for every 1 percent increase in income as a result of trade liberalization, pollution concentrations fall by 1 percent' because 'the adoption of clean technologies spread through trade more than offsets emissions resulting from increased transportation or production.'

Acclaimed economists like Dani Rodrik and Paul Krugman have, of course, disputed the validity of these data, arguing that increasing returns are postulated on general equilibrium models designed to yield expected results, wrong assumptions in terms of price convergence and shaky datasets.[16] Even assuming good financial returns, there is a wealth of interdisciplinary research focusing on the intersection between social, economic and environmental factors demonstrating the numerous negative externalities of global trade, with impacts on the life support structures of natural ecosystems. In the vertical structure of the GDP economy, trade plays a crucial role because it contributes to separating production and consumption even further, not only in terms of national value chains but across continents. This has an important influence on environmental awareness because it 'causes a geographic separation of consumers and the pollution emitted in the production of consumable items'.[17] For a strictly self-interested *homo economicus*, the shifting of local pollutants to distant lands may be seen as a rational choice, as it allows for ever-growing consumption without suffering some of the negative externalities therein. It was this kind of reasoning that led Larry Summers, then chief economist at the World Bank, to sign a memo in the early 1990s that openly advocated dumping toxic waste produced in industrialized countries on 'underdeveloped' countries.[18] He also concluded that 'underpopulated countries in Africa are vastly underpolluted; their air quality is vastly inefficiently low compared to Los Angeles or Mexico City.' The reference to 'efficiency' is obviously linked to the GDP framework of value, which sees pollution as an important contributor to the marginal utility of 'mature' economies. In the words of Russell Mokhiber and Robert Weissman, authors of *Corporate Predators: The Hunt for Mega-Profits and the Attack on Democracy*, the memo 'was not an aberration stemming from a lapse of good judgment'. Much to the contrary, it was perfectly coherent with the overall GDP approach to international trade which postulates that 'developing countries should concentrate their effort on exports, rather than production for local needs' and 'allow foreign capital to move into and out of the country without restraint'. 'The notion that poor countries should import pollution and waste is just an unsavory application of the economic theory of the US Treasury Department, shared also by the International Monetary Fund (IMF) and, to a lesser extent, the World Bank.'[19]

Yet, when it comes to global pollutants such as greenhouse gases, which have become a primary international concern in the past decade, consumers ultimately bear the costs of a globalized system of production regardless of where production occurs. As a consequence, one would expect the implications of international trade to feature prominently in climate change negotiations, with environmental considerations also taking centre stage in trade debates. However, references to international trade in climate documents are very sporadic and marginal, usually included to ensure that environmental decisions will *not* limit the prerogatives of movement of goods and services. For instance, the Kyoto Protocol's Article 2.3 states that parties 'shall strive to implement policies and measures [. . .] in such a way as to minimize adverse effects [. . .] on international trade'. The recent negotiations between the European Union and the United States for a new trade agreement known as the Transatlantic Trade and Investment Partnership (TTIP) make no mention whatsoever of the deal's impacts on climate change, as revealed in a draft text leaked in May 2016.[20] This disregard for the trade–climate nexus flies in the face of decades of research which has concluded that the problems undermining the effectiveness of global deals on climate 'are manifested in international trade [. . .] and perhaps ironically, restructuring international trade may help mitigation and accelerate sustainable development'.[21] As of 2008, 23 per cent of global CO_2 emissions (the equivalent of 5.7 gigatonnes) were embodied in international trade, with more 'developed' economies (the so-called Annex B countries) being net importers of CO_2 emissions due to carbon leakage, that is, the process whereby carbon-intensive production is shifted offshore and written off national accounts yet is ultimately motivated by domestic consumption.[22] In 2015, a research paper published in the *Proceedings of the National Academy of Sciences* (*PNAS*) argued that current statistics of resource productivity linked to GDP are grossly misleading as they hide the actual footprint of nations in a system of globalized trade.[23] The concept of 'decoupling', which postulates the capacity of delinking economic growth from environmental impacts through technological innovation, is often heralded as the way forward for economic progress. The argument is based on the recognition that many 'developed' countries have managed to reduce their use of natural resources per unit of GDP (relative decoupling), paving the way for innovations that will allow economies to grow while reducing the overall reliance on natural resources (absolute decoupling). For example, the EU has adopted the principle of 'resource productivity', which results from dividing domestic material consumption (DMC) by GDP, as a key approach to economic prosperity.[24] Its statistical office, Eurostat, is tasked with monitoring the ratio between DMC and GDP as the headline indicator for the resource-efficiency targets of the Europe 2020 strategy, with member states and companies being rated on their resource productivity attainments.[25] The OECD and the UN Environmental Programme also use the ratio between GDP and DMC as a measurement of their green-growth strategies.

Yet these measures of resource use and environmental impacts rely on production indicators, providing an incomplete picture of ecological footprint in a system in which the most polluting processes in global value chains have moved to 'emerging' and 'developing' countries. When production-based metrics are replaced with consumption-based indicators like the material footprint, the results call the decoupling argument into question, as the *PNAS* article unequivocally shows: 'By calculating raw material equivalents of international trade, we demonstrate that countries' use of nondomestic resources is, on average, about threefold larger than the physical quantity of traded goods. As wealth grows, countries tend to reduce their domestic portion of materials extraction through international trade, whereas the overall mass of material consumption generally increases.'[26]

Indeed, there appears to be a direct relationship between GDP growth and material footprint: 'With every 10% increase in gross domestic product, the average national MF increases by 6%.'[27] Conventional metrics only focus on the amount of materials directly used by an economy, that is, the raw materials extracted from the domestic territory plus all physical imports minus all physical exports. They do not include 'the upstream raw materials related to imports and exports originating from outside of the focal economy': 'This truncation might mislead assessments of national resource productivity and supply security of natural resources as the increasing spatial separation of production and consumption in global supply chains leads to a shift of resource use and associated environmental pressures among countries.'[28]

In the past two decades, the member states of the OECD and the EU have increased their GDP while keeping their domestic material consumption under control only because of statistical systems hiding the pollution embedded in the international value chain. In absolute terms, the United States is by far the largest importer of primary resources embodied in trade, while China is the largest exporter. When the responsibility for the material footprint is shifted from the country of production to that of consumption, the alleged evidence of decoupling evaporates, despite much talking about sustainable development and green growth. In particular, international trade itself has generated additional costs and impacts, with 'two-fifths of all global raw materials' being extracted and used 'just to enable exports of goods and services to other countries'.[29]

The current system of international trade generates a 'resource productivity' paradox. The environmental costs of production are outsourced to 'developing' countries, largely disappearing from the accounting books of those nations in which the ultimate consumers reside. As we have seen, this is because resource-use statistics attribute ecological impacts to producing rather than consuming countries. Yet most of the value calculated in GDP is not added during the early production phases, which are usually heavier on the environment but cheaper in transaction terms. The bulk of the market value derives from the final stages of marketization, which – either through marginal finishes or simple repackaging – takes places in importing countries. Although most production in today's world takes place in the Far East and in the so-called emerging markets of the global South, the bulk of value is ultimately appropriated by the 'rich' global North. This double accounting process, which leaves environmental footprints with the countries responsible for the dirtier lower-value stages of production and credits most income to those performing the relatively cleaner high-value final steps before distribution, is by and large responsible for the apparent resource productivity of modern economies. By retaining the most profitable stages in the value chain, these nations appear very efficient in economic terms, with high volumes of growth apparently generated with little ecological impact.

The costly and detrimental effects of international trade have been demonstrated not only for material consumption and greenhouse gas emissions but also for a variety of other areas that have a direct bearing on economic prosperity. For instance, international trade helps mask the fact that high-GDP countries require more biologically productive land per capita than low-GDP countries. In specific terms, a nation's footprint in terms of land area increases 'by a third for each doubling of income' per capita.[30] Here is another paradox: while high-income countries can therefore devote more domestic land to natural use, the shifting of agricultural, food and forestry production processes results in a net displacement of land use to low-income countries, amounting to 6 per cent of the global land demand, with Europe and

Japan in the lead. Through imports of embodied pressures, the average European consumer is responsible for the production of 13.3 tonnes of CO_2 equivalent emissions, the appropriation of 2.53 global hectares of land with average biological productivity and the consumption of 179 cubic metres of blue water, against global averages of 5.7 tonnes of CO_2 equivalents, 1.23 global hectares and 163 cubic meters of water (as of 2004 data).[31] Recent analyses of the evolution and structure of international trade have also revealed that 'developed' countries increasingly import water embodied in goods from the rest of the world to alleviate pressure on domestic water resources against the backdrop of a global volume of 'virtual water trade' that has more than doubled since the early 1990s.[32] Moreover, international trade chains were found responsible for accelerated 'habitat degradation far removed from the place of consumption', accounting for '30 percent of global species threats'.[33]

The TTIP is officially presented as a historic opportunity to reignite growth in international trade, after the relatively sluggish performance experienced since the global financial crisis. According to a study commissioned by the European Commission, the trade agreement will increase the size of the EU economy by about 0.5 per cent of GDP (that is, roughly, 120 billion euros) and that of the United States by about 0.4 per cent (about 95 billion euros). The study also posits that an acceleration of 'economic growth in the United States and the EU means more purchases by consumers and business of other countries' products', thus benefiting not only the two parties but the entire world.[34] Other studies have questioned these positive projections, arguing that the agreement would lead to a contraction instead of an increase in GDP.[35]

Because of its institutional power, analysts and advisers make reference to 'GDP effects' to support or oppose policies. Yet there are arguably more important indicators and parameters that should be looked at to gauge the desirability of international trade. Besides the environmental impacts mentioned above, there are also critical social effects that should be taken into consideration. Classical textbook theories, like the Heckscher–Ohlin and the Stolper–Samuelson models, show that trade may trigger inequality because it is driven by differences in factor abundance, especially the so-called skill premium, that is, the ratio of wages between skilled and unskilled workers.[36] As lower-income countries absorb sectors of global production destined for sales in higher-income countries, unskilled workers in the latter are likely to lose out. In the early 1990s, new research showed that the trade-driven downward spiral in wages may not be as severe as initially thought, given emerging economies' capacity to catch up and reach similar labour conditions to more 'developed' nations, thus losing most of their comparative advantage. Yet, as Krugman notes, these more optimistic accounts focus on historic data stemming from economies like Japan, South Korea and other 'Asian Tigers', which have quickly caught up with global wage standards. Currently, however, international value chains are mostly based in nations like China and India, which are endowed with a massive number of low-skilled workers.[37] Interestingly, research conducted on trade dynamics since the mid-1990s' liberalizations shows consistently that income inequalities emerge not only in high-income countries (as predicted by classical models) but also in low-income nations, mostly because modern trade agreements include more than provisions for exchanges of good and services: they provide clear regulatory guidelines for welfare reforms, intellectual property and state–business relations, thus generating 'within industry effects due to heterogeneous firms, the effects of offshoring of tasks, effects on incomplete contracting, and the effects of labour-market frictions'.[38]

Civil society's concerns about the impacts of the TTIP have largely been confirmed by the draft negotiation documents which appear to have dropped traditional clauses such as the 'general exceptions' enshrined in the WTO rules, which allow countries to regulate trade with a view to protecting the environment and health, as well as the precautionary principle, a key provision upheld by the EU founding treaties. Besides pointing out the lack of reference to the trade agreement's impact on the climate, let alone the objective of keeping global temperatures within 1.5°C in line with the 2015 Paris agreement, research also shows the likelihood of growing health-related conditions, given the changes in legislation and service provision required by the treaty.[39] In particular, specialists warn against negative impacts on access to medicines and health-care services, the increase in consumption of tobacco and alcohol (due to a relaxation in labelling regulations and restrictions) and the risks associated with diet-related diseases, food insecurity and environmental health. The treaty's chapters on intellectual property may lead to an expansion of patent monopolies and limit or delay the availability of generic drugs, resulting in an underutilization of needed medications among vulnerable populations. The so-called 'ratchet clause', which is designed to support private health insurance, is also likely to undermine public health-care services, ultimately limiting access to universal health care among the most vulnerable sectors of the population.

If the detrimental impacts on social dynamics and environmental sustainability are to be addressed successfully, then the very principles of globalized trade must be called into question. This can be done by re-scaling international exchanges. For instance, research shows that the emissions embodied in trade are much lower in exchanges that occur regionally than they are in the case of global transactions, so that 'one way to reduce the impact of trade on individual countries may be to encourage coalition formation,' that is, regional networks of countries.[40] Some have invoked the concept of 'messy' federalism, first introduced by James Madison in the drafting of the US legal system with a view to shifting trade regulations from the global scene to a web of overlapping regional and local systems of collaboration.[41] In the next section, I will explain why new forms of regional cooperation and horizontal governance across borders are the most practical and promising ways forward in redesigning globalization.

From globalization to regionalization

The transition to a post-GDP world is happening at a time of major political, social and economic shifts. As I have discussed in the preceding sections, this process may provide a fertile terrain for countries that have been traditionally marginalized by the GDP-based system of global governance to play a more prominent role in international politics. Moreover, the focus on post-GDP indicators of performance is increasingly questioning the efficiency of globalization, especially its anchor on international trade. Since the global financial crisis, international trade volumes have grown at a much slower pace than before, despite technological innovation and decreasing energy costs. While GDP-fuelling trade has incentivized countries to increase economic interdependence, it has also made economic systems in nations and continents vulnerable to systemic shocks. There is also enough evidence that the cycle of debt and consumption, which is supported by the GDP approach to economic development, was one of the main causes of the economic collapse in 2007–2008.[42] With declining profits expected from global trade, the stalling of international negotiations at the WTO and the slowing down of China's powerhouse, global market integration is unlikely to continue, let alone accelerate. Moreover, a globalized system of market governance has rendered national governments unable to tackle socio-economic imbalances, especially when they are caused by global economic dynamics, with issues like tax havens and rising global inequalities becoming predominant in public discourse.[43] Although Europe appears to have lost momentum in its pledge to establish a financial transaction tax, it is likely that some coalitions of governments may agree on some restrictive policies to encourage less speculative and more productive investment, which will in turn reduce the volume of global economic transactions.[44]

Despite the hesitation with which the international community has been pushing the post-Kyoto agenda on climate change, the Paris conference in 2015 and a series of other commitments at the global level suggest that new regulations will be introduced to limit the emissions of greenhouse gases in both industrialized nations and 'developing' countries. Some nations have already introduced carbon taxes, which are likely to become more stringent and punitive in the near future.[45] In many regards, the climate change debate at the international level is likely to replace the traditional global trade negotiations as the defining architecture of international relations in the twenty-first century. As the climate change regime supersedes the current world trade system, the exchange of goods and services is likely to experience a slow but steady relocalization, in which 'mileage' will begin to make a difference. Geographical distances will matter ever more in the process of designing a climate-compatible trading system, which means that what can be produced and consumed regionally/locally will become more profitable than what is shipped across the planet. As discussed in chapter 3, innovative reforms in corporate governance are also attesting to a (gradual) shift in the way in which businesses operate in a post-GDP world.[46] As natural capital accounting, transport costs and environmental impacts become central in the new business paradigm, production and consumption may become increasingly regional.

It is not only the movement of goods that is likely to regionalize but also that of people. Although migration is a global phenomenon, 'the largest global migrant flows take place within individual world regions, not across continents'.[47] The UN Department of Economic and Social Affairs shows the regionalization effect in migration flows, corroborated by a 2014 study published in *Science* connecting official data with modern tracking systems and dynamic visualizations: since the mid-1990s, about 0.6 per cent of the global population has migrated, with most people moving not only within the same continent but also within the same sub-region, especially in South and West Asia, in North America and in Africa.[48] Refugees are also increasingly bound to explore regional routes, not only because of obvious mobility constraints but also because of international principles, such as that of 'first country of asylum', which compel neighbouring nations to provide hospitality. The flow of asylum seekers moving across the European Union that began in 2015 is a clear example of a regional movement of people affecting mostly the south-eastern shores of Europe, which are more easily accessed via land or sea from the troubled Middle East and North Africa. While migratory movements can be affected by global dynamics, including climate change, conflict and economic crises, the repercussions are usually regional, thus requiring stronger institutional mechanisms at that level of governance.

A stronger regional focus is also motivated by trends in energy supply. As we know, the sudden increase in oil prices in 2007, which drove up food prices and exerted a ripple effect through the global economy, was a critical driver of the global economic crisis.[49] Although prices have been much lower ever since, they will inevitably pick up again as global growth resumes. But higher prices will most probably constitute a drag on trade and may potentially sink the economy again. According to estimates produced by the International Energy

Agency (IEA), the near future will require a fundamental shift in global transportation systems as crude oil, which is the most suitable form of energy for the long-distance movement of goods, will be much harder to find. In particular, the IEA believes that conventional crude output from existing fields is set to fall 'by more than 40 million barrels per day by 2035'. As a consequence, of the 790 billion barrels of total production required to meet projected demand, 'more than half is needed just to offset declining production'.[50] As regards natural gas, the IEA forecasts significant growth over the next decade, particularly in the United States, but with uncertainty about 'whether gas can be made available at prices that are attractive to consumers while still offering incentives for the necessary large capital-intensive investments in gas supply'.[51] Defenders of globalization may of course dispute these projections, arguing that fossil fuel energy is currently enjoying a low-price phase, which will continue to power global trade for the foreseeable future. Even if one accepts such contrarian arguments (which are often not substantiated by any evidence), the fact remains that the climate change imperative still makes it unlikely that these polluting resources will continue driving worldwide transportation business as usual. In this regard, natural gas is certainly not a solution, given the fact that its extraction generates methane, a greenhouse gas that is not only more polluting than CO_2 but has more serious impacts in the short term, thus making the target of limiting the rise in average temperatures to 2°C (or 1.5°C as agreed in Paris) even less likely than with the current consumption of oil and coal.[52] On the other hand, renewable energy systems like solar, wind, hydro and geothermal (which have been growing exponentially in the past few years and will become more dominant in the future) can hardly come to the rescue of globalization as they are not easily amenable to long-distance transportation. Against this backdrop, the IEA believes the climate-compatible carbon budget will be exhausted by 2040, requiring profound transformation in the energy and transportation sectors.[53] This prospect is likely to be challenged by oil-producing states and companies, which routinely use the projected future sales of proven reserves to access credit and increase their stock value, a process known as reserve-based lending. Should carbon taxes, polluter-pays schemes, natural capital accounting, energy depletion as well as environmental profit-and-loss provisions fail to reform globalization, it will probably be the soaring insurance costs for worldwide freight and transportation, due to climate variability, that make transport-intensive produce prohibitively expensive as compared to local production networked across borders at a regional level.

While renewable energy will not be able to sustain the system of transport and international freight that we have now, it will allow businesses to produce energy locally and exchange it within short-distance networks. Indeed, renewable energy systems require perfect integration between production and consumption of power because extra output is difficult to store and inefficient to transport. Proximity is an essential variable for the effective use of renewable energy, which of course requires a different approach to geography and space. As more energy production is diversified through networks of small producers and consumers and localized according to the specific needs and productive capacities of different territories, systems of exchange will need to adapt to the specifics of each geographical area. Unlike fossil fuels and other non-renewable sources of energy, renewable energy can be produced anywhere on the planet: some territories enjoy significant solar exposure, others have winds or tides, while others have geothermal sources and biomasses. This horizontal availability reduces the need for giant, top-down infrastructures and makes long-distance distribution systems redundant and inefficient, given the risk of energy dispersion through large grids. As discussed in chapter 4, micro-grids integrated across community borders and off-the-grid solutions are the most viable systems for energy exchange in 'developing' countries. In 'developed' societies, too, wasteful macro-grids will need to be upgraded through smart technology capable of transforming existing top-down infrastructure into a network of 'prosumers' feeding and sharing energy horizontally, much as internet connectivity has done for the traditional, top-down telephone line infrastructure.

All these factors (economic inefficiencies, movements of people, shifts in energy supply and climate change) are mutually reinforcing in their collective contribution to undermining the current form of globalization. Climate change makes it imperative to switch to renewable and less polluting forms of energy, which are, however, not suitable to sustain global trade. The growth of environmental regulations will mean that globalized markets are unlikely to stay profitable in the long run, forcing businesses to develop alternative forms of exchange, mostly through the integration of local value chains.

As the global market becomes less profitable, business will have an incentive to trade locally and regionally. In some cases, it will be more profitable to negotiate with neighbouring communities in a foreign country than with other faraway communities within the same nation. In the current top-down regulatory framework, regional trade has only prevailed in Europe, where a common market has become a daily reality for goods, services and workers. In South America, Asia and especially Africa, by contrast, most trade volumes are directed outside the region. Although regionalization has generated new avenues for intra-region trade, the profitability of global markets has discouraged a serious refocusing of business activities within regions.

A transition to localized forms of production and consumption does not necessarily mean a resurgence in national protectionism. If facilitated by the right policies and incentives, the post-GDP economy will become deeply embedded in the cultural, geographic, climatic and ecosystemic conditions of each territory. In this regard, national borders cannot be efficient boundaries as they can easily pose an obstacle to the organic growth of cooperative networks following social and environmental continuities. Many people share customs, languages and social habits across national borders. Many communities have more in common with their trans-frontier equivalents than with other groups in their own countries of residence. Similarly, territorial characteristics and ecosystemic dynamics do not recognize border posts. Natural biomes, that is, the natural communities defined by similar flora and fauna, which are so crucial to enable efficient use of natural resources, are almost by definition cross-national. A governance system aligned with these principles will need to adapt to human and natural integrated systems, thus transcending national borders. In this post-GDP world, regional cross-border exchanges may very well become more common than they are now. Through energy systems organized by similar geophysical characteristics, as well as trade and financial mechanisms aligned with cultural affinities, economically and politically self-sufficient communities will benefit from integration across borders, creating a hybrid and adaptable form of regional governance. This drive for regional integration may be particularly strong in large nations where distances from the periphery to the centre are wider than those between cross-border peripheries. As territorial continuity will drive bottom-up integration processes, geographically homogenous localities will have an incentive to build common infrastructure, regardless of whether they reside within the same nation or cut across multiple countries. As has been the case with more traditional, top-down forms of regional integration like the EU, the spreading of community-driven micro-regions may lead to a spillover effect from the economic to the political and social fields. While nations will remain the key locus of governance, they will most likely transition from being monopolists of regulation to being facilitators of bottom-up integration. In turn, they will find themselves connected with each other through a global web of micro-regions spanning their borders.

A world of bioregions

In a changing world, where continuous evolutions challenge traditional decision making and (nation-)states find it increasingly difficult to govern political and economic processes that are ever more cross-boundary in nature, supranational regional governance has proven a powerful tool to address such a growing complexity. As a meso-level between the state and the international system, regions have been purposefully created to deal with phenomena and processes transcending the borders of national communities. Nowadays, there is a virtually endless list of regional organizations operating in various sectors, entrusted with varying degrees of power and decision-making authority. Although most of them only perform specific functions (e.g. natural resources management, conflict prevention, customs control, financial stability, policing, etc.), there has been an increase in the establishment of 'general purpose' regional organizations, of which the European Union is the best-known and most developed example. Some of them have evolved out of specific trade arrangements, such as the Common Market of the South (Mercosur), while others have been created with a view to guaranteeing security and development, such as the Association of Southeast Asian Nations (ASEAN) and the African Union (AU).

Back in 1945, Winston Churchill had envisaged an international community made up of regional councils. Such an idea was reinforced by scholars advocating regional coalitions to advance the interests of developing countries and by those analysing regional conflict-resolution mechanisms as the best way to maintain the global order, the so-called 'peace in parts'.[54] Although a 'world of regions' has not yet materialized, nobody disputes that regional governance has become an integral part of global political mechanisms, with pivotal roles in some continents and also with explicit arrangements made with international institutions such as the UN.[55]

Along with the mushrooming of regional organizations, the study of regionalism has also evolved. While until the 1980s, the concept was simply subsumed under the broader field of international relations, since the end of the Cold War a renewed focus on the role of regional organizations has given birth to a specific field of study which highlights the increasing complexity of regional formations and their multi-level/multi-sectoral purposes.[56] A wealth of comparative analyses and in-depth case studies has thus shown the ambivalence, for instance, of concepts such as 'regional cooperation' and 'regional integration', traditionally considered as elements of a continuum process of economic regionalization.[57]

More recently, a 'new' regionalism approach has produced important insights into the study of regional politics by emphasizing also the peculiarities of regionalism beyond the traditional European context.[58] Most scholars of regionalism today would agree that regionalism is not the monopoly of states but also encompasses interactions among non-state actors, as well as between states and non-state actors within a given policy area.[59] Moreover, it is generally understood that regionalism indicates a multi-level process, where social and cultural processes can precede, strengthen or even replace economic integration. There is also an increasing recognition, by and large prompted by the application of constructivism to the study of regionalism, that regions are not a geographically given but are socially constructed through human interactions, political discourse and cultural evolution.[60] This has emphasized the role of domestic and transnational factors, which are important determinants in the emergence and development of regional institutions, and has increasingly contributed to the understanding of regionalism as an eminently political, rather than technocratic, process.

As remarked by Oxford-based expert Louise Fawcett, the concept of regionalism has had 'a complex history because of its essentially contested and flexible nature'.[61] The former director of the UN University Institute on Comparative Regional Integration Studies, Luk van Langenhove, notes that a region can refer to 'a geographical space, economic interaction, institutional or governmental jurisdiction, or social or cultural characteristics'.[62] According to Richard Hartshorne, who approached the theme from a geographer's perspective, 'a "region" is an area of specific location which is in some way distinctive from other areas and which extends as far as that distinction extends'.[63] For others, the region is a 'rubbery concept', stretching above and below the administrative boundaries of states.[64] As such, regions are not predefined: they are subject to change over time in line with the prevailing political, economic and social discourse taking place in each society. Political economist Andrew Hurrell reminds us that there are no 'natural' regions: definitions of region and indicators of 'regionness' vary according to the particular problem or question under investigation.[65] As American essayist Gary Snyder points out, 'We are accustomed to accepting the political boundaries of counties and states, and then national boundaries, as being some sort of regional definition; and although, in some cases, there is some validity to those lines [. . .] the lines are quite often arbitrary and serve only to confuse people's sense of natural associations and relationships.'[66]

Political and economic research on regionalism has traditionally focused on vertical structures of power, often dominated by elites. Their analysis has been limited to formal organizations, such as the EU and the like, although it is clear that there is more to regionalism than meets the eye. Similarly to the overall approach our societies have endorsed in economic and political governance, we have developed an understanding of regionalism that is highly selective and largely limited to state-centric forms of top-down regulation. The 'lens' through which we have understood regionalism has confined our analysis to formal institutional processes, political boundaries and governance structures characterized by a high degree of top-down control. If we expand our conceptualization of regionalism to include a variety of forms of cross-border cooperation, then the future may very well be characterized by an exponential evolution in regional governance. These forms could encompass cross-border informal networks and business partnerships operating across national borders as well as civil society-driven forms of interaction uniting social movements, trade unions, environmental organizations and indigenous groups across neighbouring countries in the management, for instance, of trans-frontier natural resources. If we accept that regions are what we humans make them to be, then it is plausible that a new approach to production, consumption, energy and governance would lead to a different vision of regionalism. This is how Snyder understands the multifaceted nature of sociobiological regions:

> correlate the overlap between ranges of certain types of flora, between certain types of biomes, and climatological areas, and cultural areas, and get a sense of that region, and then look at

more or less physical maps and study the drainages, and get a clearer sense of what drainage terms are and correlate those also. All these are exercises toward breaking our minds out of the molds of political boundaries or any kind of habituated or received notions of regional distinctions. [. . .] People have to learn a sense of region, and what is possible within a region, rather than indefinitely assuming that a kind of promiscuous distribution of goods and long-range transportation is always going to be possible.[67]

In the GDP world, a top-down approach to industrialization, vertical institutional control and large-scale economic development has created artificial boundaries for human action, mostly (if not entirely) disconnected from the natural characteristics of the ecosystems that people inhabit. As economist Paul Burkett points out, this economic approach has become dominant thanks to a social separation of producers from the natural conditions of production, leading to a manufactured dependence of any form of subsistence on the commodity market.[68] Because of this 'institutionalized separation', which is a fundamental component of the operating logics of the GDP growth paradigm, neither the producer nor the consumer has an understanding of the totality of humanity's productive relationship with nature, as he/she focuses only on segments and specifically confined steps in the production process. Such a disconnection is indispensable for the GDP economy to transcend natural limits and hold the promise of eternal growth in output. Surpassing the localization of the economy is thus indispensable to project a vision of endless expansion, which would be impossible if production and consumption were localized and reunited. In this framework, globalization provides the perfect framework to mask the origins of produce and the impact it has on nature and society. As discussed in the previous sections of this chapter, 'the impression that local adaptive fitness has been replaced by global adaptive fitness is achieved through the exporting of production and pollution to either uninhabited areas or developing countries.'[69]

A post-GDP development trajectory will require high levels of adaptability to natural conditions and flexible horizontal governance systems. As political scientist Les Milbrath argued in his book *Envisioning a Sustainable Society*, 'economic, social and political life should be organised by regions that are defined by natural phenomena'.[70] In this context, the concept of 'bioregion', defined as a specific territory characterized by similar biophysical and cultural traits, provides the 'scale of decentralisation best able to support the achievement of ecological integrity while maintaining cultural and social progress'.[71] Indeed, the bioregional boundaries 'reflect the self-producing and self-withdrawing characteristic of living systems'.[72] The realignment of political and natural boundaries creates a fertile terrain to build societies driven by the quest for permanence rather than short product cycles and planned obsolescence: 'following the necessities and pleasures of life as they are uniquely presented by a particular site, and evolving ways to ensure long-term occupancy of that site.'[73]

As some have argued, bioregions are a socio-political spin-off of complexity theory, as opposed to the linear top-down structure underpinning Newtonian physics. Just like 'fractals', these regions are patterns of patterns, fully integrated with each other so that what happens at the large scale depends on what occurs at a smaller scale. Rather than through linear influence, these phenomena can emerge at different scales at once, similar to the way crystals develop in a super-saturated solution:

[as] we have become so sharply aware of the organic interconnectedness of earth systems – whether ecological, economic

or cybernetic – we have also begun to inhabit layers and layers of other organic forms. Continentalism is now a fact of life. It is not going to disappear, and neither is bioregionalism, or city-regionalism, or a steadily expanding emphasis on neighborhoods. At every level, in true fractal form, we are witnessing the emergence of organic forms of human relatedness and governance.[74]

Bioregional initiatives have grown since the 1970s in several areas of the world as an attempt to reconnect social and economic processes with the appropriate space for sustainable development. This process of 'reinhabitation', originally developed in some of the alternative epicentres of academic research in North America and Europe, has gradually sprawled to urban neighbourhoods, rural communities and industrial districts across many regions, 'developing intersecting webs of bioregional connection that now stretch across the planet'.[75] The nexus between horizontal collaboration, technological empowerment and spatial development has always been at the heart of bioregionalism as an approach to governance. One of the first treatises focusing on the issue was titled *Renewable Energy and Bioregions: A New Context for Public Policy*, which made the case for a bioregional distribution of energy systems as early as 1980. A year later, another pamphlet, titled *Reinhabiting Cities and Towns: Designing for Sustainability*, explored the intersection between ecological design practice, technology-based support systems and alternative forms of urbanization.[76] In 1985, the Sierra Club, a prominent environmental organization, published a book titled *Dwellers in the Land: The Bioregional Vision*, which launched the bioregional project onto a global scale proposing the adoption of decentralized structures of governance and the integration of urban, rural and wild environments.[77] Since then, bioregionalism has been intimately associated with a restructuring of political power away from centralized vertical bureaucracies towards cross-border collaboration in renewable energy sources, land trusts, organic farming and agroecology initiatives driven by citizens and non-state actors, including small businesses, civil society organizations and social movements.[78]

Geographers classify bioregions into several sub-categories, including overlapping concepts such as: 'georegion', a space characterized by common geological dynamics; 'climatic region', mostly determined by rainfall patterns and temperatures; 'toporegion', structured along physiographic features, like water catchments, mountain ranges and the like; 'ecoregion', according to flora and fauna characteristics; 'economic region', in terms of agricultural dynamics, trade and availability of minerals; and 'socioregion', based on cultural factors like language, ethnicity and religion.[79] According to these principles, for instance, Australia has been divided into 80 bioregions. Often-cited bioregions in North America include the Sonoran Desert Bioregion, covering three Mexican states and southern California and Arizona, the bioregion of Cascadia spanning the North Pacific Rim of America, including the states of Idaho, Oregon, Washington, north-western California, Montana to the West of the divide, two-thirds of British Columbia and south-east Alaska, as well as the Wild Onion Bioregion, lying at the south-western end of Lake Michigan. The Notranjski National Park, in Slovenia, was also delineated by using a bioregionalist approach, as well as Dartia, a bioregion in the county of Devon, United Kingdom.[80]

Traditionally, these ecologically homogenous regions have been identified by scientists and geographers through the collection of natural data integrated into geographical information systems (GIS). For instance, an article published in *BioScience* in 2001 divides the world into 867 distinct units, which would provide a workable starting point for the definition of new systems of bioregional governance aligned with natural ecosystems, as shown in Figure 5.1.

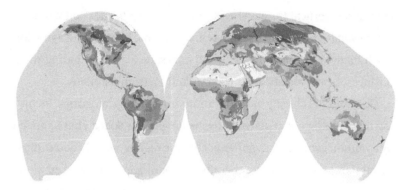

Figure 5.1 Terrestrial ecoregions of the world
Source: Olson et al. (2001).

In the past few years, new technologies have been employed to co-define bioregions through participatory processes, combining knowledge of the people 'living-in-place' with 3D and 4D GIS mapping, which a variety of stakeholders (from community groups to fishermen) can use to collaboratively identify the intersection between human dynamics and ecological dimensions in line with the bioregional governance model. For instance, in the Bonavista Bay in Newfoundland, local fishing communities, government departments and conservation groups have been using participatory methods supported by GIS mapping to achieve a shared understanding of the bioregion upon which the various communities have been operating for years with a view to establishing common rules of action to preserve depleted fisheries and identifying new income opportunities for local communities, in line with the principles of a commons economy. In South Africa, 3D GIS mapping has been used to involve local communities in establishing the bioregional contours of land distribution and use by local communities.[81]

Breaking boundaries in the post-GDP world

The shift towards a post-GDP system of production and consumption may fundamentally redesign global governance. The current model of globalization, with its reliance on fossil fuel energy, has been encouraged by the GDP framework, especially as far as this metric of economic performance does not take into consideration the social and environmental costs of pollution, long-distance transportation and natural resources consumption. As Marvin Brown reminds us, 'if globalization refers to the economic integration of different parts of the world through trade, then it began with the triangular trade of the Atlantic': a trade of slaves that powered the economic growth of modern states and ushered Europe into an age of material wealth, which however cost millions of Africans indescribable suffering.[82]

A post-GDP system would question the sustainability of a glo-balized economy and would force governments to re-invent it on a different scale. Leadership may also change. Indeed, alternative indi-cators suggest that, if GDP was to be replaced (or even complemented) by different measures of economic progress, this new form of account-ing may have an impact on the global pecking order. Conventional powers, both in the West and in the East, would rank way below countries that have been more efficient at building equitable and sus-tainable economies. If global clubs like the G7 and the G20 were to take into account factors such as well-being, sustainability and prosper-ity, their composition would change dramatically. Regionally, South America would climb to the top, together with Europe and the South Pacific. At the EU level, a post-GDP scenario should logically result in a revision of the Maastricht criteria and a different set of poli-cies on, for instance, the post-crisis austerity measures. As discussed in the previous chapters, the measured income of many European economies would increase significantly if a post-GDP set of indicators were to include the value of the informal economy and the variety of household and community services provided free of charge.[83] The infamous acronym PIGS, describing the allegedly inefficient economies of Portugal, Ireland, Greece and Spain, may also need some rethinking. As the OECD argues, these alternative calculations are 'particularly significant for comparisons of "richer" and "poorer" countries'.[84] When global rankings are revised to account for social capital, community work and household activities, many allegedly poor countries appear quite wealthy, while many rich economies fall down the ranks.

Ultimately, globalization may give way to a new form of 'deep' regionalism, building on the type of formal regional integration that we have seen emerging during the twentieth century but capable of transcending its top-down institutional structure. These new regions would be driven by bottom-up pressures and rise organically in accordance with cultural and natural spatial factors, pushed by networks of small and medium enterprises as well as hybrid networks composed of cooperatives, community organizations, social enterprises and local government institutions. The shift to localized economic empowerment would reinforce bioregionalism as the main locus of sustainability. Nations would have an incentive to support the establishment of 'sustainability corridors' across borders in terms of infrastructural development, energy production and exchange, as well as market interaction. As local webs of energy and economic interdependence grow within these micro-regions, nation-states would find themselves reciprocally entangled in macro-webs of territorial continuity. Some of these may very well be as large as entire continents, in a gradual shift 'from globalization to continentalization'.[85]

Conclusion: Data of the People, for the People and by the People

Is democracy possible without the power to decide what the ultimate goals of collective decisions should be? It is certainly true that many citizens around the world are given the right to vote at regular intervals. The reality, however, is that the democratic vote is at best a superficial exercise if citizens do not have the power to define the objectives of political life. GDP has standardized these goals, leaving citizens and their governments with the ancillary freedom of deciding *only* how to get there: they are never asked if the GDP goals are really in line with their expectations, desires and values. Left or right, progressive or conservative, people are at best allowed to choose the means to achieve GDP growth, not the objective itself. This state of affairs calls to mind Henry Ford's remark that 'any customer can have a car painted any colour that he wants, so long as it is black.' By transposition, we may say that citizens are free to choose whatever they want – as long as it is GDP.

Throughout this book, I have discussed the many ways in which this number guides governance decisions and processes. Rather than a simple descriptive statistic, GDP is a powerful institution that shapes the way in which society sees value while moulding the expectations and behaviours of politicians, businesses and people at large. In many regards, it represents the most powerful ideology of the twentieth century, equally revered by capitalists and communists; sacrosanct for neoliberal as well as Keynesian economists; and worshipped by governments, trade unions, rating agencies, stock markets and multi-national corporations the world over.

Current governance systems suffer from a 'GDP paradox': the flaws of this number have been discussed at length since its invention, yet its power has remained unchallenged.[1] This is the result of a combination of factors. Bounded rationality makes most people (especially policy makers and the media) unable to digest multifaceted information, which favours the GDP's reduction of complex economic and social realities to a single aggregate 'thermometer'. Moreover, social dynamics such as 'conformism, docility, socialization and imitation', as well as 'groupthink', reinforce its acceptance across society.[2] This is further supported by the economic literature, especially academic textbooks, which routinely presents GDP growth as a unanimously accepted fact, which in turn gives the discipline of economics a solid measurement basis, thus elevating it to a 'quasi' natural science. Elites also have a direct interest in preserving the GDP approach to growth. First of all, as I have discussed at length, large corporations have benefited a great deal. In particular, they have to thank GDP for having washed away all their negative externalities (whether in terms of environmental degradation or social distress) through the statistical 'laundromat'. Secondly, the idea of an endlessly growing 'pie' of resources made available through material growth provides a powerful antidote to demands for redistribution of wealth.[3] Finally, the integration of GDP into formal institutional processes provides this number with unparal-leled 'hard power' in terms of direct coercion against whatever form of deviance, thus silencing critics.

As remarked by environmental economist Jeroen Van Den Bergh,

GDP not only provides misleading information about social welfare but also exerts a large influence on economic reality, and therefore on the daily life and well-being of all people. One can frame this phenomenon as a serious form of information failure, which is an instance of the general case of market failures, or given the fact that the government generates GDP information, as an instance of government failure. [. . .] Because of the misleading nature of GDP information, economic agents take wrong decisions from the perspective of social welfare.[4]

Since the turn of the millennium, however, the GDP paradox has been increasingly challenged, opening an unprecedented opportunity to end this number's reign. For starters, the flaws of GDP have become a topic of public debate, exiting the confines of traditional expert circles. Popular books, special commissions, political debates, public conferences and institutional reforms have become more and more common in the wake of the realization that the convergence of economic, social and environmental crises demands a fundamental rethinking of the very basics of contemporary social order. As we have seen throughout the previous chapters, the structural changes in our economic systems make GDP not only misleading and selective but also indefensibly obsolete. In an increasingly digital economy, where most goods and services are 'prosumed' horizontally, the very meaning of prosperity can no longer be equated to the vertically dominated accumulation of material things. The inability to capture the value of free services as well as collaboration and sharing practices, especially if aided by technological innovations that reduce prices while increasing social benefits, has proven to be GDP's most fatal weakness.

GDP critics can now be found almost anywhere. In May 2016, the *Economist* featured the 'prosperity puzzle' as its cover page, running a series of stories focusing on the flaws of GDP.[5] The British magazine highlighted all the problems discussed at length in this book, including the arbitrary determination of production, consumption and asset boundaries, the pricing of high-tech as well as non-marketed goods and services, as well as the continuous rewriting of history because of patchy data, wrong estimates and continuous imputations. Not only did Britain experience a crisis in the 1970s that never really was, as I mentioned in chapter 4, but countries the world over continuously expand and rebase their GDP calculations, making leaps and bounds that have profound political consequences. In 2014, Nigeria's GDP was revised upward by 89 per cent, making it the largest economy in Africa. The same year, Kenya jumped by 25 per cent and Ghana, in 2010, climbed up the development ladder by 60 per cent in one single shift. Since 2014, European countries have begun to measure the value of prostitution and illegal drugs to 'upgrade' their statistical systems. It is estimated that most OECD countries, despite their well-developed statistical systems, revise GDP estimates by about 0.4 per cent on a regular basis.[6] In times of economic contraction, marginal variations can have significant impacts, leading to formal recessions or alleged recoveries. When Italy re-based its GDP by estimating outputs in the informal economy in the late 1980s, it became the world's fifth-largest economy, ahead of Britain, paving the way for a stronger role in the G7, the OECD and other relevant international institutions. The media, politicians and people on the streets of Rome publicly celebrated what came to be known as the 'overtaking'. Then, in 1997, Britain managed to regain its position vis-à-vis Italy, leading to comparable celebrations in the United Kingdom until a second short-lived 'overtaking' in 2009, which was publicly praised by the Italian embassy in London.[7]

Mainstream media outlets like the *Financial Times* and even *Forbes* routinely feature articles critical of GDP. Silicon Valley giants, too, have highlighted the inherent obsolescence of institutional statistical accounting. As remarked by Charles Bean, a former chief economist of the Bank of England tasked by the UK government to undertake an official review of economic statistics,

> the methods we use to measure our economies are becoming increasingly out of date. The statistical conventions on which we base our estimates were adopted a half-century ago, at a time when the economy was producing relatively similar physical goods. Today's economy is radically different and changing rapidly [as a] result of technological innovation, the rising value of intangible, knowledge-based assets, and the internationalization of economic activity.[8]

The contribution of companies like Google, Skype and Facebook (which also controls WhatsApp), to name a few, which provide a number of services at a fraction of the cost of other traditional communication systems, is structurally undervalued by GDP, leading to senseless debates about 'productivity paradoxes', as discussed in chapter 3. New platforms like Uber and Airbnb, as well as the many open-source systems supporting the 'sharing economy', are equally under-counted by the vertical approach of the GDP economy and its accounting machinery. Similarly, GDP has marginalized the non-profit community, the world of cooperatives, community-based groups, households, small businesses and informal economic activity, as if these were lesser realities compared to the giant, inefficient, polluting corporations that have dominated the twentieth century. Bean's research confirms the overall inadequacy of GDP in the new century:

> The digital revolution is also disrupting traditional business models. The reduced search and matching costs offered by a range of online platforms are unlocking the market for skills

(known as the 'gig economy') and the market for underutilized assets (known as the 'sharing economy'). This, too, causes conceptual and practical measurement challenges for established GDP calculus. The traditional statistical distinction between productive firms and consuming households leaves little room to account for households as value creators.[9]

Adam Smith famously argued that most 'respectable orders in society', including the king and the aristocrats around him, 'no matter how prestigious they are made out to be, do not possess any intrinsic economic value'.[10] His analysis of 'wealth' took power away from the old, unproductive regimes and put it in the hands of modern capitalism. Post-GDP indicators serve a similar purpose: they help to break the institutional privileges granted by the GDP system and make the 'invisible visible', thus eroding the prestige of the mainstream economic model. They reveal not only the unaccounted aberrations of vertically dominated economic structures in terms of negative externalities whose cost is ultimately charged to society and the planet, but they also show the tremendous positive externalities of horizontally structured system of cooperation, most of which will inevitably escape any form of monetary accounting. In so doing, they provide a powerful link between top-down reforms (including the SDGs, climate change regulations and energy policies) and the bottom-up pressures exerted by new economic practices, communities, social movements and civil societies the world over. From Google and Facebook to the environmental movements fighting climate change and the civil society groups mobilizing against international trade agreements, there is a broad 'invisible' coalition of social forces that share one crucial enemy: GDP.

I agree with Van Den Bergh's argument that 'without the availability of a GDP indicator decisions will be more aimed at welfare improvement, since the systematic and cumulative error resulting from economic behavioural responses to misleading GDP information will be gone':

> The removal of GDP information (without necessarily replacing it with an alternative indicator) will mean the substitution of the systematic, cumulative error by a white noise type of error (random drift). Panic responses and economic instability due to the threat of stagnating GDP growth are no longer possible. One will less dogmatically deal with stimulating developing countries to enter a transition to a formal economy [. . .] Without GDP, there will also be less resistance against policies which improve social welfare at the cost of GDP growth. Whereas from a GDP perspective such policies might look as a sacrifice, from a social welfare angle they would seem very logical.[11]

I also share the view that replacing GDP does not necessarily mean developing another, equally standardized and potentially dangerous indicator. Rather, the post-GDP world should embrace the inherent complexity of horizontal social and economic systems that cannot be efficiently understood, studied, monitored and evaluated using standardized vertical control. As Philip Ball points out, 'complex systems can't usually be *forced* to behave in a certain way by top-down measures': 'Instead, they must be guided [. . .] by "bottom up" control: by tweaking the conditions or the rules of interactions. It's like guiding the course of a river: you have to work with the flow, or it will just rearrange the banks.'[12]

As I have discussed in the book, statistical accounting has been traditionally approached as a technocratic affair, thus avoiding public deliberations and civic involvement. While number crunching is certainly a technical matter, the definition of values, principles and goals is not. Unless we democratize numbers, there is a risk that whatever post-GDP system technocrats will develop may replicate some of the pitfalls of the current top-down hierarchical reality. As March and Olsen warn us, 'a common anomaly of adaptive processes is the competency trap': 'Competency traps are inhibitors of change and instruments of induced change. They inhibit change by building competency barriers to new strategies, procedures or technologies.'[13]

Dirk Philipsen has called for 'an open and deliberate conversation about the direction of economic activity'.[14] The UN report on the 'data revolution' is also in favour of statistical democratization.[15] It points to the need for using 'the most advanced tools and features for exploring and analysing and re-using data' and calls for 'best practices in the engagement with data users through the provision of guidance and educational resources for data re-use'. A dedicated platform should also 'represent a laboratory for fostering private–public partnerships and community-led peer-production efforts for data collection, dissemination and visualisation'. For the panel, the future of data is about engaging 'think-tanks, academics and NGOs as well as the whole UN family in analysing, producing, verifying and auditing data', with a view to 'integrating different data sources, including qualitative data, perceptions data and citizen-generated data, and eventually produc[ing] a "people's baseline" for new goals'.

There are a number of pioneering initiatives in this regard. For instance, the My World project, which is run jointly by the UN Development Programme, the UN Millennium Campaign and the Overseas Development Institute, has thus far collected the opinions of approximately ten million people worldwide about expectations and development priorities for themselves and their families.[16] The data, which have been collected through interviews, mobile phones and online surveys, are publicly available on the internet, allowing users to disaggregate results by country, gender, age, education and other parameters. As reported by the UN panel on the data revolution, 'My World has shown how international organisations, together with civil society groups, can use data to feed people's perceptions and priorities into the heart of political processes.'[17] One of the experts I work with, Enrico Giovannini, who is also the chair of the data revolution panel, launched the Equitable and Sustainable Wellbeing survey when he was president of the Italian National Statistical Institute, using a methodology designed in consultation with academia, civil society and social movements.[18] My colleague Katherine Trebeck from Oxfam GB developed the Humankind Index for Scotland, which involved citizens (especially those whose voices are 'seldom heard') in determining the components of the survey.[19] Another colleague of mine, Dirk Helbing from ETH Zurich, is developing a game-changing initiative called Nervousnet, which enables anyone to measure and analyse aspects of the world in real time. Through a dedicated app, users can activate smartphone sensors that measure a wide range of phenomena, from stress, to noise and light exposure, with more functions being developed by about a dozen research groups in Europe, Japan and the United States. Unlike other 'internet of things' initiatives launched by for-profit technology corporations, Nervousnet is a 'citizen web', inspired by the pioneering forms of horizontal collaborations described in this book. Users contribute datasets, share codes and develop new ideas for applications, using a generic programming interface.[20]

As Nervousnet initiators maintain, ruling modern societies 'like a "benevolent dictator" or "wise king" cannot work because there is no way to determine a single metric or goal that a leader should maximize'. Moreover, centralized top-down control of data is more vulnerable to hacking and corruption, suffers from 'limitations in data-transmission rates and processing power', creates 'filter bubbles' that can increase 'polarization and conflict' and loses precious information, given that 'our economies and societies are like ecosystems with millions of interdependencies': 'Better is pluralism. It hedges risks, promotes innovation, collective intelligence and well-being. Approaching complex problems from varied perspectives also helps people to cope with rare and extreme events that are costly for society – such as natural disasters, blackouts or financial meltdowns.'[21]

The matching of top-down reforms and bottom-up pressures through post-GDP indicators, with the aid of new technologies, is opening an historic opportunity to change the world. Different social actors, from high-tech companies to small businesses, civil society and local communities, have a common interest in redefining the meaning and measurement of prosperity. But trading GDP for a new powerful number would be sub-optimal. We need to avoid submitting to a new emperor, perhaps supported by proprietary technologies developed in Silicon Valley. This book's institutional critique of statistics shows that there can be no real democracy without a system of data of the people, for the people and by the people. The complexity of contemporary social systems, the multidimensional challenges we face and the interconnectedness of biological life on the planet demand nothing short of a radical reorganization of our societies to usher humanity into a truly transformed post-GDP world.

Notes

Introduction

1 West (2010), pp. 578–80.
2 Trumbull (1982).
3 Ibid.
4 J. Smith (2014).
5 Cavill (2015).
6 Trumbull (1982).
7 Ibid.
8 Department of Economic Development and Environment (2003).
9 Shenon (1995).
10 Streib (2007). Check also Laurance (2011).
11 King and Rewers (1993).
12 Shenon (1995).
13 OECD Observer (2004).
14 Coyle (2014).

Chapter 1 The Making of a Post-GDP World

1 Repetto et al. (1989).
2 Fioramonti (2013); Philipsen (2015)
3 Stiglitz, Sen and Fitoussi (2010).
4 Details here: http://ec.europa.eu/environment/beyond_gdp/background_en.html (accessed 30 June 2016).
5 See http://www.gaboronedeclaration.com/ (accessed 30 June 2016).

6 A summary can be found here: https://www.weforum.org/focus/beyond-gdp (accessed 30 June 2016). The citation is from Blanke (2016).

7 Ban (2012).

8 See http://www.degrowth.de/en/ (accessed 30 June 2016).

9 More details can be found here: https://www.transitionnetwork.org/ (accessed 30 June 2016).

10 See Klein (2015).

11 Sukhdev (2012).

12 All books explicitly cited in this section are listed in the References.

13 Fukuyama (1992).

14 Meadows et al. (1972).

15 Diamond (2005).

16 Latouche (2009).

17 Rockström et al. (2009); Raworth (2012).

18 For an account of the wager, see Sabin (2013).

19 Simon (1983).

20 Lomborg (2007).

21 Makeover (2009).

22 Rifkin (2011).

23 Anderson (2012).

24 Rifkin (2014)y.

25 Karabell (2014).

26 Barnes (2006), p. 8.

27 Polanyi (1957), p. 3.

28 Abramovitz (1989), p. 345.

29 North (1990), p. 3.

30 March and Olsen (1989), p. 22.

31 North (1990), p. 3.

32 March and Olsen (1989), p. 21.

33 Parsons (1951, 1968).

34 Dawkins (1982).

35 Fioramonti (2014), *How Numbers Rule the World.*

36 March and Olsen (1989), pp. 160–1.

37 Mugge (2016), p. 412.
38 Carstensen and Schmidt (2016).
39 Ostrom (1990).
40 Campbell (2004), p. ii.
41 March and Olsen (1989), p. 54.
42 Campbell (2004).
43 Tushman and O'Reilly (2002); Gersick (1991).
44 Kuhn (1962).
45 Hodgson (2002), p. xxi.
46 P. Ball (2012), p. 2.
47 Ibid., p. xi.
48 March and Olsen (1989), p. 61.
49 Fioramonti (2016).
50 Broome and Quirk (2015).
51 Anderson (2012); Rifkin (2011, 2014).
52 Alinsky (1971), p. xxiii.
53 March and Olsen (1989), p. 62.
54 Ibid., p. 63.
55 Fioramonti (2013); Philipsen (2015).
56 See: http://ec.europa.eu/eurostat/web/ess/-/istat-equitable-and-sustainable-well-being-bes-report (accessed 30 June 2016).

Chapter 2 The Rise and Fall of GDP Ideology

1 Philipsen (2015), pp. 7–8.
2 See Fioramonti (2014), *How Numbers Rule the World*.
3 I provide details about Petty's approach in Fioramonti (2013). See also Philipsen (2015).
4 Fioramonti (2014), *How Numbers Rule the World*.
5 Smith (1904 [1776]), Book II, Chapter III, Section II.3.4.
6 Ibid., Section II.3.1.
7 Marx (1909 [1885]), Vol. II: The Process of Circulation of Capital, III.XIX.39.
8 For a detailed history, see Fioramonti (2013); Coyle (2014); Philipsen (2015); Masood (2016).

9 Philipsen (2015).

10 Ibid.

11 Galbraith (1980), p. 80.

12 Cobb, Halstead and Rowe (1995)

13 Philipsen (2015), p. 117.

14 Costanza, Hart, Posner and Talbert (2009). See also Costanza, Hart, Kubiszewski and Talbert (2014).

15 Costanza, Hart, Posner and Talbert (2009).

16 Schmelzer (2016).

17 Ibid. See also Coyle (2014).

18 See Fioramonti (2014), *How Numbers Rule the World*.

19 Fioramonti (2013).

20 Cobb, Halstead and Rowe (1995), p. 6.

21 The Compact has been criticized by both conservative and progressive economists. See Krugman (2012) and Feldstein (2012).

22 See Fioramonti (2014), *How Numbers Rule the World*.

23 US Department of Commerce (2000), p. 6.

24 Ibid., p. 13.

25 Cited in US Department of Commerce (2000), p. 7.

26 March and Olsen (1989), p. 62.

27 Greenspan's speech is reported in US Department of Commerce (2000), p. 12.

28 Fioramonti (2013); Philipsen (2015). In July 2013, the procedure for the promotion of party officials traditionally linked to GDP rates came under the scrutiny of the top leadership: see News of the Communist Party of China (2013).

29 Roxburgh et al. (2010).

30 *The Economist* (2011).

31 Ibid.

32 See Bush (2001). See also Jones and Smith (2001).

33 Vardy and Wattie (2001).

34 'America's New War: Giuliani on Local Radio Show', 21 September 2001, transcripts provided by CNN.com at http://transcripts.cnn.com/TRANSCRIPTS/0109/21/se.20.html (accessed 30 June 2016).

35 Fioramonti (2014) 'Africa Rising? Think Again'.
36 Kuznets (1962), p. 29.
37 See *The Economist* (2016).
38 See Boskin Commission's report: Boskin et al. (1996). See also the points raised by Stiglitz, Sen and Fitoussi (2009), p. 23.
39 World Bank (2016).
40 Fahey (2016).
41 Worstall (2016).
42 Hern (2016).
43 Aeppel (2015).
44 See Fukuyama (1996); Putnam (2000).
45 Folbre (2001, 2008).
46 Abraham and Mackie (2005).
47 Miranda (2011).
48 Ahmad and Koh (2011).
49 UN Statistics Division (2009), p. 7.
50 Ibid., p. 8.
51 Ibid., p. 8.
52 Smith (2016).
53 Coyle (2016), p. 8.
54 Details can be found here: https://www.airbnb.com/press/news/new-study-airbnb-community-generates-502-million-in-economic-activity-in-the-uk (accessed 30 June 2016).
55 Coyle (2016), p. 11.
56 UN Statistics Division (2009), p. 6.
57 Ibid., p. 6.
58 Ibid., p. 7.
59 Ibid., p. 7.
60 Ibid., p. 7.
61 Ibid., p. 7.
62 Ibid., p. 7.
63 Ibid., p. 7.
64 Ibid., p. 7.
65 Ibid., p. 7.
66 Ibid., p. 7.

67 Blades (1989), p. 215.
68 Repetto et al. (1989), p. 2.
69 From the preface by James Gustave Speth, in Repetto et al. (1989), p. vi.
70 Ibid., p. v.
71 The citations are from Hamilton (2006). For more details, see World Bank (2006).
72 Repetto et al. (1989), p. 2.
73 Fioramonti (2014) 'Africa Rising? Think Again'.
74 '10 Most Expensive Cities' available online at http://money. cnn.com/gallery/luxury/2014/07/10/most-expensive-cities/ (accessed 30 June 2016).
75 Stiglitz (2012), p. 124.
76 Cobb, Halstead and Rowe (1995), p. 6.
77 Byrnes (2006).
78 'GDP Growth More Quality Oriented'. *China Daily*, 27 July 2012. Available online: http://usa.chinadaily.com.cn/business/ 2012-07/27/content_15625093.htm (accessed 30 June 2016).
79 European Union (2008), p. 4.
80 Trucost (2013).
81 Fioramonti (2014), *How Numbers Rule the World*.
82 Van Den Bergh (2009).
83 Ostry, Ghosh and Espinoza (2015).
84 Miranda (2011).
85 Cited in Kaiser (2010).
86 Kuznets (1946).
87 Lundberg (1971).
88 OECD (2008; 2011, *Divided We Stand*).
89 Kuznets (1962), p. 29.
90 Nordhaus and Tobin (1973).
91 Daly and Cobb (1989).
92 All details and methodology are described at http://inclusive wealthindex.org/ (accessed 30 June 2016).
93 Pearce and Atkinson (1993); see also World Bank (2015).
94 Stiglitz, Sen and Fitoussi (2009), p. 9.

95 See also OECD (2011), *How's Life?*

96 Ceroni (2014).

97 Details are available at: http://www.gnhcentrebhutan.org/what-is-gnh/four-pillars-and-nine-domains/ (accessed 30 June 2016).

98 Helliwell, Layard and Sachs (2016).

99 See http://www.socialprogressimperative.org/network/initiatives/social-progress-framework-in-action-tackling-extreme-poverty-in-paraguay (accessed 30 June 2016).

100 Porter, Stern and Green (2015).

101 Confino (2015). See also http://ec.europa.eu/regional_policy/en/newsroom/news/2016/02/16-02-2016-moving-beyond-gdp-new-regional-social-progress-index (accessed 30 June 2016).

102 Rabinovitch (2010).

103 Wallace (2016), p. 11.

104 Ibid., p. 17.

105 Chew (2015).

106 Lelyveld (2012).

107 News of the Communist Party of China (2013).

108 Wildau (2014).

109 Lelyveld (2015).

110 Fioramonti et al. (2015).

Chapter 3 Post-GDP Economics

1 Philipsen (2015), p. 65.

2 Lopez (2016).

3 Lopez (2015).

4 Block (1990), pp. 8–9.

5 Trucost (2013).

6 World Bank (2013), p. vi.

7 Trucost (2013), p. 11.

8 Ibid., p. 32.

9 MacGregor (2016).

10 Bakan (2004).

11 Sukhdev (2012), p. 6.

12 Ibid., p. 7.

13 Ibid.

14 IMF (2013).

15 Ibid., p. 1.

16 GOC (2013).

17 Biron (2014).

18 Cited in Biron (2014).

19 Trucost and FAO (2015), p. 6.

20 Ibid.

21 Patel (2009), p. 49.

22 Nidumolu (2013), p. 16.

23 Sukhdev (2012), p. 12.

24 Ibid., p.14.

25 Smith (1904 [1776]), Book I, ch. 2.

26 Hardin (1968), p. 1245.

27 Olson (1965).

28 Hardin (1968), p. 1245.

29 Rose (1986), p. 720.

30 Ostrom (1990), p. 25.

31 Ibid.

32 For details, check here: http://www.centerforneweconomics.org/content/BALLE (accessed 30 June 2016).

33 The citation is taken from their 'theory of change' document, which can be viewed here: https://bealocalist.org/theory-change (accessed 30 June 2016).

34 The WHO's definition of 'social determinants of health' is available here: http://www.who.int/social_determinants/en/ (accessed 30 June 2016).

35 See their website at http://greatergood.berkeley.edu/about (accessed 30 June 2016).

36 Hillemeier, Lynch, Harper, and Casper (2015). See also 'County Health Rankings & Roadmaps', University of Wisconsin Population Health Institute, available online: http://www.countyhealthrankings.org/Our-Approach (accessed 30 June 2016).

37 Norris and Howard (2015).

38 Dignity Health's annual report cites these figures at p. 39 of this document: https://www.dignityhealth.org/cm/media/documents /Mission-Integration-Annual-Report.pdf (accessed 30 June 2016).

39 Philipsen (2015).

40 See *EcuRed, Conocimiento con Todos y Para Todos*: http:// www.ecured.cu/index.php/Producto_Interno_Bruto_en_Cuba (accessed on 30 June 2016).

41 BALLE (2016), p. 4.

42 Sen (1977), p. 336.

43 Helbing, Szolnoki, Perc and Szabó (2010).

44 Helbing (2015), p. 209.

45 See Charness and Rabin (2005), as well as Falk and Fischbacher (2006).

46 Jung, Nelson, Gneezy and Gneezy (2015).

47 Ibid.

48 Mellström and Johannesson (2008).

49 For an overview, see Arieli (2008) and Sandel (2012).

50 Liberman, Samuels, and Ross (2004).

51 Singer et al. (2006).

52 Hegtvedt and Killian (1999).

53 Alesina, Di Tella and MacCulloch (2004).

54 King-Casas et al. (2005).

55 Decety et al. (2004).

56 Dawkins (1976), p. 3.

57 Novak (2006), p. 1560.

58 Gintis and Helbing (2015), p. 20.

59 Smith (2007 [1759]), I.I.1.

60 Block (1990), p. 10.

61 Ostrom (1996), p. 1073.

62 Campbell-Kelly and Garcia-Swartz (2009).

63 See the summary offered by Frydman (2009).

64 See the official announcement of CEO Elon Musk here: https:// www.teslamotors.com/blog/all-our-patent-are-belong-you (accessed 30 June 2016).

65 Tapscott and Williams (2006). For an idea of macro-economic impacts of mass collaboration through new technologies, see also Tapscott and Williams (2010).

66 US Department of Transportation (2015).

67 Sundararajan and Fraiberger (2015).

68 Details can be found here: http://www/airbnb.com/press/news/new-study-airbnb-community-generates-502-million-in-economic-activity-in-the-uk (30 June 2016).

69 Ghiselli and Siegel (1972).

70 Sornette, Maillart and Ghezzi (2014).

71 Ibid., p. 1.

72 Davis (2013), p. 298.

73 Spring (2016).

74 Gray (2016).

75 Davis (2013), p. 299.

76 Rifkin (2011) and http://www.economist.com/node/21553017 (accessed 30 June 2016).

77 De Clercq (2013).

78 Check NRECA's 'Coops facts and figures' available online: http://www.nreca.coop/about-electric-cooperatives/co-op-facts-figures/ (accessed 30 June 2016).

79 Spear (2014).

80 Ioannou (2014).

81 Davis (2013).

82 Sheffi (2005).

83 Roeland (2013).

84 Reprinted in Keynes (1963), pp. 358–73.

85 Rifkin (1995).

86 Ford (2015).

87 MGI (2011).

88 Davis and Cobb (2010).

89 Schneider and Enste (2002).

90 Ibid.

91 Ibid.

92 Miranda (2011).

93 Marçal (2015).

94 Becker (1965).

95 Frazis and Stewart (2011).

96 Bridgman et al. (2012).

97 NRECA's 'Coops facts and figures' available online: http://www. nreca.coop/about-electric-cooperatives/co-op-facts-figures/ (accessed 30 June 2016).

98 ICA Housing (2012).

99 Bajo (2013).

100 UNU-IHDP and UNEP (2014).

101 Jackson and Victor (2011).

102 Ayres (2008).

103 McKibben (2007).

104 Jackson (2009).

105 Baumol (2012).

106 Timmer, O'Mahony and Van Ark (2007), p. 10, Table 1.

107 Jackson (2012).

108 Eisenstein (2011), p. 12.

109 Ryan-Collins, Greenham, Werner and Jackson (2012).

110 Whitlock (2014).

111 Laetier and Dunne (2013), p. 9.

112 Ibid.

113 Michel and Hudon (2015).

114 Van Gelder (1997).

115 Ibid.

116 Schroeder, Miyazaki and Fare (2011).

117 Thiel (2011).

118 More details about cryptocurrencies can be found here: http://www.hongkiat.com/blog/bitcoin-alternatives/ (accessed 30 June 2016).

119 Details about FairCoin can be found here: https://fair-coin.org/ (accessed 30 June 2016).

120 Boik (2014).

121 Helbing (2015), p. 206.

122 Rifkin (2014); Anderson (2012).

123 Eisenstein (2011), p. 17.
124 Rifkin (2014), p. 25.
125 Cited in Day (2013).

Chapter 4 Post-GDP Politics

1 Tawney (1958 [1926]).
2 Independent Expert Advisory Group (2014), p. 2.
3 Fioramonti (2013); Philipsen (2015).
4 Coyle (2014), p. 36.
5 Philipsen (2015).
6 See the statistics reported by IBM here: http://www-01.ibm.com/software/data/bigdata/what-is-big-data.html (accessed 30 June 2016).
7 Independent Expert Advisory Group (2014); see also MGI (2013).
8 Ibid., p. 11.
9 Ibid., p. 14.
10 Chui, Farrell and Jackson (2014).
11 Independent Expert Advisory Group (2014), p. 8.
12 Details available here: https://flunearyou.org/ (accessed 30 June 2016).
13 Holden (2016).
14 Independent Expert Advisory Group (2014), p. 17.
15 Helbing and Pournaras (2015).
16 Genschel and Zangl (2008).
17 Castells and Cardoso (2006).
18 Rosenau (1990), p. 11.
19 Dingwerth and Pattberg (2009).
20 Karns and Mingst (2004).
21 Ostrom (1990).
22 Daft, Murphy and Willmott (2010), p. 452.
23 Kanter (1983), p. 20.
24 Garcia (2009), p. 89.
25 Kuhlmann, Shapira and Smits (2010), p. 1.

26 Clegg, Kornberger and Pitsis (2008), p. 388.

27 Burke (2011), p. 56.

28 Gersick (1991).

29 Donahue (1999).

30 Drucker (1985).

31 Darroch and Miles (2015).

32 Tushman and O'Reilly (2002), p. 21.

33 Ibid., p. 167.

34 Landry, Amara and Lamari (2002), p. 686.

35 Kingdon (1995).

36 Huston and Sakkab (2006), p. 60.

37 Coleman, Katz and Menzel (1966).

38 Rogers (2003), p. 26.

39 Kaldor, Selchow and Henrietta (2012).

40 Salamon and Sokolowski (2004).

41 Henderson (1993), p. 329.

42 Rao (2008), p. 5.

43 Del Savio and Mameli (2014).

44 Edwards (2009).

45 Dowling (2011).

46 Robins-Early (2016).

47 Croucher (2015).

48 For the sources of the data cited in this section, please check: http : / / www . participatorybudgeting . org / about - participatory - budgeting/examples-of-participatory-budgeting/ (accessed 30 June 2016).

49 See Prabhu and Rao (1960).

50 Cited in Cady (2005), p. 43.

51 Prabhu and Rao (1960), p. 411.

52 Gandhi (1959), p. 9.

53 Prabhu and Rao (1960), p. 378.

54 Alstone, Gershenson and Kammen (2015).

55 Heap (2015).

56 Khama and Roche (2016).

57 Ministry of Rural Development (2015).

58 For all these details, see the sections 'Benchmarks' and 'Instruments' at www.smartvillages.org (accessed 30 June 2016).

59 Heap (2015), p. 24.

60 Ibid., p. 60.

61 Ibid.

62 Parth (2014).

63 Hani (2007).

64 Cited in Parth (2014).

65 Phaahla (2015).

66 Oyuke, Halley Penar and Howard (2016).

67 Africa Progress Panel (2015), p. 18.

68 Ibid.

69 Ibid.

70 Heap (2015), p. 53.

71 Ibid., p. 13.

72 Ibid., p. 26.

73 Ibid.

74 Hopkins (2013). Check also https://www.transitionnetwork.org/initiatives/by-number?page=15 (accessed 30 June 2016).

75 For a general review, see Delli Carpini, Cook and Jacobs (2004).

76 Pateman (1970).

77 Cited in Fung (2005).

78 Ibid., p. 47.

79 Ibid., p. 48.

80 Ibid., p. 53.

81 Nelson (2006), p. 1.

82 Bromley (2006), p. 180.

83 Brown (2010), p. 11.

84 UN Statistical Commission et al. (2012), *Central Framework*.

85 UN Statistical Commission et al. (2012), *Experimental Ecosystem Accounting*.

86 Cited in Burdon (2015), p. 75.

87 Postel (2012); see also Howard (2015).

88 See http://www.govisitcostarica.com/travelInfo/nationalParks.asp (accessed 30 June 2016).

89 See https://www.rewildingeurope.com/ (accessed 30 June 2016).

90 Fioramonti et al. (2015).

91 Check http://www.tourism.gov.bt/about-bhutan/environment (accessed 30 June 2016).

92 Asch (1951).

Chapter 5 Post-GDP World

1 Speich (2008).

2 Rist (2010).

3 O'Neill (2001).

4 O'Neill (2013).

5 Watch Michael Green's TEDx talk about the Social Progress Index here: http://ideas.ted.com/why-we-shouldnt-judge-a-country-by-its-gdp/ (accessed 30 June 2016).

6 See http://www.happyplanetindex.org (accessed 30 June 2016).

7 https://www.rt.com/business/326605-costa-rica-renewable-electricity/ (accessed 30 June 2016).

8 See http://www.worldbank.org/en/news/feature/2012/05/09/Korea-s-Global-Commitment-to-Green-Growth (accessed 30 June 2016).

9 Botswana and Mauritius are indeed the best-performing countries on the Ibrahim Index of African Governance and Transparency International's Corruption Perceptions Index.

10 From the WTO's trends in globalization reports available here: https://www.wto.org/english/res_e/booksp_e/anrep_e/wtr08-2b_e.pdf (accessed 30 June 2016).

11 See World Trade Report 2015 available here: https://www.wto.org/english/res_e/booksp_e/wtr15-1_e.pdf (accessed 30 June 2016).

12 Frankel and Romer (1999), p. 394.

13 The speech is available in the Federal Reserve's archives: https://www.federalreserve.gov/newsevents/speech/bernanke 20070501a.htm (accessed 30 June 2016).

14 Ibid.

15 Council of Economic Advisers (2015).

16 Rodrik (2007); Krugman (2013).

17 Peters and Hertwich (2008), p. 1401.

18 Mokhiber and Weissman (1999).

19 Ibid.

20 See https://ttip-leaks.org/ (accessed 30 June 2016).

21 Peters and Hertwich (2008), p. 1401.

22 Ibid.

23 Wiedmann et al. (2015).

24 See, for instance, http://ec.europa.eu/resource-efficient-europe/ (accessed 30 June 2016).

25 EUROSTAT's approach is described here: http://ec.europa.eu/ eurostat / web / environment / material - flows - and - resource - pro ductivity (accessed 30 June 2016).

26 Wiedmann et al. (2015), p. 6271.

27 Ibid.

28 Ibid.

29 Ibid., p. 6272.

30 Weinzettel, Hertwich, Peters, Steen-Olsen and Galli (2013), p. 433.

31 Steen-Olsen, Weinzettel, Cranston, Ercin and Hertwich (2012).

32 Lenzen et al. (2013).

33 Lenzen, Moran, Kanemoto, Foran, Lobefaro and Geschke (2012), p. 109.

34 CEPR (2013), p. 2.

35 Capaldo (2014).

36 See Stolper and Samuelson (1941).

37 Krugman (2008).

38 Harrison, McLaren and McMillan (2011).

39 De Vogli and Renzetti (2016).

40 Peters and Hertwich (2008), p. 1406.

41 Victor, House and Joy (2005).

42 Roubini and Mihm (2010).

43 Piketty (2014); see also Credit Suisse (2014).

44 Dendrinou (2015).

45 Randers (2012).

46 Sukhdev (2012).

47 Minguels (2016).

48 UNDESA (2012); Abel and Sander (2014).

49 Rubin (2009).

50 IEA (2013), p. 4.

51 IEA (2014), p. 3.

52 Howarth, Santoro and Ingraffea (2011).

53 IEA (2014), p. 2.

54 Nye (1971).

55 Fawcett (2013).

56 Fawcett (1995).

57 Schulz, Soderbaum and Ojendal (2001).

58 Warleigh-Lack, Robinson and Rosamond (2011).

59 Fioramonti (2012), *Regionalism in a Changing World*; Fioramonti (2014), *Civil Society and World Regions.*

60 Langenhove (2011).

61 Fawcett (2013), p. 5.

62 Langenhove (2003), p. 4.

63 Hartshorne (1959), p. 130.

64 Hooghe, Marks and Schakel (2010), p. 4.

65 Hurrell (1995).

66 Snyder (1980), pp. 24–5.

67 Ibid.

68 Burkett (1999).

69 Davidson (2007), p. 323.

70 Milbrath (1989), p. 211.

71 Ball (2002), p. 110.

72 McGinnins (1999), p. 73.

73 Berg and Dasmann (1977), p. 399.

74 Gimmis (1999), p. xiv.

75 Aberley (1999), p. 13.

76 Todd and Tukel (1981).

77 Republished as Sale (2000 [1991]).

78 Haenke (1984).

79 Ball (2002).

80 Ibid.

81 Ibid.

82 Brown (2010).

83 Miranda (2011).

84 Ahmad and Koh (2011).

85 Rifkin (2011), p. 61.

Conclusion: Data of the People, for the People and by the People

1 Van Den Bergh (2009).

2 Fioramonti (2013); Van Den Bergh (2009), p. 121.

3 The link between growth and redistribution was originally noted by Daly (1973); see also Dietz and O'Neill (2013).

4 Van Den Bergh (2009), pp. 125–6.

5 The weekly issue was 30 April–6 May 2016. The lead article is available here: http://www.economist.com/news/briefing/21697845 - gross - domestic - product - gdp - increasingly - poor - measure-prosperity-it-not-even (accessed 30 June 2016).

6 Ibid.

7 Conway and Porter (2009).

8 Bean (2016).

9 Ibid.

10 Smith (1904 [1776]), Book II, Chapter III, Section II.3.1.

11 Van Den Bergh (2009), p. 126.

12 Ball (2012), p. xi.

13 March and Olsen (1989), p. 63.

14 Philipsen (2015), p. 248.

15 Independent Expert Advisory Group (2014), p. 27.

16 See http://data.myworld2015.org/ (accessed 30 June 2016).

17 Independent Expert Advisory Group (2014), p. 16.

18 Details can be found here: http://www.istat.it/en/well-being-measures (accessed 30 June 2016).

19 Carrell (2012).

20 Helbing and Pournaras (2015).

21 Ibid.

References

Abel, G. J. and Sander, N. (2014) 'Quantifying Global International Migration Flows'. *Science* 343(6178): 1520–2.

Aberley, D. (1999) 'Interpreting Bioregionalism', in M. V. McGinnis (ed.), *Bioregionalism* (London and New York: Routledge).

Abraham, K. and Mackie, C. (2005) *Beyond the Market: Designing Nonmarket Accounts for the United States* (Washington, DC: The National Academies Press).

Abramovitz, M. (1989) *Thinking about Growth* (Cambridge: Cambridge University Press).

Aeppel, T. (2015) 'Silicon Valley Doesn't Believe US Productivity Is Down'. *The Wall Street Journal*, 16 July.

Africa Progress Panel (2015) *People, Power, Planet: Seizing Africa's Energy and Climate Opportunities* (Geneva: Africa Progress Panel).

Ahmad, N. and Koh, S. H. (2011) 'Incorporating Estimates of Household Production of Non-Market Services into International Comparisons of Material Well-Being'. *Statistics Directorate, Working Paper No. 42* (Paris: OECD Publishing).

Alesina A., Di Tella, R. and MacCulloch, R. (2004) 'Inequality and Happiness: Are Europeans and Americans Different?' *Journal of Public Economics* 88: 2009–42.

Alinsky, S. D. (1971) *Rules for Radicals: A Practical Primer for Realistic Radicals* (New York: Random House).

Alstone, P., Gershenson, D. and Kammen, D. M. (2015) 'Decentralized Energy Systems for Clean Electricity Access'. *Nature Climate Change* 5: 305–14.

Anderson, C. (2012) *Makers* (London: Random House).

Arieli, D. (2008) *Predictably Irrational: The Hidden Forces that Shape Our Decisions* (New York: Harper Collins).

Asch, S. E. (1951) 'Effects of Group Pressure upon the Modification of Distortion of Judgments', in H. Guetzkow (ed.), *Groups, Leadership, Men* (Oxford: Carnegie Press).

Ayres, R. (2008) 'Sustainability Economics: Where Do We Stand'. *Ecological Economics* 67: 281–310.

Bajo, S. (2013) 'Placing Cooperatives in Up-to-Date Theoretical Debates', in B. Roeland (ed.), *Cooperative Growth for the 21st Century* (Brussels: International Cooperative Alliance).

Bakan, J. (2004) *The Corporation: The Pathological Pursuit of Profit and Power* (New York: The Free Press).

Ball, J. (2002) 'Towards a Methodology for Mapping "Regions of Sustainability" Using PPGIS'. *Progress in Planning* 58: 81–140.

Ball, P. (2012) *Why Society Is a Complex Matter* (Heidelberg: Springer).

BALLE (2016) *The Future of Health Is Local* (Oakland: Business Alliance for Local Living Economies).

Ban, K. (2012) 'Secretary-General's Remarks at High Level Meeting on "Happiness and Well-Being: Defining a New Economic Paradigm"'. *United Nations*. Available online: http://www.un.org/sg/STATEMENTS/index.asp?nid=5966 (accessed 30 June 2016).

Barnes, P. (2006) *Capitalism 3.0: A Guide to Reclaiming the Commons* (San Francisco: Berrett-Koehler Publishers).

Baumol, W. J. (2012) *The Cost Disease: Why Computers Get Cheaper and Health Care Doesn't* (New Haven: Yale University Press).

Bean, C. (2016) 'Measuring the Value of Free'. *Project Syndicate*, 3 May.

Becker, G. (1965) 'A Theory of the Allocation of Time'. *Economic Journal* 75(299): 493–517.

Berg, P. and Dasmann, R. (1977) 'Reinhabiting California'. *The Ecologist* 7: 399–401.

Berg, P. and Tukel, G. (1980) *Renewable Energy and Bioregions: A New Context for Public Policy* (San Francisco: Planet Drum Foundation).

Biron, C. L. (2014) 'Global Agricultural Subsidies Near $500b, Favoring Large-Scale Producers'. *MintPress News*, 22 March.

Blades, D. (1989) 'Revision of the System of National Accounts: A Note on Objectives and Key Issues'. *OECD Economic Studies No. 12* (Paris: OECD).

Blanke, J. (2016) 'What Is GDP, and How Are We Misusing It?' *World Economic Forum*, 13 April.

Block, F. (1990) *Postindustrial Possibilities: A Critique of Economic Discourse* (San Francisco: University of California Press).

Boik, J. (2014) 'First Micro-Simulation Model of a LEDDA Community Currency-Dollar Economy'. *International Journal of Community Currency Research* 18(A): 11–29.

Boskin, M. J. et al. (1996) *Toward a More Accurate Measure of the Cost of Living: Final Report to the Senate Finance Committee* (Washington, DC: US Government Printing Office).

Bridgman, B., Dugan, A., Lal, M., Osborne, M. and Villones, S. (2012) 'Accounting for Household Production in the National Accounts, 1965–2010'. *Survey of Current Business* 92(5): 23–36.

Bromley, D. W. (2006) *Sufficient Reason: Volitional Pragmatism and the Meaning of Economic Institutions* (Princeton and Oxford: Princeton University Press).

Broome, A. and Quirk, J. (2015) 'The Politics of Numbers: The Normative Agendas of Global Benchmarking'. *Review of International Studies* 41(5): 813–18.

Brown, M. (2010) *Civilizing the Economy: A New Economics of Provision* (Cambridge: Cambridge University Press).

Burdon, P. (2015) *Earth Jurisprudence: Private Property and the Environment* (London: Routledge).

Burke, W. W. (2011) *Organisation Change: Theory and Practice* (London: Sage).

Burkett, P. (1999) *Marx and Nature: A Red and Green Perspective* (New York: St Martin's Press).

Bush, G. W (2001) 'Speech given to airline employees at O'Hare International Airport (Chicago, Illinois)', 27 September. Available online: http://georgewbush-whitehouse.archives.gov/news/releases/2001/09/20010927-1.html (accessed 30 June 2016).

Byrnes, S. (2006) 'Person of the Year: The Man Making China Green'. *The New Statesman*, 18 December: 60–1.

Cady, D. L. (2005) *Moral Vision. How Everyday Life Shapes Ethical Thinking* (Lanham: Rowman and Littlefield).

Campbell, J. (2004) *Institutional Change and Globalization* (Princeton: Princeton University Press).

Campbell-Kelly, M. and Garcia-Swartz, D. D. (2009) 'Pragmatism, not Ideology: Historical Perspectives on IBM's Adoption of Open-source Software'. *Information Economics and Policy* 21(3): 229–44.

Capaldo, J. (2014) 'The Trans-Atlantic Trade and Investment Partnership: European Disintegration, Unemployment and Instability'. GDAE Working Paper 14-03. Available online: http://ase.tufts.edu/gdae/policy_research/TTIP_simulations.html (accessed 30 June 2016).

Carrell, S. (2012) 'Oxfam Launches Humankind Index to Measure Wellbeing'. *The Guardian*, 24 April.

Carstensen, M. B. and Schmidt, V. A. (2016) 'Power through, over and in Ideas: Conceptualizing Ideational Power in Discursive Institutionalism'. *Journal of European Public Policy* 23(3): 318–37.

Castells, M. and Cardoso, G. (2006) *The Network Society: From Knowledge to Policy* (Washington, DC: Centre for Transatlantic Relations).

Cavill, A. (2015) 'Report Condemns Nauru Detention Centre Conditions'. *SBS News*, 23 March.

CEPR (2013) *Transatlantic Trade and Investment Partnership: The Economic Analysis Explained* (Brussels: Centre for Economic Policy Research).

Ceroni, M. (2014) 'Beyond GDP: US States Have Adopted Genuine Progress Indicators'. *The Guardian*, 23 September.

Charness, G. and Rabin, M. (2005) 'Expressed Preferences and Behavior in Experimental Games'. *Games and Economic Behavior* 53: 151–69.

Chew, J. (2015) 'Chinese Officials Admit They Faked Economic Figures'. *Fortune*, 14 December.

Chui, M. Farrell, D. and Jackson, K. (2014) *How Government Can Promote Open Data* (New York and London: McKinsey & Company).

Clegg, S., Kornberger M. and Pitsis, T. (2008) *Managing and Organisations: An Introduction to Theory and Practice*, 2nd edn (London: SAGE).

Cobb, C., Halstead, T. and Rowe, K. (1995) 'If the GDP Is Up, Why Is America Down?' *Atlantic Monthly*, October.

Coleman, J. S., Katz, E. and Menzel, H. (1966) *Medical Innovation: A Diffusion Study* (New York: Bobbs Merrill).

Confino, J. (2015) 'European Commission Agrees to Investigate Using Social Progress Tool Alongside GDP'. *The Guardian*, 9 April.

Conway, E. and Porter, A. (2009) 'UK Economy Overtaken by Italy'. *The Telegraph*, 23 October.

Costanza, R., Hart, M., Kubiszewski, I. and Talbert, R. (2014) 'A Short History of GDP: Moving towards Better Measures of Human Well-being'. *Solutions* 5(1): 91–7.

Costanza, R., Hart, M., Posner, S. and Talbert, R. (2009) 'Beyond GDP: The Need for New Measures of Progress'. *The Pardee Papers* 4, January.

Council of Economic Advisers (2015) *The Economic Benefits of US Trade* (Washington, DC: White House).

Coyle, D. (2014) *GDP: A Brief but Affectionate History* (Princeton: Princeton University Press).

Coyle, D. (2016) 'The Sharing Economy in the UK', Report for Sharing Economy UK and AirBnb, 25 January. Available online: http://www.sharingeconomyuk.com/perch/resources/210116thesharingeconomyintheuktpdc.docx1111.docx-2.pdf (accessed 30 June 2016).

Credit Suisse (2014) *Global Wealth Report 2014* (Zurich: Credit Suisse).

Croucher, S. (2015) 'Spain: What Is Podemos?' *International Business Times*, 21 December.

Daft, R. L., Murphy, J. and Willmott, H. (2010) *Organisation Theory and Design* (Andover: South-Western Cengage).

Daly, H. (ed.) (1973) *Toward a Steady-State Economy* (New York: W. H. Freeman & Co).

Daly, H. and Cobb, J. (1989) *For the Common Good: Redirecting the Economy toward Community, the Environment and a Sustainable Future* (Boston: Beacon Press).

Darroch, J. and Miles, M. P. (2015) 'Sources of Innovation'. *Wiley Encyclopedia of Management* 13: 1–8.

Davidson, S. (2007) 'The Troubled Marriage of Deep Ecology and Bioregionalism'. *Environmental Values* 16(3): 313–32.

Davis, G. F. (2013) 'After the Corporation'. *Politics & Society* 41(2): 283–308.

Davis, G. F. and Cobb, J. A. (2010) 'Corporations and Economic Inequality around the World: The Paradox of Hierarchy'. *Research in Organizational Behavior* 30: 35–53.

Dawkins, R. (1976) *The Selfish Gene* (Oxford: Oxford University Press).

Dawkins, R. (1982) *The Extended Phenotype: The Gene as the Unit of Selection* (Oxford: Freeman).

Day, P. (2013) 'Imagine a World without Shops or Factories'. *BBC News*, 11 October.

De Clercq, G. (2013) 'Analysis: Renewables Turn Utilities into Dinosaurs of the Energy World'. *Reuters*, 8 March.

De Vogli, R. and Renzetti, N. (2016) 'The Potential Impact of the Transatlantic Trade and Investment Partnership (TTIP) on Public Health'. *Epidemiologia e Prevenzione* 40(2): doi: 10.19191/ EP16.2.AD01.037

Decety, J. et al. (2004) 'The Neural Bases of Cooperation and Competition: An fMRI Investigation'. *Neuroimage*, 23: 744–51.

Del Savio, L. and Mameli, M. (2014) 'Anti-Representative Democracy: How To Understand the Five Star Movement'. *OpenDemocracy*, 4 July.

Delli Carpini, M. X., Cook, F. L. and Jacobs, L. R. (2004) 'Public Deliberation, Discursive Participation, and Citizen Engagement: A Review of the Literature'. *Annual Review of Political Science* 7: 315–44.

Dendrinou, V. (2015) 'Ten EU Countries Agree on Some Aspects of Financial Transactions Tax'. *The Wall Street Journal*, 8 December.

Department of Economic Development and Environment (2003) *First National Report to the United Nations Convention to Combat Desertification* (Nauru: Republic of Nauru).

Diamond, J. (2005) *Collapse: How Societies Choose to Fail or Succeed* (New York: Viking).

Dietz, R. and O'Neill, D. (2013) *Enough Is Enough: Building a Sustainable Economy in a World of Finite Resources* (San Francisco: Berrett & Koehler).

Dingwerth, K. and Pattberg, P. (2009) 'Actors, Arenas and Issues in Global Governance?', in J. Whitman (ed.), *Palgrave Advances in Global Governance* (Basingstoke: Palgrave Macmillan).

Donahue, J. D. (ed.) (1999) *Making Washington Work: Tales of Innovation in the Federal Government* (Washington, DC: Brookings Institution Press).

Dowling, S. (2011) 'Pirate Party Snatches Seats in Berlin'. *The Guardian*, 18 September.

Drucker, P. (1985) 'The Discipline of Innovation'. *Harvard Business Review* 63(3): 67–72.

Durkheim, E. (1997 [1893]) *The Division of Labour in Society* (New York: Simon & Schuster).

Economist (2011) 'The Hopeful Continent: Africa Rising', 3 December.

Economist (2016) 'The Trouble with GDP', 30 April.

Edwards, C. (2009) 'Sweden's Pirate Party Sails to Success in European Elections', *The Guardian*, 11 June.

Ehrlich, P. (1968) *The Population Bomb* (New York: Buccaneer Books).

Eisenstein, C. (2011) *Sacred Economics: Money, Gift and Society in the Age of Transition* (Berkeley: Evolver Editions).

European Union (2008) *The Economics of Ecosystems and Biodiversity: An Interim Report* (Brussels: European Commission).

Fahey, M. (2016) 'Facebook Turns 12 – Trillions in Time Wasted'. *CNBC News*, 4 February.

Falk, A. and Fischbacher, U. (2006) 'A Theory of Reciprocity'. *Games and Economic Behavior* 54: 293–315.

Fawcett, L. (1995) 'Regionalism in Historical Perspective', in L. Fawcett and A. Hurrell (eds), *Regionalism in World Politics: Regional Organisation and International Order* (Oxford: Oxford University Press).

Fawcett, L. (2013) 'The History and Concept of Regionalism'. *UNUCRIS Working Paper, W-2013/5*. Available online: http://www.cris.unu.

edu/fileadmin/workingpapers/W-2013-5_revised.pdf (accessed 30 June 2016).

Feldstein, M. (2012) 'Europe's Empty Fiscal Compact'. *Project Syndicate*, 27 February.

Fioramonti, L. (ed.) (2012) *Regionalism in a Changing World: Comparative Perspectives in the New Global Order* (London: Routledge).

Fioramonti, L. (2013) *Gross Domestic Problem: The Politics Behind the World's Most Powerful Number* (London: Zed Books).

Fioramonti, L. (2014) 'Africa Rising? Think Again'. *Perspectives: Political Analyses and Commentary* 1 (February): 6–9.

Fioramonti, L. (ed.) (2014) *Civil Society and World Regions: How Citizens Are Reshaping Regional Governance in Times of Crisis* (Lanham: Lexington).

Fioramonti, L. (2014) *How Numbers Rule the World: The Use and Abuse of Statistics in Global Politics* (London: Zed Books).

Fioramonti, L. (2016) 'A Post-GDP World? Rethinking International Politics in the 21st Century'. *Global Policy* 7(1): 15–24.

Fioramonti, L. et al. (2015) 'Say Goodbye to Capitalism: Welcome to the Republic of Wellbeing'. *The Guardian*, 2 September (accessed 15 May 2016).

Folbre, N. (2001) *The Invisible Heart: Economics and Family Values* (New York: New Press).

Folbre, N. (2008) *Valuing Children: Rethinking the Economics of the Family* (Cambridge, MA: Harvard University Press).

Ford, M. (2015) *The Rise of the Robots: Technology and the Threat of a Jobless Future* (New York: Basic Books).

Frankel, J. A. and Romer, D. (1999) 'Does Trade Cause Growth?' *American Economic Review* 89(3): 379–99.

Frazis, H. and Stewart, J. (2011) 'How Does Household Production Affect Measured Income Inequality?' *Journal of Population Economics* 24(1): 3–22.

Frydman, G. (2009) 'Patient Driven Research: Rich Opportunities and Real Risks'. *Journal of Participatory Medicine* 1(1): e12.

Fukuyama, F. (1992) *The End of History and the Last Man* (New York: Avon Books).

Fukuyama, F. (1996) *Trust: The Social Virtues and the Creation of Prosperity* (New York: The Free Press).

Fung, A. (2005) 'Deliberation's Darker Side: Six Questions for Iris Marion Young and Jane Mansbridge'. *National Civic Review* 93(4): 47–54.

Galbraith, J. K. (1980) 'The National Accounts: Arrival and Impact', in N. Cousins (ed.), *Reflections of America: Commemorating the Statistical Abstract Centennial* (Washington, DC: US Department of Commerce, Bureau of the Census).

Gandhi, M. K (1959) *Panchayat Raj* (Ahmedabad: Navajivan Mudranalaya).

Garcia, R. (2009) 'Types of Innovation', in V. K. Narayanan and G. C. O'Connor (eds), *Encyclopedia of Technology and Innovation Management* (Oxford: Wiley-Blackwell).

Genschel, P. and Zangl, B. (2008) 'Transformations of the State: From Monopolist to Manager of Political Authority'. *TranState Working Paper* 76: 1–27.

Gersick, C. J. G. (1991) 'Revolutionary Change Theories: A Multilevel Exploration of the Punctuated Equilibrium Paradigm'. *The Academy of Management Review* 16(1): 10–36.

Ghiselli, E. E. and Siegel, J. P. (1972) 'Leadership and Managerial Success in Tall and Flat Organization Structures'. *Personnel Psychology* 25(4): 617–24.

Gimmis, D. (1999) 'Preface', in M. V. McGinnins (ed.), *Bioregionalism* (London and New York: Routledge).

Gintis, H. and Helbing, D. (2015) 'Homo Socialis: An Analytical Core for Sociological Theory'. *Review of Behavioral Economics* 2(1–2): 1–59.

GOC (2013) 'Elimination of Harmful Fisheries Subsidies Affecting the High Seas'. *Policy Options Paper* 6 (New York: Global Ocean Commission).

Gray, R. (2016) 'Will Astronauts Be Living on the Moon by 2030? European Space Agency Is Leading Plans to 3D Print a "Lunar Village" to Replace the International Space Station'. *Mail Online*, 4 January.

Haenke, D. (1984) *Ecological Politics and Bioregionalism* (Drury: New Life Farm).

Hamilton, K. (2006) 'Where Is the Wealth of Nations?' WiderAngle, UNU-Wider, United Nations University. Available online: https://www.wider.unu.edu/publication/where-wealth-nations (accessed 30 June 2016).

Hani, Y. (2007) 'Homegrown Art'. *The Japanese Times*, 26 August.

Hardin, G. (1968) 'The Tragedy of the Commons'. *Science* 162: 1243–8.

Harrison, A., McLaren, J. and McMillan, M. (2011) 'Recent Perspectives on Trade and Inequality'. *Annual Review of Economics* 3: 261–89.

Hartshorne, R. (1959) *Perspective on the Nature of Geography* (Chicago: Rand McNally).

Heap, B. (ed.) (2015) *Smart Villages: New Thinking for Off-Grid Communities Worldwide* (Cambridge: Smart Villages Initiative).

Hegtvedt, K. A. and Killian, C. (1999) 'Fairness and Emotions: Reactions to the Process and Outcomes of Negotiations'. *Social Forces* 78: 269–303.

Helbing, D. (2015) *The Automation of Society Is Next: How to Survive the Digital Revolution* (Zurich: CreateSpace Independent Publishing).

Helbing, D. and Pournaras, E. (2015) 'Society: Build Digital Democracy'. *Nature* 527: 33–4.

Helbing, D., Szolnoki, A., Perc, M. and Szabó, G. (2010) 'Evolutionary Establishment of Moral and Double Moral Standards through Spatial Interactions'. *PLoS Computational Biolology* 6(4): 1–9.

Helliwell, J., Layard, R. and Sachs, J. (eds) (2016) *World Happiness Report 2016* (New York: UNSDSN).

Henderson, H. (1993) 'Social Innovation and Citizen Movements'. *Futures* 25(3): 322–38.

Hern, A. (2016) 'Whatsapp Drops Subscription Fee to Become Fully Free'. *The Guardian*, 18 January.

Hillemeier, M., Lynch, J., Harper, S. and Casper, M (2015) *Data Set Directory of Social Determinants of Health at the Local Level* (Atlanta: Centers for Disease Control and Prevention).

Hodgson, G. M. (ed.) (2002) *A Modern Reader in Institutional and Evolutionary Economics* (Cheltenham: Edward Elgar).

Holden, J. (2016) 'The Top 10 Sources of Data for International Development Research'. *The Guardian*, 16 March.

Hooghe, L., Marks, G. and Schakel, A. (2010) *The Rise of Regional Authority* (London: Routledge).

Hopkins, R. (2013) *The Power of Just Doing Stuff* (Cambridge: UIT Cambridge).

Howard, E. (2015) 'Hague Climate Change Judgement Could Inspire a Global Civil Movement'. *The Guardian*, 24 June.

Howarth, R., Santoro, R. and Ingraffea, A. (2011) 'Methane and the Greenhouse-Gas Footprint of Natural Gas from Shale Formations'. *Climatic Change* 106(4): 679–90.

Huntington, S. (1996) *The Clash of Civilizations and the Remaking of World Order* (New York: Touchstone).

Hurrell, A. (1995) 'Explaining the Resurgence of Regionalism in World Politics'. *Review of International Studies* 21(4): 331–58.

Huston, L. and Sakkab, N. (2006) 'Connect and Develop: Inside Procter & Gamble's New Model for Innovation'. *Harvard Business Review* 84(3): 58–66.

ICA Housing (2012) *Profiles of a Movement: Co-operative Housing Around the World* (Brussels: CECODHAS Housing Europe).

IEA (2013) *World Energy Outlook 2013. Executive Summary* (Vienna: International Energy Agency).

IEA (2014) *World Energy Outlook 2014: Executive Summary* (Vienna: International Energy Agency).

IMF (2013) *Energy Subsidy Reform: Lessons and Implications* (Washington, DC: International Monetary Fund).

Independent Expert Advisory Group (2014) *A World That Counts: Mobilising the Data Revolution for Sustainable Development* (New York: United Nations).

Ioannou, L. (2014) 'A Decade to Mass Extinction in S&P 500'. *CNBC*, 5 June.

Jackson, T. (2009) *Prosperity without Growth: Economics for a Finite Planet* (London: Earthscan).

Jackson, T. (2012) 'Let's Be Less Productive'. *The New York Times*, 26 May.

Jackson, T. and Victor, P. (2011) 'Productivity and Work in the "Green Economy": Some Theoretical Reflections and Empirical Tests'. *Environmental Innovation and Societal Transitions* 1: 201–8.

Jones, G. and Smith, M. (2001) 'Britain Needs You to Shop, Says Blair'. *The Telegraph*, 28 September.

Jung, M. H., Nelson, L. D., Gneezy, A. and Gneezy, U. (2015) 'Paying More When Paying for Others'. *Journal of Personality and Social Psychology* 107: 414–31.

Kaiser, E (2010) 'Special Report: US Data Dogs on Quest for Sexier Statistics'. *Reuters*, 6 July.

Kaldor, M., Selchow, S. and Henrietta, L. M. (eds) (2012) *Global Civil Society Yearbook 2012* (Basingstoke: Palgrave).

Kaletsky, A. (2010) *Capitalism 4.0: The Birth of a New Economy* (London: Bloomsbury).

Kanter, R. M. (1983) *The Change Masters: Corporate Entrepreneurs at Work* (London: Unwin).

Karabell, Z. (2014) *The Leading Indicators* (New York: Simon & Schuster).

Karns, M. P. and Mingst, K. A. (2004) *International Organisations: The Politics and Processes of Global Governance* (Boulder: Lynne Rienner).

Kennedy, P. (1987) *The Rise and Fall of the Great Powers* (London: Random House).

Keynes, J. M. (1963) *Essays in Persuasion* (New York: W. W. Norton).

Khama, P. and Roche, E. (2016) 'Narendra Modi Targets 100 Smart Villages by 2016'. *Live Mint*, 22 February.

King, H. and Rewers, M. (1993) 'Diabetes in Adults Is Now a Third World Problem: The WHO Ad-Hoc Diabetes Reporting Group'. *Bulletin of the World Health Organization* 69(6): 643–8.

King-Casas, B. et al. (2005) 'Getting to Know You: Reputation and Trust in a Two-Person Economic Exchange'. *Science* 308: 78–83.

Kingdon, J. W. (1995) *Agendas, Alternatives, and Public Policies* (New York: Addison, Wesley Longman).

Klein, N. (2015) *This Changes Everything: Capitalism vs the Climate* (New York: Simon & Schuster).

Krugman, P. (2008) 'Trade and Wages, Reconsidered'. *Brookings Papers on Economic Activity*, Spring.

Krugman, P. (2012) 'Europe's Economic Suicide'. *The New York Times*, 15 April.

Krugman, P. (2013) 'Should Slowing Trade Growth Worry Us?' *The New York Times*, 30 September.

Kubiszewski, I. et al. (2013) 'Beyond GDP: Measuring and Achieving Global Genuine Progress'. *Ecological Economics* 93: 57–68.

Kuhlmann, S., Shapira P. and Smits, R. (2010) 'Introduction: A Systemic Perspective: The Innovation Policy Dance', in R. Smits, S. Kuhlmann and P. Shapira (eds), *The Theory and Practice of Innovation Policy: An International Research Handbook* (Cheltenham: Edward Elgar).

Kuhn, T. (1962) *The Structure of Scientific Revolutions* (Chicago: Chicago University Press).

Kuznets, S. (1946) *National Income – A Summary of Findings* (New York: National Bureau of Economic Research).

Kuznets, S. (1962) 'How to Judge Quality'. *The New Republic*, 20 October.

Laetier, B. and Dunne, J. (2013) *Rethinking Money: How New Currencies Turn Scarcity into Prosperity* (San Francisco: Berrett-Koehler).

Landry, R., Amara, N. and Lamari, N. (2002) 'Does Social Capital Determine Innovation? To What Extent?' *Technological Forecasting and Social Change* 69(7): 681–701.

Langenhove, L. (2003) 'Theorizing Regionhood'. *UNU-CRIS E-Working Papers, W-2003 1*. Available online: http://www.cris.unu.edu/file-admin/workingpapers/paper%20regionhood.pdf (accessed 30 June 2016).

Langenhove, L. (2011) *Building Regions: The Regionalisation of World Order* (London: Routledge).

Latouche, S. (2009) *Farewell to Growth* (Cambridge: Polity Books).

Laurance, J. (2011) 'How Tiny Nauru Became the World's Fattest Nation'. *The Independent*, 4 February.

Lelyveld, M. (2012) 'China's "Green GDP" Resurfaces'. *Radio Free Asia*, 13 February.

Lelyveld, M. (2015) 'China May Abandon GDP Growth Goal'. *Radio Free Asia*, 2 November.

Lenzen, M., Moran, D., Kanemoto, K., Foran, B., Lobefaro, L. and Geschke, A. (2012) 'International Trade Drives Biodiversity Threats in Developing Nations'. *Nature* 486: 109–12.

Lenzen, M. et al. (2013) 'International Trade of Scarce Water'. *Ecological Economics* 94: 78–85.

Liberman, V., Samuels, S. M. and Ross, L. (2004) 'The Name of the Game: Predictive Power of Reputations Versus Situational Labels in Determining Prisoner's Dilemma Game Moves'. *Personality and Social Psychology Bulletin* 30(9): 1175–85.

Lomborg, B. (2007) *Cool It: The Skeptical Environmentalist's Guide to Global Warming* (New York: Alfred Knopf).

Lopez, L. (2015) 'China Is in the Midst of a Triple Bubble'. *Business Insider*, 9 July.

Lopez, L. (2016) 'Everyone Is Worried that a Third China Bubble Is about to Burst'. *Business Insider*, 24 March.

Lundberg, E. (1971) 'Simon Kuznets' Contribution to Economics'. *Swedish Journal of Economics* 73(4): 444–59.

MacGregor, A. (2016) 'Can Business Generate Profit for the Economy, for the Planet and for Society?' *The Huffington Post*, 9 June.

Makeover, J. (2009) *Strategies for the Green Economy* (New York: McGraw Hill).

Malthus, T. (1798) *An Essay on the Principle of Population* (London: J. Johnson).

Marçal, K. (2015) *Who Cooked Adam Smith's Dinner? A Story about Women and Economics* (London: Portobello Books).

March, J. and Olsen, J. P. (1989) *Rediscovering Institutions: The Organizational Basis of Politics* (New York: The Free Press).

Marx, K. (1909 [1885]) *Capital: A Critique of Political Economy* (Chicago: C. H. Kerr & Co.).

Mason, P. (2015) *Post-Capitalism: A Guide to Our Future* (London: Allen Lane).

Masood, E. (2016) *The Great Invention: The Story of GDP and the Making (and Unmaking) of the Modern World* (New York: Pegasus Books).

McGinnins, M. V. (1999) 'Boundary Creatures and Bounded Spaces', in M. V. McGinnins (ed.), *Bioregionalism* (London and New York: Routledge).

McKibben, B. (2007) *Deep Economy: Economics as if the World Mattered* (Oxford: Oneworld).

Meadows, D. H., Meadows, D. L., Randers, J. and Behrens, W. W. (1972) *The Limits to Growth: A Report to the Club of Rome* (New York: Universe Books).

Mellström, C. and Johannesson, M. (2008) 'Crowding Out in Blood Donation: Was Titmuss Right?' *Journal of the European Economic Association* 6: 845–63.

MGI (2011) *An Economy That Works: Job Creation and America's Future* (New York: McKinsey Global Institute).

MGI (2013) *Lions Go Digital: The Internet's Transformative Potential in Africa* (New York and London: McKinsey Global Institute).

Michel, A. and Hudon, M. (2015) 'Community Currencies and Sustainable Development: A Systematic Review'. *Ecological Economics* 116: 160–71.

Milbrath, L. W. (1989) *Envisioning a Sustainable Society: Learning Our Way Out* (New York: SUNY Press).

Minguels, G. (2016) 'Global Migration? Actually, The World is Staying Home'. *Spiegel Online*, 17 May.

Ministry of Rural Development (2015) *Saansad Adarsh Gram Yojana*, May 2015. Available online: http://support.saanjhi.in/support/solutions / articles / 6000003515 - 7 - activities - in - an - adarsh - gram (accessed 30 June 2016).

Miranda, V. (2011) 'Cooking, Caring and Volunteering: Unpaid Work around the World'. *OECD Social, Employment and Migration Working Papers No. 116* (Paris: OECD Publishing).

Mokhiber, R. and Weissman, R. (1999) 'Memo Misfire: World Bank "Spoof" Memo on Toxic Waste Holds More Irony Than Laughs'. *Global Policy Forum*, May. Available online: https://www.global-policy.org/component/content/article/209/43247.html (accessed 30 June 2016).

Mokhiber, R. and Weissman, R. (2002) *Corporate Predators: The Hunt for Mega-Profits and the Attack on Democracy* (Monroe: Common Courage Press).

Mugge, D. (2016) 'Studying Macroeconomic Indicators as Powerful Ideas'. *Journal of European Public Policy* 23(3): 410–27.

Nelson, J. A. (2006) *Economics for Humans* (Chicago: University of Chicago Press).

News of the Communist Party of China (2013) 'President Xi Promises to Shake Off GDP Obsession in Promoting Officials', 1 July. Available online: http://english.cpc.people.com.cn/206972/206974/8305576. html (accessed 30 June 2016).

Nidumolu, R. (2013) 'Organizational Change for Natural Capital Management: Strategy and Implementation'. TEEB for Business Coalition, Natural Capital Series. Available online: http://www. naturalcapitalcoalition.org/news/article/organisational-change-for-natural-capital-management-strategy-and-implementation. html (accessed 30 June 2016).

Nordhaus, W. D. and Tobin, J. (1973) 'Is Growth Obsolete?', reprinted from M. Moss (ed.), *The Measurement of Economic and Social Performance*, special issue of *Studies in Income and Wealth* 38, NBER: 509–32.

Norris, T. and Howard, T. (2015) *Can Hospitals Heal America's Communities?* (Washington, DC: Democracy Collaborative).

North, D. (1990) *Institutions, Institutional Change and Economic Performance* (Cambridge: Cambridge University Press).

Novak, M. (2006) 'Five Rules for the Evolution of Cooperation'. *Science* 314: 1560–3.

Nye, J. (1971) *Peace in Parts: Integration and Conflict in Regional Organisation* (Boston: Little Brown and Company).

O'Neill, J. (2001) 'Building Better Global Economic BRICs'. *Global Economics Paper No. 66* (New York: Goldman Sachs).

O'Neill, J. (2013) *The BRIC Road to Growth* (London: London Publishing Partnership).

OECD (2008) *Growing Unequal: Income Distribution and Poverty in OECD Countries* (Paris: OECD).

OECD (2011) *Divided We Stand: Why Inequality Keeps Rising* (Paris: OECD).

OECD (2011) *How's Life? Measuring Well-Being* (Paris: OECD).

OECD Observer (2004) 'Is GDP a Satisfactory Measure of Growth?' *OECD Observer* (2004–2005): 246–7.

Olson, D. M. et al. (2001) 'Terrestrial Ecoregions of the World: A New Map of Life on Earth'. *BioScience* 51(11): 933–8.

Olson, M. (1965) *The Logic of Collective Action* (Harvard: Harvard University Press).

Ostrom, E. (1990) *Governing the Commons* (Cambridge: Cambridge University Press).

Ostrom, E. (1996) 'Crossing the Great Divide: Co-Production, Synergy and Development'. *World Development* 24(6): 1073–87.

Ostry, J. D., Ghosh, A.R. and Espinoza, R. (2015) 'When Should Public Debt Be Reduced?' *IMF Staff Discussion Note*, SND/15/10, June. Available online: http://www.imf.org/external/pubs/ft/sdn/2015/sdn1510.pdf (accessed 30 June 2016).

Oyuke, A., Halley Penar, P. and Howard, B. (2016) 'Off-grid or 'Off-on': Lack of Access, Unreliable Electricity Supply Still Plague Majority of Africans'. *Afrobarometer Dispatch no. 75*, 14 March.

Parsons, T. (1951) *The Social System* (London: Routledge & Kegan Paul).

Parsons, T. (1968) *The Structure of Social Action* (New York: The Free Press).

Parth, S. (2014) 'Another Lesson from Japan: How to Make Smart Villages'. *Governance Now*, 11 October.

Patel, R. (2009) *The Value of Nothing: How to Reshape Market Society and Redefine Democracy* (London: Portobello Books).

Pateman, C. (1970) *Participation and Democratic Theory* (Cambridge: Cambridge University Press).

Pearce, D. W. and Atkinson, G. D. (1993) 'Capital Theory and the Measurement of Weak Sustainable Development: An Indicator of Weak Sustainability'. *Ecological Economics* 8: 103–8.

Peters, G. P. and Hertwich, E. G. (2008) 'CO_2 Embodied in International Trade with Implications for Global Climate Policy'. *Environmental Science & Technology* 42(5): 1401–7.

Phaahla, E. (2015) 'Costs, Delays Spiralling – No Completion in Sight'. *Biz News*, 6 August.

Philipsen, D. (2015), *The Little Big Number: How GDP Came to Rule the World and What to Do about It* (Princeton: Princeton University Press).

Piketty, T. (2014) *Capital in the 21st Century* (Cambridge, MA: Belknap Press).

Polanyi, K. (1957) 'The Economy as Instituted Process', in M. Granovetter and R. Swedberg (eds), *The Sociology of Economic Life* (Boulder, CO: Westview Press).

Porter, M., Stern, S. and Green, M. (2015) *Social Progress Index 2015* (Washington, DC: Social Progress Imperative).

Postel, S. (2012) 'A River in New Zealand Gets a Legal Voice'. *National Geographic*, 4 September.

Prabhu, R. K. and Rao, U. R. (eds) (1960) *The Mind of Mahatma Gandhi* (Ahmedabad: Navajivan Mudranalaya).

Putnam, R. (2000) *Bowling Alone: The Collapse and Revival of American Community* (New York: Simon & Schuster).

Rabinovitch, S. (2010) 'China's GDP is "Man-made", Unreliable: Top Leader'. *Reuters*, 6 December.

Randers, J. (2012) *2052: A Global Forecast for the Next Forty Years* (White River Junction: Chelsea Green).

Rao, H. (2008) *Market Rebels: How Activists Make or Break Radical Innovations* (Princeton: Princeton University Press).

Raworth, K. (2012) 'A Safe and Just Operating Space for Humanity'. *Oxfam Discussion Paper*. Available online: http://www.oxfamtrailwalker.org.nz/sites/default/files/reports/dp-a-safe-and-just-space-for-humanity-130212-en.pdf (accessed 30 June 2016).

Repetto, R., Magrath, W., Wells, M., Beer C. and Rossini, F. (1989) *Wasting Assets: Natural Resources in the National Income Accounts* (Washington: World Resources Institute).

Rifkin, J. (1995) *The End of Work* (New York: G. P. Putnam's Sons).

Rifkin, J. (2011) *The Third Industrial Revolution* (New York: Palgrave Macmillan).

Rifkin, J. (2014) *The Zero Marginal Cost Society* (New York: Palgrave Macmillan).

Rist, G. (2010) *The History of Development: From Western Origins to Global Faith*, 3rd edn (London: Zed Books).

Robins-Early, N. (2016) 'This Radical Protest Party Is Now Leading Iceland Polls'. *The Huffington Post*, 11 April.

Rockström, J. et al. (2009) 'A Safe Operating Space for Humanity'. *Nature* 461: 472–5.

Rodrik, D. (2007) 'The Globalization Numbers Game'. *Dani Rodrik's Weblog*, 7 May.

Roeland, B. (ed.) (2013) *Cooperative Growth for the 21st Century* (Brussels: International Cooperative Alliance).

Rogers, E. M (2003) *Diffusions of Innovation* (New York: Free Press).

Rose, C. (1986) 'The Comedy of the Commons: Custom, Commerce, and Inherently Public Property'. *The University of Chicago Law Review* 53(3): 711–81.

Rosenau, J. (1990) *Turbulence in World Politics: A Theory of Change and Continuity* (Princeton: Princeton University Press).

Roubini, N. and Mihm, S. (2010) *Crisis Economics: A Crash Course in the Future of Finance* (New York: Penguin).

Roxburgh, C. et al. (2010) *Lions on the Move: The Progress and Potential of African Economies* (New York and London: McKinsey Global Institute).

Rubin, J. (2009) *Why Your World Is About to Get a Whole Lot Smaller: Oil and the End of Globalization* (New York: Random House).

Ryan-Collins, J, Greenham, T., Werner, R. and Jackson, A. (2012) *Where Does Money Come From?* (London: New Economics Foundation).

Sabin, P. (2013) *The Bet: Paul Ehrlich, Julian Simon and Our Gamble over the Earth's Future* (New Haven: Yale University Press).

Salamon, L. and Sokolowski, S. W. (2004) *Global Civil Society: Dimensions of the Nonprofit*, Vol. 2 (Bloomfield: Kumarian Press).

Sale, K. (2000 [1991]) *Dwellers in the Land: The Bioregional Vision* (Athens and London: The University of Georgia Press).

Samuelson, P. A. and Nordhaus, W. D. (2009 [1948]) *Economics* (New York: McGraw Hill).

Sandel, M. (2012) *What Money Can't Buy: The Moral Limits of Markets* (New York: Farrar, Straus and Giroux).

Schmelzer, M. (2016) *The Hegemony of Growth: The OECD and the Making of the Economic Growth Paradigm* (Cambridge: Cambridge University Press).

Schneider, F. and Enste, D. (2002) 'Hiding in the Shadows: The Growth of the Underground Economy'. *Economic Issues 30.* Available online: http://www.imf.org/external/pubs/ft/issues/issues30/ (accessed 30 June 2016).

Schroeder, R. Miyazaki, Y. and Fare, M. (2011) 'Community Currency Research: An Analysis of the Literature'. *International Journal of Community Currency Research* 15: 31–41.

Schulz, M., Soderbaum, F. and Ojendal, J. (eds) (2001) *Regionalization in a Globalizing World: A Comparative Perspective on Forms, Actors and Processes* (London: Zed Books).

Sen, A. (1977) 'Rational Fools: A Critique of the Behavioral Foundations of Economic Theory'. *Philosophy and Public Affairs* 6(4): 317–44.

Sheffi, Y. (2005) *The Resilient Enterprise* (Boston: MIT Press).

Shenon, P. (1995) 'A Pacific Island Nation Is Stripped of Everything'. *The New York Times,* 10 December.

Simmel, G. (1978) *The Philosophy of Money* (London: Routledge).

Simon, J. (1983) *The Ultimate Resource* (Princeton: Princeton University Press).

Singer, T. et al. (2006) 'Empathic Neural Responses Are Modulated by the Perceived Fairness of Others'. *Nature* 439: 466–9.

Smith, A. (1904 [1776]) *The Wealth of Nations* (London: Methuen & Co.).

Smith, A. (2007 [1759]) *The Theory of Moral Sentiments* (New York: Cosimo Books).

Smith, A. (2016) 'Shared, Collaborative and On Demand: The New Digital Economy'. *Pew Research Center,* 19 May.

Smith, J. (2014) 'Nauru's Road from Bird Droppings to Bust'. *Financial Times,* 30 September.

Snyder, G. (1980) *The Real Work: Interviews and Talks 1964–1979* (New York: New Directions Books).

Sornette, D., Maillart, T. and Ghezzi, G. (2014) 'How Much Is the Whole Really More than the Sum of Its Parts? 1 + 1 = 2.5: Superlinear Productivity in Collective Group Actions'. *PLoS ONE* 9(8): 1–15, e103023.

Spear, S. (2014) 'Samso: World's First 100% Renewable Energy-Powered Island Is a Beacon for Sustainable Communities'. *EcoWatch*, 1 May.

Speich, D. (2008) 'Travelling with the GDP through Early Development Economics' History'. *Working Papers on the Nature of Evidence: How Well Do 'Facts' Travel?* No. 33/08, ETH Zurich.

Spring, S. (2016) 'How the Alien Suit in Colony Was 3D Printed on a MakerBot Replicator Z18'. *MakerBot*, 24 March.

Steen-Olsen, K., Weinzettel, J., Cranston, G., Ercin, A. E. and Hertwich, E. G. (2012) 'Carbon, Land, and Water Footprint Accounts for the European Union: Consumption, Production, and Displacements through International Trade'. *Environmental Science & Technology* 46(20): 10883–91.

Stiglitz, J. E. (2012) *The Price of Inequality* (London: Penguin).

Stiglitz, J. E., Sen, A. and Fitoussi, J. P. (2009) *Report by the Commission on the Measurement of Economic Performance and Social Progress*. Available online: http://www.insee.fr/fr/publications-et-services/ dossiers _ web / stiglitz / doc - commission / RAPPORT _ anglais . pdf (accessed 15 May 2016).

Stiglitz, J. E., Sen, A. and Fitoussi, J. P. (2010) *Mismeasuring Our Lives: Why GDP Doesn't Add Up* (New York: The New Press).

Stolper, W. and Samuelson, P. (1941) 'Protection and Real Wages'. *Review of Economic Studies* 9(1): 58–73.

Streib, L. (2007) 'World's Fattest Countries'. *Forbes*, 2 August.

Sukhdev, P. (2012) *Corporation 2020: Transforming Business for Tomorrow's World* (Washington, DC: Island Press).

Sundararajan, A. and Fraiberger, S. P. (2015) 'Peer-to-Peer Rental Markets in the Sharing Economy'. NYU Stern School of Business Research Paper, 6 October. Available online: http://papers.ssrn. com/sol3/Papers.cfm?abstract_id=2574337 (accessed 30 June 2016).

Tapscott, D. and Williams, A. D. (2006) *Wikinomics: How Mass Collaboration Changes Everything* (New York: Penguin).

Tapscott, D. and Williams, A. D. (2010) *Macro-Wikinomics: New Solutions for Our Connected Planet* (New York: Penguin).

Tawney, R. H. (1958 [1926]) *Religion and the Rise of Capitalism* (New York and London: Harcourt Brace).

Thiel, C. (2011) 'Complementary Currencies in Germany: The Regiogeld System'. *International Journal of Community Currency Research* 15: 17–21.

Timmer, M., O'Mahony, M. and Van Ark, B. (2007) EU KLEMS Growth and Productivity Accounts – Overview November 2007. Groningen: University of Groningen.

Titmuss, R. M. (1996 [1970]) *The Gift Relationship: From Human Blood to Social Policy* (New York: The New Press).

Todd, J. and Tukel, G. (1981) *Reinhabiting Cities and Towns: Designing for Sustainability* (San Francisco: Planet Drum Foundation).

Trucost (2013) *Natural Capital at Risk: The Top 100 Externalities of Business* (London: Trucost and TEEB).

Trucost and FAO (2015) *Natural Capital Impacts in Agriculture* (Rome: Food and Agriculture Organization).

Trumbull, R. (1982) 'World's Richest Little Isle'. *The New York Times*, 7 March.

Tushman, M. L. and O'Reilly, C. A. (2002) *Winning Through Innovation: A Practical Guide to Leading Organisational Change and Renewal* (Boston: Harvard Business School Press).

UN Statistical Commission et al. (2012) *System of Environmental-Economic Accounting 2012: Central Framework* (New York: United Nations).

UN Statistical Commission et al. (2012) *System of Environmental-Economic Accounting 2012: Experimental Ecosystem Accounting* (New York: United Nations).

UN Statistics Division (2009) *System of National Accounts 2008* (New York: United Nations).

UNDESA (2012) *Trends in International Migrant Stock: Migrants by Destination and Origin* (New York: United Nations).

UNU-IHDP and UNEP (2014) *Inclusive Wealth Report 2014: Measuring Progress toward Sustainability* (Cambridge: Cambridge University Press).

US Department of Commerce (2000) 'GDP: One of the Great Inventions of the 20th Century'. *Survey of Current Business,* January: 6–14.

US Department of Transportation (2015) *Transportation and Housing Costs* (Washington DC: US Department of Transportation).

Van Den Bergh, J. (2009) 'The GDP Paradox'. *Journal of Economic Psychology* 30: 117–35.

Van Gelder, S. (1997) 'Beyond Greed and Scarcity'. *Yes Magazine,* 30 June.

Vardy, J. and Wattie, C. (2001) 'Shopping is Patriotic, Leaders Say'. *The National Post,* 28 September.

Victor, D. G., House, J. C. and Joy, S. (2005) 'A Madisonian Approach to Climate Policy'. *Science* 309(5742): 1820–1.

Wallace, J. L. (2016) 'Juking the Stats? Authoritarian Information Problems in China'. *British Journal of Political Science* 46(1): 11–29.

Waring, M. (1990) *If Women Counted: A New Feminist Economics.* San Francisco: Harper Collins.

Warleigh-Lack, A., Robinson, N. and Rosamond, B. (2011) *New Regionalism and the European Union. Dialogues, Comparisons and New Research Directions* (London and New York: Routledge).

Weinzettel, J., Hertwich, E. G., Peters, G. P., Steen-Olsen, K. and Galli, A. (2013) 'Affluence Drives the Global Displacement of Land Use'. *Global Environmental Change* 23: 433–8.

West, B. A. (2010) *Encyclopedia of the Peoples of Asia and Oceania* (New York: Facts on Life).

Whitlock, M. (2014) *Human Politics, Human Value* (Totnes: Mindhenge Books).

Wiedmann, T. O. et al. (2015) 'The Material Footprint of Nations'. *Proceedings of the National Academy of Sciences* 112(2): 6271–6.

Wildau, G. (2014) 'Small Cities Steer Away from GDP as a Measure of Success'. *Financial Times,* 13 August.

World Bank (2006) *Where Is the Wealth of Nations? Measuring Capital for the 21st Century* (Washington: World Bank).

World Bank (2013) *Little Green Data Book 2013* (Washington, DC: World Bank).

World Bank (2015) *Little Green Data Book 2015* (Washington, DC: World Bank).

World Bank (2016) *World Development Report 2016: Digital Dividends* (Washington, DC: World Bank).

Worstall, T. (2016) 'Facebook Doesn't Waste Trillions in Time: That's the Value Facebook Adds for Us'. *Forbes*, 4 February.

Index